Reflections on Toscanini

ALSO BY HARVEY SACHS

Toscanini

Virtuoso

Music in Fascist Italy

Reflections on Toscanini

Harvey Sachs

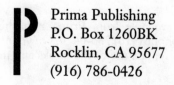

Prima Publishing
P.O. Box 1260BK
Rocklin, CA 95677
(916) 786-0426

This edition is reprinted by permission of Grove Weidenfeld.

Interior design by Joyce Weston
Cover design by The Dunlavey Studio, Sacramento

Library of Congress Cataloging-in-Publication Data
Sachs, Harvey, 1946–
   Reflections on Toscanini / Harvey Sachs.
     p. cm.
   Originally published: New York : Grove Weidenfeld, 1991. With new introd.
   Includes bibliographical references.
   ISBN 1–55958–315–0 (pbk.) : $14.95
   1. Toscanini, Arturo, 1867–1957. 2. Conductors (Music) — Biography.
I. Title.
[ML422.T67S338   1993]
784.2′092 — dc20   93–926
[B]   CIP
                                              MN

93 94 95 96 97 RRD 10 9 8 7 6 5 4 3 2 1
Printed in the United States of America

How to Order:
Quantity discounts are available from Prima Publishing, P.O. Box 1260BK, Rocklin, CA 95677; telephone (916) 786-0426. On your letterhead include information concerning the intended use of the books and the number of books you wish to purchase.

To Emanuela di Castelbarco,
Walfredo Toscanini,
and the people dearest to them,
in friendship.

—Harvey Sachs
Author

To Walter Levin,
founder of La Salle Quartet.

—Ben Dominitz
Publisher

Contents

Author's Note

MY biography of Arturo Toscanini was first published in 1978, in Great Britain and the United States. During the intervening years I have often been invited by magazines and newspapers to write essays and articles about him—discussions of newly discovered caches of documents, analyses of newly released or re-released Toscanini recordings, critiques of writings about him, and general pieces. Some of the items in this book are revised versions of articles that originally appeared in American periodicals. Others, originally written in Italian for Italian periodicals, are printed here for the first time in English. A few pieces are new. Only one essay, "Toscanini and Mussolini," has previously appeared in a book—my own *Music in Fascist Italy*, published in London in 1987 and in New York in 1988; both editions are out of print, and I wanted to make the piece available to readers who are interested in Toscanini but may not have been interested in the subject of musical life under Mussolini's regime. My thanks to Weidenfeld and Nicolson of London and W. W. Norton of New York for permission to reprint it. I also thank BMG Music (RCA Red Seal Division) for permission to use, in Chapter 10, excerpts from the notes I wrote for the Toscanini Television Concerts, released in 1990 on video cassettes and laser disks. Parts of some of the other essays have appeared in the following newspapers and periodicals (listed in alphabetical order): *Antologia Vieusseux* (Florence), *Atti e memorie della Accademia Petrarca* (Arezzo), *Croma* (Parma), *Grand Street* (New York), the *Guardian* (London), *Le Monde de la Musique* (Paris), *Musica* (Milan), *Musica e Dossier* (Rome), *Neue Zeitschrift für Musik* (Mainz), the *New Republic* (Washington), *Nuova rivista musicale italiana* (Rome), *Ovation* (New York), and *La Stampa* (Turin).

The first chapter is introductory and, in part, polemical; the following six concern specific periods or episodes in Toscanini's life and are arranged in roughly chronological order so as to form, together, something of an intermittent biography; the eighth chapter describes, in brief, the contents of the Toscanini family's archives at the New York Public Library; the ninth is a book review; and the last two are analyses—technical, in part—of aspects of Toscanini's work. At the end of each essay I have placed a note about its origins, and to a few I have added afterthoughts. Inevitably, some of the background information in each essay repeats facts given in my biography of Toscanini. I have tried, however, to keep the repetition to a minimum, and I have also made what I hope are judicious cuts and adaptations in the individual chapters, to minimize overlap among them.

I do not possess what has been called the gift of faith. This may seem an odd confession to make in the preface to a book of essays about a conductor, but it is surprisingly apt. I know partisans of several performing musicians—Caruso, Callas, Horowitz, Furt-wängler, Karajan, and, of course, Toscanini—whose fanatical admiration for their idols evidently satisfies a need to believe in a source of pure greatness. Toscanini is the conductor whose recorded performances stimulate, convince, and move me more often than those of any other conductor, and I consider him the most original and gripping performing musician I have heard. But I know many fine musicians and serious listeners whose musical ideas and physical reactions to music differ from mine, and I have no reason or desire to proselytize—much less to indulge in the childish game of "Who's Greater Than Whom." When I criticize some of Toscanini's critics—as, for example, in this book's first and ninth chapters—I do so not because I disagree with their opinions of his music-making, but because I believe that they have grossly misrepresented his approach to general or specific musical problems, or have inadvertently or intentionally ignored facts in the complicated Toscanini story. There is still much to be learned about—and from—that story.

H. S., Loro Ciuffenna
February 1991

Numbered endnotes indicate only sources of quotations. Footnotes of substance are indicated with asterisks and are printed *in situ*.

Major Events in
Toscanini's Life

1867 March 25: born in Parma, Italy, the son of Claudio Toscanini
      (1833–1906) and Paola Montani (1840–1924)
1876 Enters Parma's Royal School of Music
1885 Graduates with highest honors in cello and composition and
      maximum points in piano, taking first prize in graduating
      class
1886 June 30: makes debut as conductor in Rio de Janeiro; Novem-
      ber 4: makes Italian debut in Turin
1892 Conducts world premiere of Leoncavallo's *I Pagliacci*, Milan,
      Teatro Dal Verme
1895 Becomes principal conductor of Teatro Regio, Turin; con-
      ducts first Italian production of Wagner's *Die Götterdäm-
      merung* there
1896 Conducts world premiere of Puccini's *La Bohème* at the Regio,
      where he also conducts his first complete symphony concerts
1897 Marries Carla De Martini (1877–1951) of Milan
1898 Son Walter born (dies 1971); Toscanini leaves the Regio to
      become principal conductor of the Teatro alla Scala, Milan
1899 Conducts first Italian production of Wagner's *Siegfried* at La
      Scala
1900 Daughter Wally born (dies 1991); Toscanini conducts Italian
      premiere of Tchaikovsky's *Eugene Onegin*
1901 Son Giorgio born (dies 1906, of diphtheria)
1901, '03, '04, '06 Conducts, during Argentine winter season, at
      Teatro de la Opera, Buenos Aires; gives Argentine premieres
      of Berlioz's *La Damnation de Faust*, Puccini's *Madama Butterfly*,
      Cilea's *Adriana Lecouvreur*, and other operas

1903   Leaves La Scala; free-lances for three years

1906   Returns to La Scala; conducts Italian premiere of Strauss's *Salome* at La Scala (contemporaneous with a version conducted by the composer in Turin)

1907   Daughter Wanda born

1908   Conducts Italian premiere of Debussy's *Pelléas et Mélisande* at La Scala; leaves La Scala and becomes a principal conductor of the Metropolitan Opera Company, New York

1910   Takes Metropolitan ensemble (excepting orchestra) to Paris for a series of performances that includes the French premiere of Puccini's *Manon Lescaut*; conducts world premiere of Puccini's *La Fanciulla del West* at the Metropolitan Opera

1912   May–September: conducts at Teatro Colón, Buenos Aires

1913   Conducts U.S. premiere of Mussorgsky's *Boris Godunov* at the Metropolitan

1915   Leaves the Metropolitan

1915–18   Conducts only benefit performances (concerts and operas) and only in Italy until the end of World War I

1920–21   Conducts marathon tour of Italy, the United States, and Canada with a new orchestra formed under the auspices of La Scala; with this orchestra makes his first phonograph records; completely reorganizes La Scala's artistic and financial administration

1921   December 26: with a performance of Verdi's *Falstaff*, Toscanini reopens La Scala, which has had no regular season since 1917

1926   First concerts as guest conductor with the New York Philharmonic; conducts world premiere of Puccini's *Turandot* at La Scala

1927   Becomes coconductor, with Willem Mengelberg, of New York Philharmonic; makes first radio broadcasts with this orchestra

1929   Gives historic performances with La Scala ensemble in Vienna and Berlin; leaves La Scala

1930   Takes New York Philharmonic on its first European tour; becomes first non–German-school conductor to appear at the Bayreuth Festival (*Tannhäuser* and *Tristan*); becomes New York Philharmonic's principal conductor

1931   Assaulted by Fascist hooligans in Bologna for refusing to perform their party's hymn before a concert, determines not to conduct again in Italy under the Fascist regime; returns to Bayreuth (*Tannhäuser* and *Parsifal*)

1933   Withdraws from Bayreuth Festival following Hitler's accession to power in Germany; makes first guest appearances with Vienna Philharmonic (returns every year through 1937)

1935   Makes first appearances with a British ensemble—the BBC Symphony Orchestra, London—and returns in 1937, '38, and '39; conducts *Fidelio* and *Falstaff* at Salzburg Festival

1936   Resigns directorship of the New York Philharmonic; adds *Die Meistersinger* to his Salzburg repertoire; goes to Palestine at his own expense to conduct inaugural concerts of new orchestra, made up of Jewish refugees from Central Europe (returns in 1938)

1937   Adds *The Magic Flute* to his Salzburg repertoire; at seventy, becomes principal conductor of National Broadcasting Company Symphony Orchestra, New York, with which he remains for seventeen years (excepting 1941–42 season)

1938   Withdraws from Salzburg Festival after first hints of Austrian government's compromise with Nazi Germany; conducts first concerts of Lucerne Festival, founded as a result of his willingness to participate in it (returns in 1939 and 1946)

1940   Takes NBC Symphony on South American tour

1946   Conducts inaugural concert at La Scala, reopened after wartime damage

1948   Makes first television appearances, with NBC Symphony

1950   Makes transcontinental U.S. tour with NBC Symphony

1952   Makes final appearances in Italy (La Scala) and in England (Philharmonia Orchestra, Royal Festival Hall, London)

1954   April 4: final concert of his career, with NBC Symphony at Carnegie Hall

1957   January 16: dies at home in Riverdale (Bronx), New York

Reflections on Toscanini

CHAPTER *1*

Toscanini Again

TO discuss Arturo Toscanini nowadays is to embark upon a foolhardy enterprise, and not only because the literature on him is already so extensive. There are many traps: antihistoricism, deconstructionism, blind partisanship that understands nothing but pardons everything, equally blind antagonism that attempts to transmute personal tastes into lapidary laws. Besides, the "Toscanini question," like so many problems that we create for ourselves, is largely the result of an equivocation: because Toscanini was much recorded in the last years of his career, and because so many of his recordings are still, or again, available, he seems almost to belong to our time. We believe that we can know him thoroughly. But when contemporary musicians or critics or knowledgeable members of the public listen to Toscanini's recordings, they often discover that the recordings don't do what was expected of them. Toscanini's music-making—or at least as much of it as was recorded—does not always fit in with contemporary canons regarding the Good, the Beautiful, and the True. It sometimes gives us a jolt.

Fifty years of changes in the conducting profession have produced an even more fundamental equivocation. Because conductors produce no sound but occupy an apparently dominant position in the orchestra, conducting has long been, for the general public, the most misunderstood musical profession; today, however, the misunderstanding seems to be spreading from the public to critics and other professional observers, and even to many conductors. The hyperbolic statements issued at the time of Herbert von Karajan's death in 1989 brought the situation into high relief—and Karajan is in many respects the right man to set at the opposite end of the spectrum to Toscanini. "Last of the greats," "last heir to the grand tradition," "last of the podium giants"—all these descriptions were applied to Karajan, and all were nonsense. That Karajan was a "great conductor," in the strict sense of the term, is beyond dispute: his musical knowledge was outstanding, and when he stood before an orchestra, he knew what he wanted and how to achieve it. But there is no case for placing him in the long line of conductors that included (in chronological order) Hector Berlioz, Richard Wagner, Hans von Bülow, Hans Richter, Artur Nikisch, Karl Muck, Gustav Mahler, Felix Weingartner, Richard Strauss, Toscanini, Willem Mengelberg, Serge Koussevitzky, Pierre Monteux, Bruno Walter, Sir Thomas Beecham, Leopold Stokowski, Ernest Ansermet, Otto Klemperer, Wilhelm Furtwängler, Fritz Busch, Erich Kleiber, and fifteen or twenty others, all born between 1800 and 1900.

All the people in this list grew up with the notion that their main task was to bring new and newish music to the attention of the public; the reinterpretation of the classics was important and desirable but secondary, although most of them let it occupy more and more of their time as they grew older. Mahler, not long before his death at the age of fifty-one, told Klemperer that one of his greatest experiences in America had been the opportunity to conduct Beethoven's "Pastoral" Symphony, which he had previously performed only twice. Toscanini first conducted the Beethoven Seventh when he was forty-nine and *Fidelio* when he was sixty, and Walter first conducted Mozart's Symphony in G Minor, K. 550, when he was fifty. Karajan cannot be blamed for the petrifaction of the repertoire, a gradual process that is no more exclusively the fault of supposedly recalcitrant performers than it is of supposedly disdainful composers or supposedly lazy audiences. Still, he made hardly any impact in or on the music written by composers born in this, his own century. He was the first of a new breed of inconsequential conductors, repertorially speaking, rather than "the last of the giants."

Even as a conductor of what has become the classical hit parade, however, Karajan belongs with his successors, good and bad, rather than with his predecessors. In the mid-1960s, George Szell said that he dreamed of a conductor who would combine the virtues of Toscanini and Furtwängler but avoid their excesses. He presumably believed that he was the most likely person to achieve that strange goal—strange, because great artists' virtues can't exist without their complementary excesses—but in the end it was Karajan who became the most successful example of conductorial hybridization. For the last thirty years of his life, he seemed to be trying to smooth away music's rough edges, to eliminate all the original, disturbing concepts that Toscanini, Furtwängler, and a handful of other conductors of the past had taken pains to bring into relief, each in his own way. Karajan seemed to have opted, instead, for an all-purpose, highly refined, lacquered, calculatedly voluptuous sound that could be applied, with the stylistic modifications he deemed appropriate, to Bach and Puccini, Mozart and Mahler, Beethoven and Wagner, Schumann and Stravinsky. Like his predecessors, and like any intelligent musician, Karajan often changed his mind about the interpretation of a work, yet many of his performances had a prefabricated, artificial quality that those of Toscanini, Furtwängler, and the other above-named conductors seem never to have had.

Nor do Karajan's recordings elicit the kind of nitty-gritty musical debate that Toscanini's and Furtwängler's still do, decades after their deaths. Most of Karajan's records are exaggeratedly polished, a sort of sonic counterpart to the films and photographs of Leni Riefenstahl. To some extent, this is the result of today's superrefined recording processes, but the main reason is more likely related to Karajan's apparent obsession with control. In interview after interview and documentary after documentary, he compared conducting a first-rate orchestra to driving a magnificent sports car or piloting a new jet: you have achieved the ultimate form of control, he kept telling us—and himself—when you can sit back and let the instrument do what you want it to do. But the greatest conductors have never been interested in remote control. They have always wanted to get into the fray.

With respect to baton technique, too, Karajan broke with the past; and in this regard one must mention Leonard Bernstein, the other podium god of recent years, on whose corpse the music world's obituary writers banqueted only fifteen months after Karajan's death. Weingartner, Toscanini, Monteux, Walter, and Klemperer held widely differing interpretive viewpoints, but they all had a functional approach to technique; even Furtwängler's celebrated unclear beat was organic, not superimposed. There are films of all these fellows at work, and it's easy to see that although they don't resemble each other, they all conducted only the orchestra, not the audience. No matter how much charisma they possessed, and no matter how overstuffed their egos may have been, they transmitted the distinguishing characteristics of their music-making almost exclusively through the sounds produced by the orchestra. "Almost all the great conductors of the past stood absolutely still," said the English conductor Sir Adrian Boult, who saw them all, from Richter on:

> The picturesque habit of walking about and miming the music like a ballet dancer is a modern development, which I dare say will appeal to some of the less sophisticated members of our audience. But it doesn't make matters easier for the players and singers, and I am inclined to think that it is only when he has complete control of himself that a conductor can hope to control other people.[1]

But Karajan and Bernstein conducted the audience as well as the orchestra. Admittedly, they were not the first conductors to do so. Stokowski, for instance, indulged in some grotesque clowning on the podium during the cinematic phase of his career, but when I saw him, in the 1960s, his gestures were clear and unostentatious. And Stokowski at his worst was a model of restraint in comparison with the nineteenth-century French conductor Louis-Antoine Jullien, who sat in a velvet chair and faced the audience, using a baton that a liveried servant had carried onstage. Karajan and Bernstein, however, through their frequent television appearances, made conducting the audience an acceptable and even, according to some people, a desirable aspect of the profession. The vast visual diffusion of Bernstein's exhibitionistic gestures and Karajan's power-exuding ones has done much to corrupt the relationships between conductor and orchestra and between orchestra and audience.

Referring to such podium shenanigans, Stravinsky said that Bernstein could get a dozen curtain calls out of the national anthem; and Klemperer wondered how so fine a musician as Karajan could be "so addicted to applause. . . . He's just the conductor for 1969," said Klemperer—in 1969, of course.[2] Today's observers might add that

Karajan and Bernstein are likely to remain "just the conductors" for many decades to come because many of their younger colleagues, under the influence of the K/B Mystique, now believe that one of their professional duties is to demonstrate, visibly, the full extent of their emotional involvement in the music. Karajan went so far as to say that audiences appreciated being guided by the conductor's expressions and gestures, and some of Karajan's and Bernstein's younger colleagues seem to believe that today's audiences can no longer do without the conductor's visual "assistance."

What are the thoughts of the people who play the instruments, the people for whose sake, presumably, the conductor is on the podium? As a rule, they are not enchanted by conductors' extra-musical carryings-on. "What's the difference between a bull and an orchestra?" goes a riddle that recently made the rounds of players' dressing rooms the world over. Answer: "On a bull the horns are at the front, and the ass is at the back." The players' attitude is not merely a result of cynicism or indifference. Although fifty orchestra musicians will have fifty different opinions of the same conductor, as a group they have a clearer idea than most audience members of the limits of the conductor's power—and another, hoarier piece of locker room lore brings those limits into focus. Weber's *Oberon* Overture begins with a slow, delicate French horn solo; legend has it that one conductor, after carefully giving the customary, preparatory upbeat, used to turn his head away and screw his face into a sour expression, in anticipation of a horrible crack or quaver on the first note. In other words, no matter what the conductor does, the sound is produced by the players.

James Levine has pointed out that many people who attend symphony concerts make two incorrect assumptions: that the conductor necessarily likes what the orchestra is doing, and that the conductor can necessarily control what the orchestra is doing. During rehearsals, stopping and starting are possible, and any reasonably competent conductor working with a decent orchestra can at least make the pieces of the puzzle mesh. But if something goes fundamentally wrong during a performance, not even the best of conductor-orchestra teams can always bring the progression of musical events back into line. Conductors who appear to be acting out a Mannerist painting of St. Teresa in ecstasy are either conducting an imaginary performance, parallel to but rarely identical with the

orchestra's, or are trying—consciously or unconsciously or both—
to impress the audience.

ALTHOUGH Toscanini's authorized recordings are being reis-
sued in good-to-excellent digitally reprocessed sound, on compact disks and even on video cassettes and laser disks, he undeniably
belongs to a rather distant musical past. When Toscanini was born,
in 1867, Rossini was still alive; Verdi was finishing *Don Carlos* and
Wagner was finishing *Die Meistersinger* (*Tristan* had had its premiere
two years earlier); Brahms was not quite thirty-four years old and
working on his *German Requiem*; Bizet, Tchaikovsky, Dvořák, Massenet, Boito, and Grieg were all in their twenties; and Puccini,
Mahler, Debussy, Mascagni, Richard Strauss, Sibelius, and Busoni
were under the age of ten. Toscanini began his studies at the Royal
School of Music in Parma, his hometown, in November 1876, the
month in which Brahms's First Symphony had its world premiere
and three months after the first Bayreuth Festival. *Boris Godunov* and
Carmen had had their premieres during the two previous years.
Arnold Schoenberg was two years old, and Bruno Walter was a
newborn babe. When Toscanini made his professional conducting
debut in 1886, Verdi was finishing *Otello*; Bartók was five years old,
Stravinsky four, Webern three; Berg was one year old and Furtwängler was five months old. Toscanini grew up in the midst of a
musical reality entirely different from our own. Most members of
today's opera audiences, for instance, have no desire whatsoever to
hear operas written within the last fifty years; thus in today's opera
world performers count for nearly everything; composers—living
ones—count for nearly nothing. But during the 1881–86 seasons,
when Toscanini played cello in the orchestra of Parma's Teatro
Regio, the house's repertoire did not include even one opera written
more than fifty years earlier. Serious musical creativity and the mass
music industry overlapped in those days in a way that is unimagin-
able today.

During the first forty years of his sixty-eight-year career, Toscanini conducted the world premieres of many operas, four of which
have become part of the popular repertoire: *I Pagliacci*, *La Bohème*,
La Fanciulla del West, and *Turandot*. He also conducted the first Italian productions of *Siegfried*, *Die Götterdämmerung*, *Salome* (at the
same time as a rival production conducted by Strauss), and *Pelléas*

et Mélisande. He gave Italy its first performances of three of Verdi's Four Sacred Pieces and various symphonic works of Brahms, Tchaikovsky, Dvořák, Debussy, Strauss, Sibelius, Elgar, Rachmaninoff, Respighi, Stravinsky, and many others among his contemporaries. In Buenos Aires, where he led five substantial seasons between 1901 and 1912, he gave the South American premieres of *Tristan*, *Madama Butterfly*, *Adriana Lecouvreur*, and several other works; and at New York's Metropolitan Opera, where he worked from 1908 to 1915, he conducted the North American premieres of *Boris Godunov* and works by Paul Dukas, Umberto Giordano, Italo Montemezzi, and Ermanno Wolf-Ferrari.

Toscanini was a reformer, especially in the opera house. He put into practice many of the changes suggested by Wagner and Verdi, and in so doing he exercised a lasting influence on operatic performance practices. At La Scala he had an orchestra pit installed in 1907; until then, the orchestra had always played at main-floor level. (How must Verdi's later operas, not to mention Wagner's works and Strauss's *Salome*, have sounded in a house that had no pit?) He also insisted on replacing the old, vertically opening, painted front drop with a modern, horizontally opening velvet curtain, and in 1900 he persuaded the Scala administration to install what was then the most modern stage lighting system in Europe. He insisted on darkening the house during performances, so that the audience's attention would be focused on the stage. And he believed that a performance could not be artistically successful unless unity of intention was first established among all the components: singers, orchestra, chorus, staging, sets, and costumes. Carlo Maria Giulini has said, "Toscanini fought terrible battles in order to achieve things that everyone today takes for granted. Even musicians who disagree with him are the direct beneficiaries of his work, of his struggle."[3]

Certain revisionist historians of singing have complained, recently, about the likes of Mahler and Toscanini, who, they say, turned a popular form of entertainment into a religion. Some of them long for the good old days, when, for instance, Milan's aristocratic families chatted, flirted, played cards, and ate dinner in their boxes during performances at La Scala and when audiences vociferously expressed their opinions of the singers. It would indeed be nice if there were still significant numbers of opera enthusiasts capable of distinguishing between vocal fool's gold and the real thing, so that bravos and catcalls would have some significance; and Toscanini, in his day, did not object to resounding demonstrations of approval or disapproval for singers. On the other hand, the opportunity to concentrate on what one is hearing and seeing at the theater seems wholly desirable, and there cannot be many audience members today who would be delighted to hear the banging of doors, the clatter of dishes, and the incessant murmur of hundreds of people during a musical performance.

There is something fundamentally wrong with the revisionists' critiques of Toscanini the opera reformer; that "something" has to do, no doubt, with the fact that Toscanini's few opera recordings were made when he was in his late seventies and eighties, and under the unnaturally tense conditions of one-shot concert versions that were simultaneously being broadcast around the world on radio— and, in one case, on television. Rodolfo Celletti, one of Italy's leading historians of singing, is right to say that it is difficult "to have an idea of what Toscanini must really have been like as an opera conductor,"[4] and that it is "dangerous" to judge him from the recordings. The degree to which Toscanini tightened up as an opera conductor in his last years is strikingly evident even when one compares such small items as the aria "Eri tu" from Verdi's *Un Ballo in Maschera* in an unpublished recording made during a live broadcast in 1943 and the same aria as it was recorded during a complete concert performance of the opera in 1954. In the earlier version the baritone, Francesco Valentini, is allowed a great degree of freedom, and there is much rubato in the orchestral accompaniment; in the later one Robert Merrill, although not hard pressed, is made to toe the line.

Celletti's criticisms of aspects of some of Toscanini's opera recordings are judicious and just. Sometimes, however, he ignores his own warning about the perils of judging Toscanini by his recordings, and plunges into dark and treacherous waters. "Toscanini's so-called 'lesson,'" he says, "insofar as it concerns performance practices for neoclassical and protoromantic operas, is used as a reference-point only by those time-beaters who are fifty to seventy years old or older." But to which lesson can he possibly be referring? Does anyone still alive remember a Toscanini performance of an opera by Rossini (the last one took place in Buenos Aires in 1906) or by Bellini (Turin, 1898)? Toscanini did not conduct any other operas that could be designated "neoclassical" or "protoromantic." Besides, anyone who has listened to Toscanini's recordings of Rossini overtures, made between 1929 and 1938 with the New York Philharmonic and the BBC Symphony (the later NBC Symphony versions are slightly less convincing), will have a hard time imagining them played more flexibly, more lyrically, more elegantly, more ironically, more neoclassically and protoromantically than in these versions, which are indeed a lesson. Toscanini was a romantic in temperament and outlook and a classicist in his approach to form; his performances of Rossini and Bellini may therefore have been excellent. But we do not know.

Celletti is not entirely averse to using evidence one-sidedly. He says, for instance, that Verdi's publisher, Giulio Ricordi, "considered Toscanini an excessively metronomical conductor" but fails to add that Ricordi was prejudiced against Toscanini for other reasons.* Verdi himself, who had discussed details of his compositions with Toscanini on several occasions and had always heard good things said about him—especially from Boito, who had been responsible for Toscanini's first engagement, in 1898, as La Scala's principal conductor—was perplexed by Ricordi's criticisms. "If Toscanini isn't skilled," he wrote to Ricordi in typically telegraphic style in 1899, "the others are even less so." Celletti cites letters in which Verdi avowed his opposition to the "tyranny of the conductors." But, with all due respect, quoting Verdi's letters is a little like quoting the Bible: you can find something to support every point of view. Celletti conveniently avoids quoting Verdi's letter of June 7, 1869, addressed to Ricordi: "So you see how important the Conductor is. In Parma, with four singers who were much liked, with the best orchestra members, with the finest scene-painter in Italy, *Don Carlos* was only moderately successful . . . and it was above all and solely the fault of the conductor's spineless soul. Just about the same was true in Florence. In the end, I have only one answer to all the questions you pose: 'Find a man who knows how to mount and conduct an opera!' "

An English commentator, David Wooldridge, has made rash assumptions about Toscanini along the same lines as Celletti's, but in

---

* I described Toscanini's relations with Ricordi at some length in Chapter III of my biography of Toscanini.

a more amateurish way. He says, for instance, that "Toscanini would have been unequivocal in his disdain of a voice like that of Alessandro Bonci," who liked to linger on high notes "with infinite and consummate artistry"; and he fulminates against what he describes—outrageously, to my way of thinking—as a lack of personality in Conchita Supervia's recording of "Una voce poco fa" from *The Barber of Seville*—a recording made "under the direct influence of Toscanini."[5] Wooldridge ought to have investigated a few facts before making such statements. Toscanini did work with Bonci but did not work with Supervia, nor could Supervia have heard him conduct anything by Rossini except, possibly, an overture or two.

From 1895, when Toscanini became what would today be called the artistic director of Turin's Teatro Regio, until 1902, when he was well into his fourth season in a similar position at La Scala, the only Verdi operas he conducted at those prestigious theaters were the late, atypical *Otello* and *Falstaff.* In recent years some critics have theorized that Toscanini's reticence to conduct Verdi's other works in Turin and Milan grew out of his belief in Wagner's concept of music drama as a *Gesamtkunstwerk*, a complete work of art, and out of his consequent disdain for operas in which the vocal element was of greater importance than any other individual production element. This opinion may be dismissed at once, because during the period and at the theaters in question Toscanini conducted works by Rossini, Bellini, and Donizetti in which the vocal element is even more dominant than in any but the very earliest of Verdi's operas. The real reason for Toscanini's reticence is much more interesting.

Before he planned one of his Turin or Milan seasons, Toscanini had to ask himself the same questions that the artistic directors of today's major opera companies have to ask themselves: "What do the people who sit in the audience want to hear? How far can I push them in the direction of my own tastes, insofar as those tastes differ from theirs? With the singers and other forces available to me, which works can be brought off decently and which ones can't?" But Toscanini faced a problem that today's artistic directors do not face. At major theaters in those days, prestige was measured largely in terms of major premieres, and audiences built their self-esteem on their ability to distinguish good music from bad—according to the taste of the time, of course—rather than to distinguish good performers from bad.* The tendency was to look down on or even reject familiar old pieces. In 1908, when *La Forza del Destino* was programmed at La Scala, the newspaper critics wrote, "It shows its age" (*Frusta teatrale*); "a hodgepodge" (*Teatro illustrato*); "it is not a beautiful opera" (*Lombardia*); "the audience . . . got no enjoyment out of it, but rather a feeling of tedium and disappointment . . . some of the cabalettas make a vulgar impression" (*Perseveranza*).[6] No wonder, then, that nearly half of the forty-four operas that Toscanini conducted during his first seven Scala seasons (1898–1903 and 1906–08) were Milanese premieres; only seven were Italian works written before his birth—and he was only forty-one at the end of that period. His reluctance to offer good old *Rigoletto*, *Trovatore*, and *Traviata* to the public resulted, in the first place, from the reluctance of a considerable portion of the public to hear them. *Il Trovatore*, for instance, was already an object of satire in Italy forty or fifty years before Hollywood came up with *A Night at the Opera*. According to the conductor Tullio Serafin, who was one of Toscanini's assistants at the turn of the century, the celebrated comic actor Edoardo Ferravilla used to do a *Trovatore* parody that made even Verdi "laugh until he cried":

> To do the role of the Conte di Luna, Ferravilla would put on a big helmet with enormous, garishly colored ostrich feathers. He would pull on a pair of green gloves and wrap himself in an ample, extremely long, white cape. So in 1902, when Toscanini wanted to bring *Trovatore* back to La Scala, where it hadn't been done for some time, the great concern was to make sure that the audience did not laugh.[7]

The *Trovatore* production was prepared with great care, and the audience did not laugh. Indeed, many music historians believe that the Verdi Restoration in Italy began with that production.

In the opinion of many of the revisionists who miss the good old days (which they never experienced) of wild and woolly vocal virtuosity, Toscanini, with his Wagner-influenced ideal of presenting every opera as a total work of art, was one of the causes of the present-day sterility in the vocal world—as if the fact that not a single Italian opera has entered the popular repertoire since 1926, when *Turandot* had its premiere (under Toscanini's baton), and the

---

* See Appendix I.

consequent fact that there is no longer a *living* Italian operatic culture, did not sufficiently explain the phenomenon! Celletti even
makes Toscanini responsible for the fact that Riccardo Muti, "im-
pregnated with youthful Toscanini-ism," did not allow the tenor in a
Florentine production of *Il Trovatore* to sing a traditional but unwritten high C. The judgment is absolutely wrong. In *Il Trovatore*,
Toscanini allowed tenors to sing not only the two unwritten high Cs
in the cabaletta "Di quella pira" but also the unwritten high B-flat at
the end of "Deserto sulla terra" and that of "Ah! sì, ben mio." He did
not, on the other hand, allow the baritone to sing the traditional but
unwritten G in the phrase "Leonora mia" because, as he reminded
baritone Benvenuto Franci, "It's a count who's talking, not a rag-
picker, not a shrieker." Every interpretive problem requires an individual solution, Toscanini believed; there are no general rules.* In all
of Verdi's operas antedating *Otello*, Toscanini often made cuts and
other substantial changes—sometimes highly debatable ones—
according to the circumstances of the production, as did all the other
conductors who were active when the Italian operatic tradition was
still alive. And he knew as well as anyone that many interpretive
decisions depend on the voices of the performers. Says Giulini:

> [Toscanini] himself once told me: "The tempo, the rhythmic scansion of
> a given musical phrase, cannot be the same for every singer. Every voice
> has its own special requirements that vary from case to case; the rhyth-
> mic pacing has to be adapted, albeit with minimal jerkiness, to the
> practical abilities of each vocal instrument, to its capacity for harmo-
> nious development in relation to the orchestra."[8]

So much for the "protoromantics" and Verdi. As to Toscanini's
suitability for the music of Italian opera composers of his own generation, the majority opinion was summed up by a remark made by Puccini in 1922, in a letter to his close friend, Riccardo Schnabl-Rossi:
"Toscanini is now really the *best* conductor in the world because he
has everything—soul, poetry, flexibility, dash, refinement, dramatic
instinct—in short, a real miracle."[9] Another of Puccini's comments,
in a letter of 1915 to the same friend, elicits a chuckle today: "In Milan

---

* There is little sense, however, in berating Riccardo Muti for opposing, in our day,
practices in regard to which Verdi himself was by no means enthusiastic.

I attended a good [performance of] *Tosca* as far as Toscanini was concerned, mediocre as far as the singers were concerned."[10] The Tosca in that performance was Claudia Muzio, who is often, and justifiably, held up as a paragon of the vocal virtues required of Puccini's heroines; but Puccini did not even deign to mention her name.

Another allegation against Toscanini—that presumed wet blanket of the opera world—is that he arbitrarily put an end to the tradition of encoring arias by popular demand during opera performances and even quit La Scala in 1903 rather than concede an encore during a performance of *Un Ballo in Maschera*. Celletti, too, evidently believes this nonsensical old legend, although it has long been known that the conductor's break with La Scala in 1903 was mainly the result of a salary dispute. Toscanini opposed encores not only because he believed that they interrupted the drama and created a *corrida*-like atmosphere, but also because many singers hated doing them. The stars certainly enjoyed the audience's approval but not the extra wear and tear on their voices, especially in an age in which they were often expected to perform the same opera four times a week, several weeks in a row. Here, for instance, is the *Corriere della Sera*'s account of the *Ballo* incident to which Celletti refers (the italics are mine): "One part of the audience wanted an encore of the aria [*sic*] 'È scherzo od è follia'; *but since the tenor [Giovanni] Zenatello did not appear willing to concede it*, Maestro Toscanini motioned to proceed."[11] Not even Toscanini could have put an end to so deeply rooted a tradition as the encore unless most singers agreed with him.

At least Celletti does not believe one of the most ridiculous judgments (passed off as incontrovertible truths) attributable to Toscanini's current detractors in the opera world: that he wanted to work only with singers who would obey him, and did not care whether a singer had character. Among the well-known singers with whom he worked were Paul Lhérie, Nicolai Figner, Medea Mej Figner, Eugenia Mantelli, Antonio Cotogni,* Romano Nannetti, Francesco Tamagno, Victor Maurel, Antonio Pini-Corsi, Virginia

---

* Antonio Cotogni (1831–1918), a baritone, was probably the oldest celebrated singer with whom Toscanini worked. Cotogni made his debut in Rome in 1852, sang in most of the great European theaters, and was chosen by Verdi to sing the role of Rodrigo at the Italian premiere of *Don Carlo* (Bologna, 1867). Toscanini conducted Cotogni, Tamagno, and Nannetti in a short but very successful season at Rome's Teatro Costanzi in 1892.

Ferni Germano, Gemma Bellincioni, Félia Litvinne, Ramón Blanchard, Cesira Ferrani, Amelia Pinto, Enrico Caruso, Giovanni Zenatello, Pasquale Amato, Antonio Scotti, Angelica Pandolfini, Adelina Stehle, Elisa Bruno, Giuseppe Borgatti, Emma Carelli, Rosina Storchio, Salomea Krusceniski, Fyodor Chaliapin, Fernando De Lucia, Maria Gay, Eugenia Burzio, Ester Mazzoleni, Giuseppe De Luca, Giovanni Martinelli, Adamo Didur, Leo Slezak, Emma Eames, Emmy Destinn, Louise Homer, Frances Alda, Geraldine Farrar, Lucrezia Bori, Alma Gluck, Jane Bathori, Marie Delna, Dinh Gilly, Albert Reiss, Angelo Badà, Edoardo Garbin, Giacomo Rimini, Virginia Guerrini, Margarethe Matzenauer, Jacques Urlus, Edoardo Ferrari-Fontana, Maria Farneti, Giuseppe Anselmi, Frieda Hempel, Nazzareno De Angelis, Marzelline Ober, Beniamino Gigli, Tito Schipa, Claudia Muzio, Alessandro Bonci, Aureliano Pertile, Mariano Stabile, Toti Dal Monte, Giacomo Lauri-Volpi, Elvira Casazza, Maria Labia, Marcel Journet, Riccardo Stracciari, Gilda Dalla Rizza, Miguel Fleta, Mercedes Capsir, Carlo Galeffi, Giuseppina Cobelli, Antonin Trantoul, Rosa Raisa, Fanny Anitua, Juanita Caracciolo, Maria Carena, Bianca Scacciati, Tancredi Pasero, Benvenuto Franci, Francesco Merli, Salvatore Baccaloni, Ebe Stignani, Gabriella Besanzoni, Ezio Pinza, Rosetta Pampanini, Giannina Arangi Lombardi, Mercedes Llopart, Lauritz Melchior, Elisabeth Rethberg, Gerhard Hüsch, Ivar Andrésen, Elisabeth Ohms, Erna Berger, Fritz Wolff, Herbert Janssen, Rudolf Bockelmann, Maria Müller, Nanny Larsén-Todsen, Deszö Ernster, Charles Kullman, Helge Roswaenge, Alexander Kipnis, Lotte Lehmann, Alfred Jerger, Willi Domgraf-Fassbaender, Richard Mayr, Friedrich Schorr, Jarmila Novotná, Bruna Castagna, Maria Caniglia, Mafalda Favero, Dusolina Giannini, Set Svanholm, Helen Traubel, Jan Peerce, Robert Merrill, Richard Tucker, Jerome Hines, Nan Merriman, Ramón Vinay, Giuseppe Valdengo, Leonard Warren, Zinka Milanov, Jussi Bjoerling, Nicola Moscona, Eleanor Steber, Rose Bampton, Licia Albanese, Herva Nelli, Cloe Elmo, Giacinto Prandelli, Renata Tebaldi, Lois Marshall, Giuseppe Di Stefano, Cesare Siepi, and Fedora Barbieri.

It is a list that begins with singers who had been chosen by Verdi (Cotogni, Lhérie, Tamagno, Maurel), Bizet (Lhérie), and Tchaikovsky (the Figner couple) to sing leading roles in their operas, and that ends with an artist who is still active in the 1990s. Few of the those who are not—Titta Ruffo, Conchita Supervia, Rosa Ponselle, and Maria Callas, for instance—are missing for logistic, contractual, or other mundane reasons (or possibly because of my oversights in compiling the list) and not because of artistic incompatibility with Toscanini. He did not get on equally well with all singers, and with some he worked only once; but that has been true of every important conductor. Erich Leinsdorf, who was Toscanini's assistant at Salzburg during the 1930s, has said, "In preparing singers, [Toscanini] was very thorough but not small-minded. When he had singers like Lotte Lehmann or Richard Mayr, who had many years' experience in the parts they were performing with him, he would very willingly let them be and not try to mold them in a new way. The same was true of solo wind players in the orchestra. He was a generous man. He was totally impatient only with the wrong mentality. If he felt that people were not serious, that they were taking things lightly, or that they were stupid—these were things he could not stand."[12]

"FORMERLY the way to show one's understanding was to praise [Toscanini], today it is to find fault with him; and the attacks reveal as little understanding of the Toscanini operation and what it produced as did most of the praise."[13] Thus wrote B. H. Haggin in a book published in 1959, two years after Toscanini's death. His observation is as apt today as it was then, because most of the praise and most of the attacks were and are based on a granitic, immutable Toscanini who never existed. The greatest danger in Toscanini criticism was inadvertently indicated by Toscanini himself, in old age. "They say that I've always been the same," he said, during a chat with a young conductor, Gianandrea Gavazzeni. "Nothing more foolish has ever been uttered about me. I've never been the same— not even from one day to the next. I knew it even if others didn't."[14] The more Toscanini recordings one gets to know, and the more one studies his artistic development, the more clearly one sees that the only constant in his story was his willingness to change.

So let's not be afraid, after all, to talk again about Toscanini; but, in so doing, let's try to maintain a sense of history, a sense of reality, and a sense of fairness.

Parts of this essay appeared in *Antologia Vieusseux* (Florence), no. 81, 1986; *La Stampa* (Turin), August 26, 1989; *Musica* (Milan), June–July 1990; and *Musica e Dossier* (Rome), January–February 1991. Other parts are new.

CHAPTER 2

The Young Toscanini— Without Zeffirelli

ARTURO Toscanini was nineteen years old when he went to Brazil in 1886 as principal cellist and assistant chorus master of a touring Italian opera company. During that trip he was catapulted for the first time into the role of conductor, a role he would fulfill with unprecedented success for nearly seven decades.

For the last three years the Italian director Franco Zeffirelli has been telling the press of his intention to create a movie based on the story of Toscanini's debut. He claims to have heard the story directly from the conductor, whom he met in the 1950s, but his recently released (1988) film, *The Young Toscanini*, has little to do with the story as Toscanini told it or as it was recounted in the newspapers of the day. If the film were a fine work of art, its historical inaccuracies would be pardonable. Unfortunately, it is a mindless, hollow, badly acted, embarrassingly saccharine confection; and its emotional and intellectual impact resemble those of an episode from a low-budget soap opera. Zeffirelli's film presents a stereotypical young musician with a characterless face, a careworn but loving mother, and a high-principled, socialist father. We are shown his audition as a potential cellist for the orchestra of Milan's Teatro alla Scala, a tempestuous incident that ended with his abrupt departure for South America; his shipboard romance with an aspiring Sister of Mercy from a well-to-do Milanese family; his human and professional concern for the aging diva Nadina Bulichoff, mistress of the Brazilian emperor Dom Pedro II; and the joint effort of Toscanini and Bulichoff to persuade the cynical monarch to put an end to slavery in his country.

These strands of the movie's plot, like most of its details, are pure if not very clever invention. Toscanini's mother was a harsh, proud, disillusioned woman; and her husband, a Mazzinian anti-monarchist and anticlericalist and a soldier of Garibaldi, but not a socialist, was an irresponsible tailor who had a drinking problem. Toscanini first set foot in La Scala after his return from Brazil, and there was nothing tempestuous about his audition there: he was accepted as second cellist and occupied that position during the 1886–87 season, which included the world premiere of Verdi's *Otello*. If he was romantically involved with anyone during the tour, his companion was probably the contralto Eugenia Mantelli (ca. 1860–1926), a member of the company who later sang regularly at New York's Metropolitan Opera. Bulichoff, the aging diva—portrayed by the fifty-six-year-old (in 1988) Elizabeth Taylor—was a twenty-six-year-old Russian soprano, neither unknown nor cele-brated. She could hardly have been the emperor's mistress: as a member of the itinerant company, she arrived in Rio with her col-leagues only a few days before the events purportedly described in the film took place. Dom Pedro II (1825–91) was one of the most enlightened South American leaders during the nineteenth century. He had put an end to Brazil's slave trade in the 1850s and had forced the country's unwilling landowners to accept a bill aimed at the total abolition of slavery, which was achieved in 1888, two years after Toscanini's visit. Bulichoff did donate her diamonds to purchase the freedom of seven slaves, but this happened at a performance later in the season—not at Toscanini's debut, as Zeffirelli has it. Her gesture was interpreted as an act of support for Dom Pedro's policies, not as a challenge to them.

Some of the details of the debut and of the whole tour are known from contemporary published accounts, but Toscanini's own account has been preserved on a tape that belongs to his family. In 1955 and 1956, the conductor, who had retired in 1954 at the age of eighty-seven, was busy approving or rejecting recordings that he had made with the NBC Symphony Orchestra. His son, Walter, and some of RCA's engineers—notably John Corbett—had set up a sound laboratory in the basement of the Toscanini home, the Villa Pauline in Riverdale (Bronx); Toscanini, however, used to listen to the recordings on speakers that had been installed upstairs, in the living room. Microphones had also been placed in the living room so that Toscanini could communicate with Walter and Corbett in the basement, and Walter sometimes taped his father's comments for future reference. One evening in 1955, Walter and his sister Wally Castelbarco invited the conductor Wilfrid Pelletier and his wife, the soprano Rose Bampton, to the Villa Pauline. Walter turned on a tape recorder, presumably without his father's knowledge, and Toscanini was then encouraged to tell the story of his debut. The tape contains a much more interesting story than the one told by Zeffirelli.

Toscanini had graduated from the conservatory in his home-town, Parma, in 1885 and had immediately begun to earn a living by playing the cello in various Italian opera orchestras. On the tape, he accurately recalls the repertoire of Parma's Teatro Regio during the 1885–86 season. All the works were by living composers: Ponchielli's *La Gioconda* and *Marion Delorme*, Gounod's *Faust*, and Verdi's *Aida*. The conductor, Nicola Bassi, was nonplussed by his youngest cellist's habit of playing everything by heart. "I never had to turn a page," Toscanini remembered with a chuckle, "and when we got to *Marion Delorme*, which was a brand-new opera, Bassi came over to me and said, 'Now we'll see if you can play this by heart!' And I said, 'Why not? Isn't this music, too?' It was there that Superti, a violinist who also conducted ballets at La Scala, engaged me for [South] America, because he saw that I never turned a page while I played."

Carlo Superti was coimpresario, assistant conductor, and chorus master of the company bound for Brazil; thus, when Parma's season had ended, Toscanini went to Genoa and boarded ship with the rest of the company, including the main impresario, Claudio Rossi. "We stopped at Cádiz," he said, "and there I spent my nine-teenth birthday," on March 25, 1886. The ensemble's season opened at São Paulo in mid-April, under the baton of Leopoldo Miguez (1850–1902), a noted Brazilian composer whose conducting abilities did not impress the Italians. At one rehearsal, the principal *basso*, Gaetano Roveri, shouted at Toscanini, " 'What are you doing? Those cellos are not keeping time!'

" 'But I can't follow the conductor's beat,' I said.

" 'For heaven's sake, just don't look at him any more!' " The public and critics were not delighted with the company's achieve-ments, and there were rows at the last São Paulo performances in mid-June. But the troupe moved on to Rio de Janeiro, as scheduled, for a two-month engagement.

"At our first performance of *Faust*," said Toscanini, "the stage band sounded as if it were at war with the orchestra in the pit. Miguez thought we had done it on purpose, to give Superti a chance to conduct *Aida*," which was scheduled for the evening of June 30. Miguez resigned and Superti was indeed designated to replace him. Toscanini, who was usually a bear for punctuality, dawdled at his boarding house that evening, "studying Schubert lieder with Eugenia Mantelli." (This, at any rate, was his official version of their activities.) "I was sitting at the piano," said Toscanini, "and at the last minute I remembered that I was first cello in *Aida*. I took the tram and arrived at the theater. . . . There was a hell of an uproar!

"I went to my place, took out my instrument, and asked what was going on. 'The audience doesn't want Superti.' . . . The ballet master, who spoke Portuguese, came out to tell the audience to be quiet and that there would be a different conductor." Someone else attempted to conduct but had "no luck at all. The impresario spoke, too, but that didn't work, either. We orchestra players were telling each other, 'Now they'll close the theater.' At that moment, it occurred to me that I'd forgotten, as usual, to pick up my pay on time and that I'd have to buy a ticket back to Italy—and that now the impresario wouldn't pay me. While all this stuff was running through my mind, a subscriber came over and said, 'Isn't there anyone in the orchestra who can conduct *Aida*?' My second cellist turned to me, and I left my cello right then and there and ran onto the stage to save my soul.

"But I'd gone from the frying pan into the fire. . . . On the stage I ran into all the women from the chorus who had studied with me [during the trip to Brazil]. Everyone knew about my memory because the singers had all had lessons with me, and I had played the piano without ever looking at the music. There was a woman named Leoni from Parma, ugly as the devil, who started to cry, and who said [in Parmesan dialect], 'Who knows if Toscanini can do it? Let him go out and conduct.' Then the impresario came; everyone was imploring me. He even wanted to give me his frock coat, since we were the same height. I was barely out of school, and I was still wearing my military-style school uniform, with gold buttons. I said, 'No, no, if I have to go and conduct, I'll go dressed as I am.'" But they persuaded him to change and, said Toscanini, "I went to conduct in a stunned state, as if I were drunk."

The audience must have been surprised to see a mere boy step onto the podium, because the protest abated. "In the beginning," said Toscanini, "when I got up on the podium and saw the orchestra below me, it didn't disturb me at all. But when I saw the curtain go up and heard [the first words] 'Sì: corre voce'—well, singers aren't like an orchestra; you always hear them a little bit late, and that disturbed me. I was afraid that my arms couldn't go on. . . . My arms were used to playing the cello, not to conducting. But as soon as the chorus entered—'Ed osan tanto?'—I conducted. I really conducted. I didn't have the technique for conducting, but I conducted. I got used to it. As you can imagine, after the second act I don't know how many people rushed onto the stage—painters who wanted to do everyone's portrait, and whatnot."

The Rio newspapers reported the young man's triumph. "Afterward," said Toscanini, "I had to continue, otherwise they would have had to close the theater. . . . I conducted [twelve] operas, including a new one by a certain [Augusto] Machado [1845–1924], *Lauriana*, which I still remember. They didn't increase my pay; I still got 920 liras a month." If Toscanini's memory is correct on this point, he was earning four times more than he would have in a similar position in Italy; but he had to pay his own boat fare and his living expenses during the tour.

In those days, each of the principal performers had a *serata d'onore* in the course of a season, a performance at which he or she received valuable gifts and floral tributes. "They put on a *serata* for me without telling me anything," Toscanini recalled. "On the theater's portico there was a big poster with my name in large letters, and I stopped in my tracks when I saw it. I didn't want to conduct." His colleagues persuaded him to change his mind. "The opera was *Faust* . . . and that evening all the artists gave me presents. The emperor, Dom Pedro II, called me to his box. He and his daughter spoke Italian, and they gave me gifts that were later stolen from me. I went back to the hotel and put everything in a drawer, and someone stole everything, plundered everything. It's not that I was stupid, but I was still a schoolboy."

Toscanini told another friend that several members of the company succumbed to food poisoning during the tour, and that he therefore ate mainly a sort of broth, which he had found to be safe.

According to the same friend, Toscanini said that a beautiful young black woman had flirted with him in Rio, but that there was something about her that he had found frightening. The friend added that this must have been one of the few times in Toscanini's life that he did not take advantage of a beautiful woman's interest in him, regardless of her race, religion, or nationality.

The tour also determined the future of one of Toscanini's fellow Parmesans and former classmates. Ferruccio Cattelani, a violinist, had ranked second, immediately after Toscanini, in their graduating class and had been engaged as concertmaster of the Rossi Company's orchestra. In Rio, Toscanini accompanied him at the piano during two or three special appearances, and Cattelani's playing was so well liked that he decided to remain in South America. By the end of the century he had settled in Buenos Aires, where he became a major force in local musical life, as a player of chamber and solo music, composer, conductor, teacher, and founder of important musical organizations. He returned to Italy in 1927 and died in 1932.

The company's principal baritone, Paul Lhérie (originally Lévy), a Frenchman, had begun his career as a tenor; in 1875 he had sung the role of Don José at the world premiere of *Carmen*, and in 1884 Verdi had chosen him to be the first Rodrigo for the revised version of *Don Carlo*. "He was an artist!" says Toscanini on the tape. "I learned things from him that I tried to teach to other baritones, but he had such a talent! He was an even greater talent than [Victor] Maurel [Verdi's first Iago and Falstaff]. He didn't have as beautiful a voice as Maurel's, but I tell you! His Rigoletto made you cry. He used to tell me, 'Look, Toscanini, here I sing slowly, but you keep going and I'll follow you.' In fact, when he sang 'Vien Leonora' in *La Favorita*—it's an adagio in A minor—I pressed forward and he followed. In Thomas's *Hamlet*, which I later did with Maurel, the way Lhérie did the scene on the battlements was something! Unfortunately, on the words 'spettro santo, ombra vendicatrice,' where the cellos have D-C-C-B, he went up to an unwritten A, but in the duet with the queen—it made your blood run cold! . . . Maurel, too, sang *Hamlet* well, but Lhérie was more refined. . . . He sang [Meyerbeer's] *Les Huguenots* with me, and what grace he had! And he sang the role of Masaniello when I conducted [Gomes's] *Salvator Rosa*. 'Who was Masaniello?' he asked me. What did he, a Frenchman, know about

Masaniello?" laughed Toscanini. "So I explained about the fisher-
man who had led the revolution in Naples. I guarantee you, he was a
great artist. There was [in the company] a certain Callioni, who had a
beautiful voice but was an imbecile of a tenor. And [Lhérie] said, 'It
seems impossible that I, who have never had much of a voice, have
always had to think about placing the C here, the D there, the E in
another place, every time I sing, while this imbecile, who doesn't
understand a thing . . . !' " Lhérie retired in 1894, at the age of fifty,
and lived until 1937.

"Yes, I conducted many operas," said Toscanini, "but when I
got back to Genoa I started to play the cello again. I didn't feel
important enough to think of myself as a conductor yet." But the
Rossi company's principal tenor, Nicolai Figner (1857–1918), a Russian who later sang the role of Gherman in the world premiere
production of Tchaikovsky's *The Queen of Spades*, could not forget
Toscanini. "Figner had studied many operas with me," said the
conductor, "even Russian operas like *Onegin*." (*Onegin* was only seven
years old in 1886. Its Italian premiere did not take place until 1900,
under Toscanini's direction at La Scala.) "When I didn't show up
in Milan," which was the hub of Italian musical life, Figner "wrote
to me, 'What are you doing in Genoa?' I answered, 'I'm playing
the cello.'

" 'What are you doing, playing the cello? After what you've
done!' But what was I supposed to do—go around telling people I
was a conductor? I was nineteen years old and looked even younger
than my age. And who was I supposed to tell? But then he called me
to Milan, gave me the money I needed, and put me up at the Hotel
San Michele, which was an annex of the Hotel Leone, at the corner
of Via Durini and the Corso. He was staying [at the Leone], and he
put me up [at the San Michele]. He began to sing auditions, and I
accompanied him. His wife [the well-known, Florence-born Medea
Mej Figner, 1859–1952], who was a mezzo-soprano, had begun to
sing soprano roles. They had learned the love duet from *Marion
Delorme*—it's so beautiful—and I knew it by heart. They took me to
La Scala [for their audition]. Faccio was there, Ricordi was there,
D'Ormeville was there, and they heard me play." Franco Faccio was
La Scala's principal conductor; Giulio Ricordi was the most power-
ful publisher in the operatic world; Carlo D'Ormeville was an im-
presario, librettist, and critic.

"After that [Figner] introduced me to Giovannina Lucca [1814–94; another important publisher, who held the Italian rights to Wagner's operas]. She had a beautiful villa above Cernobbio, on Lake Como, and she invited us to lunch. There, Figner began to aggrandize my abilities, to talk about what I had done in America. . . . He had been given a contract to sing in *Edmea* [an opera by Alfredo Catalani, published by Lucca] in Turin, and he maintained that I could conduct it. I had been sitting, playing the piano—I knew *Lohengrin*, I knew *Tannhäuser*—and when he talked about having me conduct, she said, 'You know, this opera has been performed at La Scala and at Trento. Alessandro Pomè [another well-known conductor] and Faccio have conducted it. This maestro is a young maestro. What can one say to a nineteen-year-old boy, just because he has conducted in America? In America lots of things can happen!' But she added, 'I'll try, I'll do what I can, but I don't have high hopes.'

"But they hit on a trick. One morning, I was in bed, and Figner called my room to say, 'Come over immediately! They've sent me the score of *Edmea*. Let's start to study it.' I went. In fact, there, in a ground-floor room of the Hotel Leone, I started to play, and on and on I went. I used to sight-read very well, really very well, and I started to play, just like that. I got to the finale of the second act—it was a grandiose finale, along the lines of that of the third act of *La Gioconda*—and I was sweating. And someone came up to me, looking at me. It was the impresario from Turin [Giovanni Depanis]. When I had finished the second act he said, 'You must have known this opera already!'

" 'No,' I said, 'I didn't know it. It just came this morning, and I'm reading it for the first time.' Then he turned and motioned to another man to come forward. It was Catalani, and Catalani had been listening to me play." On the basis of this audition, Toscanini was engaged for Turin's Teatro Carignano, where he made his Italian debut with *Edmea* on November 4, 1886, not more than five weeks after his return from Brazil. "So I owe Figner my career," said Toscanini, "because if he hadn't called me to Milan I would have continued to play the cello. Maybe I would have become a conductor. I thought about becoming a conductor at twenty-seven or twenty-eight, but not at nineteen."

That, however, is the beginning of a different story; and if there is a sequel to *The Young Toscanini*, may it be done with greater intelligence, accuracy, taste, and liveliness than characterize Zeffirelli's pastiche.

While writing my biography of Toscanini in the 1970s, I had a chance to listen only once to the tape quoted in this article; only later was I given a copy of the tape, which I was able to transcribe and translate with care. This essay is a greatly enlarged version of an article written in 1988 for the *New York Times*, which did not publish it because Zeffirelli's film was not accepted at the time by a major movie distributor in the United States (possibly because *The Young Toscanini* had been a critical disaster at the 1988 Venice Film Festival). Different versions of the article were published in *Croma* (Parma), vol. 4, no. 9, November 1989; *La Stampa* (Turin), December 11, 1990 (when Zeffirelli's film was shown on Italian television); and the *Guardian* (London), December 21, 1990.

CHAPTER 3

"Worthiest Among the Worthy": Toscanini in Turin

IN 1902, the impresario and critic Gino Monaldi published *Memorie di un suggeritore* (A Prompter's Memoirs), a book that describes the rough-and-tumble working conditions within Italian opera ensembles during the last quarter of the nineteenth century. According to Monaldi, even the straightforward business of getting an orchestra to begin the first rehearsal of a season sometimes presented insurmountable difficulties:

> The conductor . . . gives the iron bar of his music stand a sharp rap with the baton [and says], "Gentlemen, take your places!" If the orchestra is a permanent one, and therefore organized and disciplined, this invitation is a mere formality. . . . But if it is an adventitious, newly formed one, with players who were engaged one by one, things don't go smoothly and rebellions are not infrequent. I can recall having been present at many scenes of this sort, including some nasty ones, usually quelled by the conductor's moral authority—if he has any. At other times, however, the question of seating rank is exacerbated to such a degree that it degenerates into violent altercations, and as a result police intervention is required. For it is impossible to imagine how exaggeratedly sharp the spur of self-esteem becomes in all these virtuosi who inhabit the theater.

Arturo Toscanini grew up within this system. Every year, in his native Parma as in other towns, the city council accepted bids from Milan-based impresarios and selected one of them to organize an opera season at the Teatro Regio. Every year, a different conductor came to town to prepare an orchestra that had been assembled for the occasion, and Toscanini played in the orchestra from the age of fourteen until he was nearly nineteen. Every year, singers arrived only a few days before the season opened. Every year, three or four operas were mounted in a hurry.

But if conditions in Parma left a great deal to be desired, the young Toscanini must have looked back on them with regret during his first years as a conductor at the theaters of such outposts as Voghera and Casale Monferrato, Macerata and Senigallia. At Voghera, a small Lombard town, the twenty-two-year-old Toscanini was engaged to take charge of a brief opera season in the fall of 1889. The contract, signed by the town council and an impresario, Vincenzo La Via, stipulated, among other things, that "the rehearser will also have to be the conductor." In the old Italian system, which was then fading away, productions were often prepared by a *maestro concertatore*, or rehearser, and were taken over at the last moment by a *direttore d'orchestra*, or conductor; the local authorities felt obliged to clarify that in this case the two jobs were to be carried out by the same person. The contract also enjoined the conductor to prepare the scores "exactly as they are written, excepting the customary changes and deletions, and the staging as indicated in the corresponding libretto." There were to be forty-six orchestra musicians (fifteen of them from out of town), "and these will have to play the parts assigned to them by the conductor at the first rehearsal." There would also be a stage band, a chorus of twenty-four male and eighteen female voices, and eight ballerinas, in addition to the members of the cast. With such forces, *Aida* and *La Favorita* were mounted and, according to newspaper reports, were wildly successful.

Conditions at theaters in medium-sized towns were not much better. Surviving documentation from an engagement in 1894 at Ravenna—where Toscanini conducted a season that consisted of only one opera, Jules Massenet's *Le Roi de Lahore*—provides an intimate glimpse into Italian musical and theatrical life toward the end of opera's most vital century. From the vantage point of people familiar with today's opera world, in which well-known performers have to be booked several years in advance, the most immediately striking details in the Ravenna material are its datelines. On March 21, 1894, the Ceruso Anguissola Theatrical Agency of Milan sent the Municipality of Ravenna a preliminary list of possible participants in a production that was scheduled to open only seven weeks later. There were five candidates for the soprano role, including the celebrated Eva Tetrazzini (elder sister of Luisa, who was soon to be even more celebrated); four for the mezzo-soprano role; five for the tenor role, including the much admired Michele Mariacher; four for the baritone role, including Toscanini's old friend, Paul Lhérie; five for the bass role; and three for the position of conductor, including the well-established Alessandro Pomè and Toscanini, whose first name appears on the proposal sheet as "Torquato." Not until April 20, however, did the municipality approve final arrangements— with a different agency, the De Comis Agency of Milan, and for the most part with performers whose names did not appear on the original list: the soprano Cesira Ferrani, who had been Puccini's first Manon Lescaut the previous year, and who was to be his first Mimì (under Toscanini's baton) in 1896 and the first Italian Mélisande (again under Toscanini) in 1908; the mezzo-soprano Maria Quaina; the tenor Franco Cardinali; the baritone Mario Sammarco, who would "create" the role of Gérard at the world premiere of Giordano's *Andrea Chénier* in 1896 and with whom Toscanini would later work on several occasions; and the bass Antonio Sabellico.

The contract* between the Municipality of Ravenna and the De Comis Agency stipulated that the performers were to be in town by April 28, only eight days after the document was signed, and that performances were to begin by May 10; in the event, they did not begin until the twelfth. Thus, within not more than fourteen days, Toscanini organized and trained the orchestra, which was made up of both local and imported players; taught roles to those singers who had not previously sung *Le Roi de Lahore*, as well as coaching all members of the cast separately and jointly; oversaw the chorus master's work and directed the staging, as there were no *régisseurs* in those days; and coordinated cast, orchestra, chorus, and stage action, including the ballet. In other words, he had to create the conditions under which the preparation of the production would be possible; having done that, he had to rehearse and assemble most of the production's components.

Even at prestigious houses in major cities, such as Milan's Teatro Dal Verme and Rome's Teatro Costanzi, Toscanini faced similar

---

* See Appendix II for a complete translation of the contract.

---

problems throughout the early years of his career: vocal ensembles and orchestras were brought together for brief seasons and then dispersed, rehearsal time was woefully inadequate, stage action was minimal, and painted backdrops were often made to look as anonymous as possible ("forest," "castle," "throne room") so that they could be used in several operas. In short, impresarios sought to maximize their earnings and minimize their expenses. Toscanini gradually developed a verbally and psychologically violent rehearsal method, to force companies to produce the best possible results under such discouraging circumstances. As Erich Leinsdorf correctly surmised:

> The anarchy of the Italian musical world explains the furious meticulousness of Toscanini, which must have come like a storm, like a shock. Toscanini went into the Italian theaters like a hurricane; people trembled, and he was able to create a semblance of order. Part of his reputation [for toughness] came from this hurricane approach, which was absolutely necessary under those conditions, and without which one couldn't put together a performance.[1]

In 1895, after nine years of itinerant music-making and of artistic and professional maturation, Toscanini assumed the direction of a major opera company. The opportunity was offered him by the city of Turin, which, then as now, was one of Italy's most important industrial, commercial, and cultural centers. And it was already a key location in Toscanini's career. He had made his Italian debut in 1886 at the city's second theater, the venerable Teatro Carignano, where, six years earlier, Eleanora Duse had made her debut as a prima donna. Toscanini had returned to the Carignano on other occasions and had also conducted at another Turin theater, the Vittorio Emanuele. In 1895, however, he reentered the city in triumph: at the age of twenty-eight, he became conductor of the principal opera house, the 155-year-old Teatro Regio.

The Regio's chief administrator was Giuseppe Depanis (1853–1942), son of Giovanni Depanis (1823–89), who had arranged Toscanini's debut at the Carignano nine years earlier. Giuseppe was a lawyer by training but an art, music, and literary critic by preference and a man of the theater by instinct. He had observed Toscanini's artistic growth from the start, and the two men shared several important goals: the strengthening of Wagnerism south of the Alps (Depanis had attended the first Bayreuth Festival and the *Parsifal* premiere and had known Wagner personally), the establishment of conditions under which a company made up of first-rate individuals could grow and improve from season to season, and the broadening of Italy's nonoperatic musical horizons. Like Wagner and Verdi, Depanis believed that unified opera productions could not be created without the overall control of gifted, determined conductors, and he had singled out the gifted and determined young Toscanini as the best person for the job of implementing a new system at the Regio. A theatrical agency and its impresario were still employed to furnish the principal performers, but the orchestra was directly financed by the municipal government. The players, selected under Toscanini's supervision, were to form the backbone not only of the opera company but also of a new musical institute and of a concert society born the following year.

Toscanini's first season at the Regio began with a project of enormous proportions: the first Italian production of *Die Götterdämmerung*. Months before the season opened, however, he and Depanis had persuaded the municipality to make improvements in the old theater. In a letter of August 2, 1895 (part of a cache of documents in Turin's Municipal Archives on which the rest of this essay is based), the mayor, Rignon, asked Toscanini for advice about some of the changes:

1. In your opinion, how many and what kind of registers should the new organ have for making the best effect, considering that the necessary expenditure must not exceed approximately 4,000 liras?
2. How would you like the orchestra's music stands to be positioned, so that we can provide for the proper diffusion of electric light? In this regard, and in view of the better effects that you were able to obtain elsewhere by grouping the four string sections in the middle, I would ask you to give me a seating *plan* for the whole orchestra, such as you wish it to be, reserving the right to improve upon the details when you come to Turin to adjudicate the competitors for positions at the Musical Institute.[2]

Toscanini's answer has not been preserved, but the minutes of Turin's City Council meeting of November 27 mention that the organ had cost 1,700 liras less than originally estimated, and that the funds left over had been used for creating an orchestra pit; the floor was lowered and the pit's walls were constructed "in thin wood":

> Maestro Toscanini, Arturo, having visited the work that is being completed on the Teatro Regio's resonating box [orchestra pit], declared that the work is being carried out impeccably, but commented that the job would remain incomplete, and in such a way as to impede good results, if the woolen rope supported by cast-iron columns were left, as in the past, as [the only] divider between the orchestra and the audience. In order that the sound not be dispersed before the sound waves have blended together, it is necessary that the orchestra be closed off, as if within an uncovered box. This could easily be achieved by constructing an internally hollow double railing, made of thin, narrow strips of lumber, to replace the current divider between the orchestra and the main-floor seats. In addition to completing the resonating box, this work, the cost of which has been estimated by the Public Works office at about 400 liras, would also help to keep the orchestra members from walking into the main-floor area and would furthermore prevent their being distracted every time a spectator walks along the front aisle.

The council approved the expenditure, and the Regio became one of the first Italian theaters to have a modern orchestra pit.

In October, Toscanini had sent the mayor a letter in which he approved the season's program as presented by the impresario, Luigi Piontelli,

> with the exception of the principal soprano Signora Annetta Vita, under contract to do the extremely important role of Brünnhilde in the *Götterdämmerung*. After having heard her recently in another theater, I am convinced that she does not have the vocal means for *the said part* or the artistic talent. I beg Your Lordship to make this objection of mine known to the Piontelli Agency as quickly as possible. A. Toscanini.

Vita was replaced by Gianna Paganini-Francescati.

The *Götterdämmerung* production opened on December 22, 1895, and was successful beyond anyone's hopes. In major Italian opera houses, productions ran as long as large numbers of people kept going to them; by the time the Regio's season was six weeks old,

Götterdämmerung had been given twenty-two times. (All operas were performed in Italian, so that the audience had a reasonable chance of understanding the words.) The season's other productions, all conducted by Toscanini, were Verdi's *Falstaff* (which was not quite three years old), the world premiere of Puccini's *La Bohème*,* a revival of Ferdinand Paër's *Le Maître de Chapelle*, and the house's first performances of operas by the now forgotten composers Natale Canti and Antonio Lozzi. At the end of the season, Toscanini conducted the first full-fledged symphony concert of his career; it consisted entirely of works barely known in Italy at the time: Schubert's "Great" C Major Symphony, Tchaikovsky's *Nutcracker* Suite, the Italian premiere of the "Tragic" Overture by Brahms, who was still alive, and the "Entrance of the Gods into Valhalla" from *Das Rheingold*.

A month later, Toscanini made his debut at La Scala in a series of four sold-out concerts that were highly praised by the critics. A letter that Depanis sent him demonstrates that on the strength of the first of those concerts—and of his reputation—Toscanini had immediately been invited by the Scala administration to assume the direction of Italy's greatest theater, and that he had asked advice of Depanis, who had gone to Milan to hear the second concert. Depanis was alarmed at the prospect of Toscanini's departure from Turin:

> May 8, '96
> Very dear friend,
>   Here I am, like Banquo's ghost, to remind you of your promise of a reply regarding the Regio business, about which I talked to you last Sunday. I won't repeat what I already told you, nor, for that matter, do I want to exert pressure on you in any way. Frankly, however, I think you would have everything to gain by a reconfirmation [at the Regio]:
> 1) for the moral effect deriving from it;
> 2) for the raise of 1,000 liras, which shows that you were in the right in your claims and which is justified by your merits;
> 3) as a pretext for [participation in] the Exposition [to be held in Turin] in '98, for which it is more likely than ever that your services will be

---

* Concerning the *Bohème* premiere, see H. Sachs, "Manon, Mimì, Artù," in *The Puccini Companion* (ed. S. Puccini and W. Weaver), New York: W. W. Norton, in press.

desired, and in regard to that eventuality we could, if you wish, even insert an appropriate clause into your contract;

4) for the orchestra, the equal of which you would be unlikely to find in Italy, especially in view of the planned [personnel] changes;

5) for the public, which knows, values, and loves you, despite—don't take offense—your irritability;

6) for the possibility, or even the probability, that Wagner's *Ring* cycle will be mounted (but let me make it clear that I cannot guarantee this);

7) for the concerts that we will find a way of organizing, and that won't stop you from conducting La Scala's.

I realize that you're aiming toward La Scala, and you're right to do so, and you have the abilities necessary for aspiring to it, since I can't think of anyone who could compete with you in that regard. But reflect, too, on the fact that another two or three years at the Regio—the Italian theater at which serious music is most likely to triumph and at which certain other kinds of music [*i.e.*, the so-called verismo operas, of which neither Depanis nor Toscanini approved] don't take root at all—will stand you in good stead at La Scala and certainly won't do you any harm. It's always good to let them, to make them want you, also because you will thus be able to lay down the law for the cliques that reign there.

In any case, think about it and decide, and above all answer me quickly. The City Council is awaiting your reply, which I had promised for yesterday. Don't delay it any longer, whatever it may be, since you yourself will understand the urgent necessity of resolving things. In your reply regarding reconfirmation, if it is favorable, add whether it is for one or two or three years. I wish and I hope that the reply will be favorable. And in this hope I heartily shake your hand. Goodbye for now, my dear friend, and believe me always

Your affectionate
Giuseppe Depanis

Five days later, Depanis wired Toscanini, "You promised reply last Thursday. I wrote Friday reminding you of promise. I beg you at least courtesy reply as decision required in this regard." Toscanini answered by telegram the next day, "If you agree pay eight thousand I accept contract. I believe easy for you find remedy beyond my request by adding to agreed-upon salary that of assistant who is of no use to me at all."

Depanis was shocked. Toscanini's salary the previous year had been 5,000 liras; although the young conductor had made it clear from the start that he considered that sum too low, Depanis deemed this great, sudden leap excessive:

May 15, 1896
Dear Toscanini,

I have just returned from the country and have found your telegram in reply to mine of Wednesday.

The Mayor is away from Turin. Thus I have not yet passed your telegram on, and I am writing to learn whether the request for *eight thousand* liras, that is, for a raise of *three thousand* liras in one fell swoop, is really definite and irrevocable.

Your telegram does not indicate the length of the contract or the dates of your arrival in town and of your departure [*i.e.*, how many weeks' work the contract would require of Toscanini]. In regard to which, if we're talking about a raise—and a substantial raise—I think it must be understood that the season, including concerts, with no respective additional pay, should last from the end of November through the whole of Lent, as is the case in Naples and Milan and as was decided upon for [the conductor Edoardo] Mascheroni in a similar case. I also bring to your attention the fact that it is within the Municipality's rights to give up making some of the improvements in the orchestra's personnel in order to have more funds available, but not to eliminate the assistant conductor; that is the Agency's business, and it may insist on keeping the thousand liras that have been set aside for the assistant. If I remember correctly, ever since last December, when the question of the six thousand liras came up, there was an attempt to make use of the assistant's one thousand liras to satisfy your desire. And the Agency formally opposed this, as it was fully within its rights to do.

I won't repeat again what I said about the Exposition year or about the other advantages that the Turin contract offers. I would be only too regretful if someone else were to take your place at the Regio (and I very much fear that that will happen if you insist on the eight thousand), and if, in the often fallacious hope of finding something better elsewhere, you were then to be left without either the better situation or the worse one. The *sure* theaters in Italy can be counted on one's fingers, and dealing [directly] with a Municipality [instead of through an agency] is not something to be overlooked. I am talking to you as an old friend who has some experience in this matter. And in the name of this friendship, I ask you to send me an answer so that I will have it not *later than Sunday*, in order that last week's uncomfortable situation won't repeat itself. Relying on your promise, I had undertaken to give the Mayor and the Council your decision—which didn't arrive. A couple of lines don't take so much time, especially now that the orchestra concerts [at La Scala] are done. [Not quite: another one took place on May 18.]

Looking forward to your reply, which you will send me in writing so that I can pass your final demands on to the Council (allow me to hope that the fee of eight thousand liras is not final), I heartily shake your hand.

Yours affectionately
[Giuseppe Depanis]

Toscanini did not answer. On May 22 Depanis sent him a telegram: "As I cannot understand your continuing silence please for my sake reply to the letter of Friday of last week. Depanis." And Toscanini answered by wire the same day: "I insist on my final demand of eight thousand. Season December first through Lent including concerts—Piontelli is offering me the same conditions [elsewhere] but is keeping the location a secret from me—This is reason my continuing silence. Greetings——Toscanini."

The next day, Depanis telegraphed Toscanini: "Council meets Tuesday—Please in name of Mayor suspend other negotiations until that day—I will telegraph immediately Tuesday morning [the results of the] Council's deliberation—Greetings Depanis." The same day, Toscanini replied that he would wait; but two days later, he again wired Depanis: "I made an error in calculating term of contract forgetting Easter falls April 18 [*i.e.*, somewhat late]. I would like reduce season December 10 [to] April 5. Greetings—Toscanini." This telegram bears a note in Depanis's hand: "I should think that we could take advantage of this telegram by proposing to Toscanini L. 7,500 from December 1 [*sic*; presumably means 10] to April 5, inclusive—otherwise insist that L.8,000 cover December 1 to April 18. Only, of course, if the Council wants to grant him the L.8,000."

Later that day, May 25, the mayor's chief secretary sent a note to Depanis: "In regard to Maestro Toscanini's noted telegram, the Mayor has given me the authority to tell you, Respected Sir, that the Council would allow 7,000 liras for the season, from December 10 to April 5, granting to Maestro Toscanini all the recompense that is his due as conductor of the concerts, which you magnified this morning to the value of eight hundred liras. . . ." This message is followed by the draft of Depanis's reply:

It's not a matter of magnifying recompense or of having given precise assurances. It's simply the case that, not having been able to obtain a reduction in the price, an attempt has been made to obtain one indirectly, by making the contract last longer. Thus the possibility that, if the concerts are held, the Concert Society will reimburse the Municipality one hundred liras per concert, in accordance with the plan, throughout the duration of Toscanini's contract:—and the other possibility that, if the Agency lengthens the season beyond one hundred days, that is, after March 19 (and Easter falls on April 18 in 1897), it, too, will have to pay the Municipality fifty liras per day, again in accordance with the plan.

A telegram must be sent to Toscanini this very day, Tuesday.

The Mayor or the Council must telegraph directly, as my job of carrying out the preliminary negotiations has been completed.

The telegram must have been sent, because the next day Toscanini wired Depanis: "I am enormously sorry I absolutely cannot accept—If my circumstances were other than what they are I would not hesitate a moment—Greetings—Toscanini." A draft of a reply, undated but clearly written the same day or the next one, from Depanis to Toscanini, says: "Business finished—Council agrees eight thousand liras coming winter season—Please at least [make] season length conform your first request December first through Lent—Greetings. Depanis." But Toscanini wired back: "Impossible change season length because fall [in] New York has been arranged I will arrive in Italy first ten days December then in April will be busy Scala concerts Greetings—Toscanini."

The minutes of the City Council meeting of that same day, May 27, summarize the negotiations and repeat that the conductor would accept no other conditions than to be present in Turin from December 10 to April 5, for a fee of 8,000 liras; and they add:

It should be mentioned that last year Maestro Toscanini did not want to sign the contract that gave him a salary of L.5,000. . . . Things being as they are, and since this is a conductor of exceptional worth, so much so that the highest authorities on the subject consider him to be absolutely the most important element in a production's success; and considering, too, that the deadline for canceling the orchestra's contract expired this past April 30, so that the Municipality already has obligations for the coming season toward the [orchestra's] various members; [. . . and as] it is held that an attempt to find another conductor under the present conditions would lead to an expense that would certainly not be lower than L.8,000, while lacking the element of security provided in the person of Maestro Toscanini, who has presided over the creation of the orchestra, the Council has decided to grant [Toscanini] the sum of L.8,000 for the aforementioned season, by taking . . . L.2,000 from Category 53, sundry expenses, of the budget for 1896, and L.1,000 pledged from the money to be taken in at the popular concerts.

For Depanis, it was a bitter victory. "Sorry I didn't have better luck with you," he wired Toscanini the same day. "I repeat business concluded eight thousand December tenth April fifth—Mayor will send contract Greetings—Please tell me how long you'll be in Milan Depanis." But Toscanini telegraphed, the next day, "I assure you that for Turin I gave up contract America five months thirty thousand liras very happy however to have settled things. I leave tomorrow—don't send me contracts Friday—send them to Trento. Greetings—Foscarini [*sic*]."

What to make of all this? Depanis was universally recognized as an upright man, and one can hardly blame him for defending his organization's interests. But 5,000 liras, approximately $1,000 at the time, although by no means a starvation wage, was indeed a ridiculously low fee for three-and-a-half months' work by one of the most sought-after conductors in Italy. Moderately well known singers earned more than twice as much in one month at major Italian theaters, but the municipality did not have to concern itself with singers' fees, which were negotiated and paid by the impresario. (Orchestra members, however, earned only 300 to 1,000 liras per season; their salaries were determined according to professional reputation and seniority, the instruments they played, and the amount of time they would be required to spend in the orchestra in the course of a season.) It is easy to believe that Toscanini had no use for an assistant conductor, since he probably had never had such a luxury before. Not until his accession to La Scala, with its crushing workload, did he learn to let assistants do some of the preliminary work for him; and to the end of his active life he often preferred to coach singers himself, from the keyboard, while his assistants stood by. Nor is there any reason to doubt that he had been offered 30,000 liras ($6,000) for five months' work in the United States. His name was already known there, and when he did eventually go to New York for the first time in 1908, as coprincipal conductor (with Gustav Mahler) of the Metropolitan Opera, he was paid 150,000 liras ($30,000) for six months' work. Why did he not accept the American offer—whatever it was—in 1896?* In Turin he had his own opera company to run; he was interested in participating in the special musical events that were to take place during the 1898 exposition and, presumably, in conducting a complete *Ring* cycle— although, in the end, the *Ring* was not mounted during his stay in the city; and he was courting eighteen-year-old Carla De Martini, with whom he had fallen in love during rehearsals for the *Götterdämmerung* production, in which her sister, Ida, had sung the role of Woglinde. The couple married in June 1897.

No sooner had Toscanini's 1896–97 contract been settled than Depanis got after him to deal with personnel changes in the orchestra. The administrator's first letter on the subject was probably written at the beginning of June (the autograph draft bears no date):

Dear Toscanini,

I, too, am happy to have you in Turin again for the coming winter season. And I hope that you will win new, splendid laurels, doing honor to yourself, in the first place, and then to the Municipality, which has spared no expense to have a first-rate conductor and orchestra.

The former we have: now we have to think about the latter. And that is why I am writing to you, with reference to the conversation we had early last month.

---

* I have found no further information regarding either this American engagement or the projected New York engagement for the fall of 1896. Neither materialized.

First and foremost, it must be understood that the Municipality set aside a total of L.48,000 last year, and that with the additional 3,000 for your salary this year the budget will be raised to L.51,000. By no means can we now consider additional increases, nor, at least for now, [the engaging] of a second harp and a third bassoon—on the contrary, the new contracts must bring with them new savings rather than increases in expenses. So much for the preliminaries. For the first violins we already have: Polo,* Guarnieri, Fanchiotti, Gallè, Massini, Romagnoli, Deleide, Porro, Percivati (who has finished the course at the Liceo [Musicale] and is becoming a full-time member at L.400— and he's worth it, because he's a good violinist). Three are needed to complete the *twelve* required. We'll negotiate with Villa to be one of them, Genesini to be another, but no longer at L.1,000 if he doesn't play the ballets [which followed the operas but were not conducted by the principal conductor], and for the third Superti [presumably Carlo Superti; see Chapter 2], or if not, who instead of him? Answer me about this. Besides the 12 permanent ones, we'll have one or two good students. . . .

Depanis continues his detailed, section-by-section analysis, and adds:

In order to provide immediately for these changes, you'll have to have the patience of a saint, give a shake to your proverbial epistolary laziness, and answer me by return of post. . . . With these planned changes, you'll have a first-rate orchestra, much better than last year's. And we'll keep trying, funds permitting, to improve it, little by little, for the Exposition. The main thing is to go step by step.

---

* Enrico Polo (Parma, 1868–Milan, 1953) had been a classmate and friend of Toscanini's at the Parma Conservatory and had later studied in Germany with Joseph Joachim. He was engaged as Toscanini's concertmaster in Turin in 1895 and remained at the Regio until 1903, when he became principal violin teacher at the Milan Conservatory, a position he held until his retirement. He was one of Brahms's first important Italian supporters, and he communicated his enthusiasm to Toscanini. Polo was a well-known chamber music player and did some conducting, too, even with soloists of the caliber of Ferruccio Busoni and Wanda Landowska. His pupils included several future concertmasters of the Scala orchestra and another influential Italian violin pedagogue, Michelangelo Abbado, father of the conductor Claudio.

Toscanini's "proverbial epistolary laziness," combined with his workload (he was conducting a short season in Trento and preparing for another in Brescia), caused him not to reply to this request or to three subsequent reminders from Depanis. Only on June 29, after the mayor had sent Toscanini a telegram in which he threatened not to make any changes in the orchestra, did the conductor put pen to paper:

My very dear Depanis,

You have been too good in not sending me a bunch of insults. They would have been like so much manna to me. You have to understand that I'm one of those brats for whom a few smacks on the head have a greater effect than any serious sort of admonition. Good God! If you knew how much I suffer as a result of this exaggerated laziness and how ashamed I am of myself, you wouldn't upset yourself but would, rather, double the dose of pity you've shown toward me so far. Enough, be as good as always, yet again—shake my hand affectionately and forget this most recent childish prank, since you mustn't interpret it any other way. And now we come to our orchestra. The first violin section will be fine when it's completed by Genesini (who, if he accepts at a lower salary will surely not want to play the ballets), Villa, and Superti. If the last doesn't accept, we could engage Prof. Minelli [*N.B.*: all professional Italian orchestra musicians are called *professori*], a most excellent first violin. The second violin section, too, seems to me complete and good. Remember to reprimand soundly *Bertazzi*, who *got drunk every Saturday*, and *Sesia*, who was late to rehearsals and deserted several performances with the aim of *carrying on behind his wife's back*.

I'm afraid that Sabbia won't accept—and I would be very sorry, because besides being an excellent player he is a dear and distinguished young man. In any case, let me know and we'll replace him as best we can. For the violas, once you've signed up De Marzi we'll be all right.

As to the cellos, I've asked Serato* in Bologna to recommend some of his distinguished pupils who could replace Melluzzi and Forzano, and in a few days I'll send you the names of these new members. In sending the contract to Guarnieri, warn him that I absolutely won't

---

* Francesco Serato (1843–1919), a well-known cellist and teacher, father of the violinist Arrigo Serato.

accept him in the orchestra except with a different instrument, because the one he had last year was impossible. Instead of *Morini* I'd like to propose *Agesilao Villani*, who is far superior to the other and who will accept the same terms. His address is simply [the town of] Correggio. The others are fine.

I hope that the question of Beniamino [flute] will be resolved to our advantage, that is, by excluding him altogether and replacing him with a competent young man who is now at *Saint Moritz*: Abelardo Albisi. Instead of making Nizza [piccolo] change instruments, I would have him change brains—but as the operation would be painful and might not work, I advise you to change the whole person by replacing him with Prof. *Gennaro Giuliani*, who is also currently under contract at Saint Moritz.

And now for pity's sake, let's not ruin the excellent quartet of horns that we would have by engaging, besides Fontana as first, Caletti, Naglia, and Pasetti. Moressi may be all that you say, a good man, good player, good-looking, and virtuous—but he has an impossible sound. He doesn't fit in, doesn't blend with the other three [horns], and what's more, he plays out of tune. If a fifth horn should be engaged, however, *Moressi* would be my preference, because he's better than Forzano and Savino. But remember for pity's sake not to touch the quartet of horns that I had last year.

Filippa, the third trombone, I can manage to swallow again if, before renewing his contract, you give him a good punch in the head and tell him that I wasn't at all happy with him either as a player or as a person—but I absolutely don't want that fourth trombone. He may be wonderful for the band and for Maestro Vaninetti [the bandmaster], but he's worthless in the orchestra—in fact he ruins things—because he has no sound, he can't hold a note for four quarter-beats without running out of breath, and furthermore he blithely plays out of tune and is always cold.

As to the first clarinet and bass clarinet, I want to hear them—because I remember the first's exam, which *wasn't very satisfactory*—therefore his nomination didn't convince me, and furthermore, I wouldn't want to make the same mistake as last year by trusting Maestro Vaninetti's assurances.

With that, I've finished the chat about the orchestra. I'll tell you now that I probably won't go to America—so it will be easy to arrange the concert business.

Write to me soon. I'm leaving for Milan tomorrow, and you can address letters to me at the usual address—Via della Maddalena, 5.

I promise to reply by return of post and not to disquiet you any more. A strong, hearty handshake from your

Affectionate A. Toscanini

Four days later, Toscanini sent a letter to the mayor of Turin:

With great sorrow, I find that I have to tell Your Lordship that Professors *Nizza*—piccolo—*Praj*—bass clarinet—*Forzano, Savino, Moressi*—horns—*Campanella*—fourth trombone—did not live up to the hopes that we had for them last season, 1895–96, or fulfill the duties of the positions they occupy. Consequently, I must make use of the option granted me by Article 59 of the Personnel Regulations and ask that they be removed for the coming season. I repeat that I am extremely sorry about this request, which is not inspired by any personal feelings whatsoever, but rather by the duty and by the responsibility that I have assumed toward the Municipality that has honored me by nominating me Conductor of the Municipal Orchestra.

With special deference I declare myself to be Your Honor's

Most devoted A. Toscanini.

P.S. To the above-named players I must add Forzano—Cello.

A request from the mayor's office asked Toscanini to reconsider Campanella. On July 8, Toscanini wrote a long letter, similar in tone to the one to Depanis, to Count Ignazio Torazzo, who was also involved in running the orchestra. After going into further detail about the new players to be engaged, Toscanini says:

I've saved the best for last!—About Campanella I again repeat what I said in my last letter. He is impossible. If he didn't make as horrible a mess in the *Götterdämmerung* as in the other operas, it was because he *preferred to remain silent* or *to read newspapers* instead of playing, and in the end I let it pass so as not to let it distract me from what I was doing, and I had pity on him—this year I don't intend to hear the same refrain—but since *the necessity of replacing him does not seem clear* (that was literally the phrase used) to the Municipality, I'll be careful not to touch a sensitive spot by insisting on the replacement of this most precious player. He'll have to play [only] in the stage band, however. Allow me to tell you that although I don't find the phrase quoted above either nice or flattering to me, it seemed well turned, novel in its genre, and it amused me.

For that matter, I had been asked which changes were necessary in order to improve the municipal orchestra and I did my duty by indicating them. Now let the others do as they please.

Other letters followed, and by August 3 Toscanini seemed satisfied with the orchestra's makeup. "And now, dear Torazzo," he wrote,

I must tell you confidentially but in all honesty that I am happy, extremely happy, to have made these changes, which were necessary, and I am very grateful to Depanis, to you, and to all those who have taken my complaints to heart, complaints that are justified by the goal toward which they aim—that is, to bring the Turin orchestra to a level of perfection such as has perhaps never been achieved in Italy.

But trouble was brewing. "From several players [from Turin] who are engaged to play with me in Genoa this fall . . . I have learned that the orchestra will be *called to Turin as of December 1 for concerts,*" continued Toscanini. "*How is it possible that I know nothing about this?*"

The answer to Toscanini's question has not survived, but it undoubtedly informed him that the composer, conductor, and pianist Giuseppe Martucci had been engaged to conduct the first two concerts of the forthcoming season. This caused Toscanini to send an unreasonable protest to Depanis on August 16:

My dear Depanis, So the business of the concerts has been resolved as I expected, which is far from the way I had wished. I cannot refrain from expressing to you my deep displeasure at having received such a slap, just like that, with no reason and without having deserved it in any way. But there is no use now in my getting bogged down in boring complaints—I only want to point out to you that even for an ingenuous person like me, the premeditated plan to keep me from conducting the concerts is clear and obvious. Look here: at the end of June I let you know, albeit by chance, that the American business might not materialize. This piece of news ought to have been well received by you and the Concert Society— the more so inasmuch as the negotiations with Maestro Martucci cannot and must not have been very far advanced at the time if everything has been settled only during the last few days. But it had the opposite effect. I knew nothing more about it because you didn't mention the subject again, although you must have been involved in it, and I believed that the idea of giving concerts had not materialized.

It was not until about three weeks ago that I heard from some players engaged for Turin that you were assembling the orchestra on November 30. I asked why—I was told that it was for concerts, for which negotiations were still pending with Maestro Martucci, who could not or would not accept before getting out of some engagements in Vienna.

So: for Martucci it was possible, or rather was considered desirable to wait *two months* in the hope of arranging things; for Toscanini, who was engaged by the Municipality of Turin, who took part in creating the municipal orchestra, who ought to have a certain right to insist that his orchestra not be conducted by others—and who had no other engagements—it was not possible, or rather it was not considered desirable to wait. It is true that I didn't answer your second letter [which has not survived], which was sent to me in Trento and in which you asked my opinion of the idea of engaging Maestro Martucci, but allow me to tell you—that between June 30 and the day before yesterday, when you made final arrangements with Martucci, there was time enough to organize things in such a way as to reach a very different solution today.

This is not to put the blame on you—I honor and appreciate you too much for that. But someone's hand has guided this affair toward its present outcome—I don't know whose, or rather I prefer not to guess. I repeat, I am much embittered by this slap, but not surprised. I decline to participate in any way in the Lenten concerts—which will make many people happy. Beyond that I won't go, because it's not my habit to play nasty tricks or to go to excessive lengths.

I have found the cellist we needed—he asked me for 7.50 per day but will accept 7. He's in Udine for the festival season—he's called Goffredo Vancini.

I greet you heartily and shake your hand.

Yours affectionately A. Toscanini
Brescia, Albergo Italia

Depanis replied on August 18:

Dear Toscanini,

I am replying to your letter of the sixteenth, and in replying let me say, to avoid any further equivocation, that there has been a guiding hand in this whole affair regarding the concerts, and it is mine, and I assume the whole and entire responsibility. I do not, therefore, deserve the praise that you direct at me personally, separating it from the condemnation inflicted upon the Administration of the Concert Society, and I don't deserve them because I was the one who proposed the name of Martucci, and I was also the one who settled the business with Martucci a few days ago. I like to keep things above board, and that is why it is important to me to clarify who, if anyone, is responsible.

I thought I'd succeeded in convincing you that neither you nor Martucci is at fault in regard to this whole mess, and that it's purely a sort of mishap if an idea that grew out of the intention to cause you as little annoyance and as little bother as possible has instead taken a tumble and done the opposite. It didn't work, and I'm sorry.

You cannot deny, however, that during your contractual negotiations with the Municipality I always pressed for the starting date of December 1 for the concerts (and the negotiations lasted a month and more, that is, from April to the end of May); that I reluctantly accepted the starting date of December 10, and that I hastened to write and tell you about my embarrassment, and that the only alternative was to turn to Martucci, in order not to turn to others. You didn't answer me for nearly a month, despite requests and incitements. It was already summer, and it was necessary to look after the business before vacation time. At that point, after having waited *two months*, and not a few days, as you state, and having waited with the hope of settling things with you; faced, on the one hand, with your categoric telegram that left not a shadow of a doubt about your engagement in New York and, on the other, with your silence, which was implicitly a confirmation of your consent, the Concert Society asked Martucci if he could come to Turin in December to conduct his [First] Symphony. Martucci replied, accepting in principle, if he could arrange the dates to work out with some of his previous engagements. We gave him until the end of July, because, among other things, we were not able to commit ourselves formally until we knew whether the orchestra would be available by November 30. In the midst of this came your letter of June 29, in which you mentioned the probability that you would no longer be going to America. Afterward, you didn't write anything more to me, nor did I write anything more to you, both because I was absorbed with negotiations for the replacements within the orchestra and because I was awaiting confirmation from you, which never came. At the end of July, however, I did not hesitate to ask for a definite reply from Martucci, and as soon as it arrived . . . I wrote you a friendly letter, even letting you know Martucci's plans! Would you have wanted me to let Martucci know, after your letter of June 29, that we no longer knew what to do with him, that we had turned to him for want of anything better, and that we considered ourselves free of any obligation toward him? . . .

The result of this is that you think there's been a trick. Well, I'm telling you that you're off the track, absolutely off the track. The person who will be most surprised by the choice of Martucci is precisely the man to whom you allude in your letter [the mayor?], who has been out of town for over a month, has had no communication with me, and is unaware of everything. You see how blind we sometimes are, and how we blind others in turn!

You talk about moral slaps, about going to excessive lengths and playing nasty tricks. I'll pass over this last expression, preferring to assume that it escaped from your pen when you weren't looking. Let anyone judge as to whether your engagement by the Municipality with a raise of three thousand liras is a moral slap or, rather, a splendid demonstration of trust. And let anyone judge as to whether the sacrifices made by everyone in order to satisfy you in regard to the orchestra's personnel are further moral slaps or, rather, the confirmation of boundless trust in you. But I absolutely deny that turning to Martucci under the circumstances . . . signifies a premeditated slap or jab from the Concert Society.

. . . You can rest assured that in the future I won't be so simpleminded as to create headaches for myself merely in order to be regarded with suspicion by the person I meant to serve. No, believe me, I'll grant you that I may be an ass; but disloyal or a mafioso—no, no, and again no.

As to the rest of your letter, allow me not to pay any attention to it. It's better for you and for me. I am writing and replying privately to a private letter.

. . . I'm leaving for Sierre (Valais) in Switzerland, Villa Baur, the day after tomorrow, and I'll stay there until early September. I need some peace and quiet.

And with that, I greet you.

Your

Giuseppe Depanis

P.S. Your displeasure over the fact that others conduct your orchestra is just and legitimate, and no one can understand it better than I because no one observed you at work more than I did, and I know all the love you put into it. But your resentment is not as just [end of letter missing].

The same day, Depanis wrote to Torazzo to summarize the contents of his letter to Toscanini. "Worse things have happened. And this, too, shall pass," he concluded. He was right: the storm blew over. The problem had arisen in the first place only because Toscanini was ingenuous, as he said in his letter; and, like many other ingenuous people, he tended to overcompensate by suspecting double-dealing even when there was no cause.

Martucci, a pioneer in broadening Italy's musical horizons in the last two decades of the nineteenth century and the first decade of the twentieth, was in any case one of the musicians Toscanini most loved and honored; he continued to conduct his music all over the world almost until the end of his life—by which time that music had been nearly forgotten even in Italy, let alone abroad. Shortly after this incident, Toscanini was invited to conduct Puccini's *Le Villi* and *La Bohème* at Bologna's prestigious Teatro Comunale in November and early December—right up to the beginning of the Turin season—and from Bologna he wrote anxiously to Polo in Turin, to find out whether Martucci was satisfied with the orchestra. All was forgiven. The long-suffering Depanis remained Toscanini's best friend, counselor, and supporter throughout the conductor's Turin years.

The Municipal Archives' few remaining documents that concern Toscanini are mostly about orchestra personnel and similar problems. He conducted concerts in Turin in the fall of 1896 (after Martucci's), the spring and fall of 1897, and the spring of 1898; and between May 8 and October 31, 1898, he conducted forty-three repertorially groundbreaking concerts during the Exposition. During the last two of his three seasons at the Regio, he conducted the Turin premiere (and second Italian production) of *Tristan*, the second

Turin production of *Die Walküre*, the Turin premiere of *Andrea Chénier*, the world premieres of two operas by now-forgotten Italian composers, new productions of Saint-Saëns's *Samson et Dalila*, Boito's *Mefistofele*, Mancinelli's *Ero e Leandro*, and Bellini's *Norma*, and remountings of *Mefistofele* and *La Bohème*. The Turin audiences continued to "know, value, and love" Toscanini, as Depanis had said, and so did the critics. "Worthiest among the worthy" is the phrase one journalist used to describe him, and it summarizes the consensus of opinion.

In the fall of 1898, La Scala again beckoned to Toscanini, and this time he responded positively. He returned to Turin to conduct the 1905–06 opera season, during a rift with La Scala, and to conduct concerts on many other occasions until 1930, with local and visiting orchestras. But from 1898 on, Toscanini's base was Milan. "Other cities envied our having Toscanini," wrote Depanis years later, "and Milan was able to attract him into La Scala's orbit. It was predestined that that happen: La Scala was worthy of Toscanini and Toscanini was worthy of La Scala. But it was a grave loss for Turin."[3]

My thanks to Anna Levi Bassan and Alberto Basso for bringing Turin's archival material to my attention. Short excerpts from this material were included in the Italian edition of my biography of Toscanini, which was published three years after the Anglo-American editions, and in the January 1982 issue of *Ovation* (New York). The rest of this chapter is new.

CHAPTER 4

Background to the Rebirth of La Scala

I have given up my position at that theater because my artistic aspirations and ideals did not find the realization that I had dreamed of achieving when I entered it in 1908. Routine is the ideal and the foundation of that theater. That may be of use *for the artisan, not for the artist.** "Renew yourself or die." Voilà tout.[1]

T HUS Arturo Toscanini explained his departure from the Metropolitan Opera Company in 1915, after seven productive seasons in New York. He may well have remembered this statement five or six years later, when he was in the midst of renewing not only himself but also one of the world's great opera ensembles, the Teatro alla Scala in Milan. Throughout the following decade, he would come as close as any great conductor has ever come to realizing his "artistic aspirations and ideals" in an opera house.

Milan's musical revolution began on July 14, 1920, the day on which La Scala's board of governors nominated Toscanini plenipotentiary director of the theater. He was fifty-three years old and had been a professional conductor for thirty-four years. No doubt he hoped to have another fifteen or twenty good working years ahead of him; in the event, his career lasted another thirty-four. Although he had conducted approximately 200 symphony concerts by 1920, most of his work had taken place in the opera house, where his labors had comprised some 350 productions of 106 operas by fifty composers. He had conducted the world premiere of fourteen operas,

---

* The italicized words are in English in the original Italian letter.

the South American premiere of eleven, the Italian premiere of ten, the North American premiere of eight, and the French premiere of one. These efforts had been carried out during seventy-two series of productions in forty-six theaters, in thirty-seven cities, in eight countries, on three continents. The number of opera performances he had conducted by 1920 has not yet been ascertained, but 3,000 is a conservative estimate.

In short, he was not lacking in experience. The concepts on which he based the new Ente Autonomo del Teatro alla Scala (Independent Administrative Body of the Scala Theater) grew out of decades of experiences within other production systems. The system he set out to create at La Scala in 1920 was based on a mixture of the highest artistic ideals and a comprehensive, thoroughly realistic understanding of the available resources. By December 26, 1921, when the Ente Autonomo opened its first season with a production of Verdi's *Falstaff*, Toscanini had selected and rehearsed a new orchestra and taken it on a seven-month tour of Italy and North America; he had seen to the renovation of La Scala's technical facilities; and he had chosen a staff of highly competent administrators, musical and production assistants, and set and costume designers. Working closely with the mayor, Emilio Caldara, a Socialist, and the Liberal senator, Luigi Albertini, editor in chief of the *Corriere della Sera*, Milan's (and Italy's) most influential newspaper, he had developed a system of financing for the theater that brought together the best aspects of subsidization, subscription, and sponsorship.

Prior to the Ente Autonomo, the most advanced production system within which Toscanini had worked was the one instituted at La Scala when he assumed its directorship for the first time, in 1898. The impresarios formerly employed to organize the house's seasons were replaced by a general manager directly responsible to the board of governors, which consisted of prominent citizens; and Toscanini was given the contractual right to choose the operas to be performed and the singers, orchestra members, and set designers with whom to realize the productions; to determine the number of rehearsals; and to set the opening date of each opera when he believed that the production was ready. At thirty-one, he had become, in effect, the first artistic director in La Scala's 120-year history. But if La Scala had greater resources at its disposal than did other Italian companies (by the turn of the century, Milan had become Italy's commercial and industrial capital), the attitudes and habits of the house's employees were essentially those of their counterparts elsewhere in the country. Tullio Serafin, who was assistant principal viola in the Scala orchestra from 1898 to 1901 and assistant conductor to Toscanini for the following two seasons, has described the general situation at the time and Toscanini's way of dealing with it:

Toscanini's methods were truly harsh, and they provoked endless mutterings and protests (whispered, of course) among my colleagues [in the orchestra]. But it didn't take me long to realize that he was right. In those years, orchestral discipline, even at La Scala, was very lax. There were quite a few fine players, but they didn't make an effort. They took no trouble to be accurate in playing rhythmic figurations, and they almost entirely ignored dynamic markings; thus, as far as interpretation was concerned, the results were often left to chance. Only rarely did the orchestra mobilize itself to obtain what Wagner, in his essay on the art of conducting, indicates as the most difficult thing of all: a long, sustained sound of even intensity.

Against this whole conglomeration of defects, made up of laxity, laziness, inattentiveness, and false tradition, Toscanini fought like a lion. He was after one thing only: respect for art. But in his anxiety to get it, or rather to force it to happen, he exercised no self-control: he shouted, imprecated, even insulted. He could have taught [the players], instead, and he could have obtained severe, indispensable discipline through his wisdom alone (he was so tenaciously studious!); and he did that, too, I must say. But his impatience made him go too far. Having said this, I must add that the effects he produced, to the advantage of musical interpretation, and the good he did for the art of performing, were of such dimensions that even the excessive aspects of his character can be understood. Not justified, but understood.

. . . It must be admitted, however, that a special pride, a point of honor, a sort of "esprit de corps" existed among La Scala's personnel from that time on. Even the least important stagehand or the most humble supernumerary felt responsible for the success of the production.[2]

Toscanini did not have an easy time during his first period at La Scala, from 1898 to 1903. He broke with the company after five embattled seasons, each of them strewn with triumphs and defeats; and he spent the following three years conducting at other major

Italian theaters and at the Teatro de la Opera in Buenos Aires. These houses' administrative structures were backward in comparison with La Scala's, but Toscanini's presence had become so desirable that he was able to lay down the law wherever he went, regardless of the prevailing system. He returned to La Scala in 1906, this time much heralded and coddled even by former opponents, many of whom had decided that, whatever their differences of opinion with Toscanini, his artistic stature was greater than that of any of his colleagues.

In 1908 he left La Scala for the Metropolitan Opera, where he had at his disposal an outstanding orchestra and chorus and one of the finest companies of singers in operatic history. There as elsewhere, however, he was dissatisfied with the organizational structure, which, at the Met, was based on the patronage of the financier Otto Kahn and other wealthy New Yorkers. It is now known that the main reasons for Toscanini's departure from the Met in 1915 were personal and patriotic: he had just made a difficult break with the soprano Geraldine Farrar, with whom he had been having an affair, and he wanted to remain in Italy, to do what he could for the war effort against Germany and the Austro-Hungarian Empire. But his dissatisfaction with conditions at the Met was real, as the letter quoted at the beginning of this chapter indicates.

By the time he left the Met, Toscanini was one of the most respected conductors in the world. The extent of his fame, not only as a musician but also as a man of the theater, is reflected in *Meister des Taktstocks* (Masters of the Baton), a groundbreaking history of conducting, by the German musicologist Carl Krebs; it was published in 1919, a full decade before Toscanini's first appearances in the German-speaking world:

Arturo Toscanini occupies first place among Italian conductors. Or rather, he is alone, in a class by himself, and one of the most important conductors of all, anywhere. He is a phenomenon reminiscent of Gustav Mahler. His memory is much fabled, as unshakable as Hans von Bülow's. . . . He is tireless, pitiless, at rehearsals. . . . At performances, if the most painstaking accuracy in every detail has been achieved, Toscanini is like a painter who has the richest array of color gradations at his disposal, like an actor burning with passion, like a sculptor whose imagination for forms brings everything under his control. He exerts his influence on the staging, too, and on the set designers' work. A German composer who saw one of his works performed under Toscanini at La Scala in Milan burst into tears from the emotion caused by the visual and aural perfection of the performance. German music is entirely suited to Toscanini, and he has become its most zealous champion in Italy.[3]

D URING World War I, Toscanini conducted only benefit performances, few of which took place at La Scala; but the house's fate never ceased to interest him. In 1916, he learned that La Scala was about to take a giant step backward, organizationally speaking, and he wrote a characteristically frank letter on the subject to Duke Uberto Visconti di Modrone, president of La Scala's board of governors. It is the most substantial document that has come to light in which Toscanini set forth his thoughts on what the lyric theater should and should not be, and it exposes several of the problems that would later be resolved by the constitution of the Ente Autonomo:

To the Most Illustrious Duke UBERTO VISCONTI DI MODRONE. SENA-TOR OF THE KINGDOM.

La Scala's official program for the coming season, which is known to have been prepared by the Impresario of the Teatro Colón of Buenos Aires, Mr. Walter Mocchi, and approved by you, Duke, has now been made public, and I am rising up to protest against you for violating a noble tradition of high moral significance, well established for years at La Scala, rooted in the conscience of the public and of the entire citizenry. The obviously secretive arrival on the scene of Mr. Walter Mocchi—the most singular exponent of theatrical speculation—* to

---

* Here is a translation of part of the entry on Walter Mocchi (Turin, 1870–Rio de Janeiro, 1955) in the *Dizionario enciclopedico universale della musica e dei musicisti* (Turin, 1988):

"Having left the Turin Military School, he moved to Naples to work as a journalist and, after having taken part in the popular uprisings of 1898, he was banished to the island of Procida. As an editor of [the Socialist Party's newspaper] *Avanti!* he founded and edited, with [Socialist leader Arturo] Labriola, *Avanguardia socialista*, dedicating himself tempestuously and enthusiastically to political activities, which he soon gave up to become an impresario. He was the husband of the singer Emma Carelli [1877–1928]. In 1907 he founded the Italo-Argentinian Theater Society (STIA) in order to unite, under a single administration, the Colón and other theaters in Argentina and in other South American countries; similarly, he founded in Italy the International and National Theater Society (STIN), which

share with you the responsibility for La Scala's artistic decency, constitutes that violation; and this is happening precisely in the theater that eighteen years ago [when Toscanini became its principal conductor, in 1898] was rescued, with noble intentions and aspirations, from the hands of the speculators, by your father Duke Guido Visconti di Modrone (whom I still honor and remember with reverent affection) together with distinguished citizens worthy of him. You could not have been more poorly advised, if you were advised at all in this rash act.

The joining of the two theaters—Scala and Colón—which, as the orchestra's contracts demonstrate, has [already] taken place, can only be the result of selfish interests, all to the disadvantage of the Milanese institution. The two theaters diverge in their ideals, and diverge in their means of achieving them.†

You are thus initiating and establishing new criteria contrary to the spirit of the concession that was given you by the Municipality and the Boxholders [who helped to guarantee La Scala's solvency], and therefore contrary to the raison d'être of the Municipal subsidy and the box rental fees; contrary to the meaning of the civic subscription and to the demands of public-spirited service; contrary to your immediate prede-

---

controlled—in addition to Rome's Teatro Costanzi, which he had bought—the San Carlo of Naples, the Massimo of Palermo, the Regio of Parma, and other important theaters, and which was artistically and commercially connected to the STIA. As a result of differences that arose within the two societies, he transformed the STIN into the 'Teatral' and assumed its direction, which he ceded to Carelli in 1912 (by which time it had been transformed into the 'Teatro Costanzi Agency'). Through this society's contacts with its South American counterpart, opera seasons and exchanges of artists continued through the [First World] war. After the war, South American opera houses continued to be dominated by Italian artists, along with whom, however, [Mocchi] succeeded in inserting singers and musicians from other European countries."

The entry fails to mention that in 1926, when Mocchi realized which way the political wind was blowing, he joined the Italian Fascist party, with which he ingratiated himself in a variety of ways. In 1937 he denounced Titta Ruffo to the Political Police, on the grounds that the celebrated baritone had made anti-Fascist statements in his presence; this information led to Ruffo's brief imprisonment and to the government's refusal to let him leave the country as long as the regime endured. During World War II, Mocchi used his journalistic experience to write Fascist propaganda, in which he even thanked the regime for its "guardianship of the Race and struggle against Judaism."[4]

---

† Toscanini knew the Colón well, having been its principal conductor in 1912.

cessors and to the tradition begun and scrupulously maintained by your father, who was admired and applauded by all; and they are criteria that offend all those who have given and who continue to give the best of themselves to Art, who have suffered, struggled, trembled for it, for the attainment of a high ideal, and who cherish in their hearts the living flame of a religious love for all those institutions which, like La Scala, are the pride not only of the city, but of the Nation. And if legal chicanery and subtleties elude the various bodies that unite to subsidize La Scala and that have the right to raise objections to Mr. Mocchi's meddling, moral reasons, which also have power and meaning in cases like these, must absolutely take precedence. The Municipality, boxholders, and subscribers are wrong in not contesting the matter. Supine acquiescence is an outrage against the law.

Eighteen years ago the wisdom of entrusting the direction of La Scala to Lawyer DI GIORGI of Palermo was argued to death, because he had at times managed that city's theaters. Then, instead of him, Engineer Giulio Gatti Casazza, who was untainted by original sin, was nominated. Ten years later there were again arguments over Mr. Temistocle Pozzali, a theater impresario, who gave an unfortunate interview, published, I believe, in the *Corriere della Sera*, which led to the choice of Maestro Vittorio Mingardi.* Mr. Walter Mocchi's arrival at La Scala is, therefore, a violation of this tradition, and it has sullied the steadfast purity of your management. It may also have prepared the way for a movie house–like trash heap of performances put together in a hurry, as [happened] last season at the Teatro Colón in Buenos Aires. He has done nothing whatsoever that would give him right of access [to La Scala's administration]. This impresario had the

---

* Toscanini's point in these last three sentences is that the management of La Scala had been kept absolutely clean during the previous eighteen years. In 1898, the mere fact that an otherwise qualified candidate had previously functioned from time to time as an impresario in Palermo, at the other end of the country, had been sufficient to prevent his nomination at La Scala and to bring about the nomination of the twenty-nine-year-old Gatti Casazza, who was a modern administrator rather than an old-fashioned impresario. (Toscanini calls him "Engineer" because Gatti Casazza had a degree in naval engineering; *Ingegnere* is a title in the same vein as Doctor or Professor.) And in 1908, when Gatti Casazza had left La Scala to go to the Metropolitan with Toscanini, the candidate most likely to replace him had disqualified himself merely by giving a newspaper interview that cast doubts on his professional reputation.

impudence to write to me that *he is creating, by agreement with you, Duke, a new technical mechanism for operating the theater and that it ought to yield above-average artistic results, in his opinion.* I have already replied to him personally: "No, Mr. Walter Mocchi, you cannot create anything, but only destroy everything—you cannot reform anything, but only deform everything—your career as a theatrical impresario demonstrates this. What happened yesterday will happen again tomorrow. You began with little honor at the [Teatro] Adriano in Rome—nor did you find greater glory later at [Milan's] Teatro Dal Verme—do you remember? And so you continued, moving from one theater to another, from one scandal to another, speculating one day on a singer's fame, the next on a composer, without ever doing anything that was artistically beautiful.

"You opened the Teatro Colón in Buenos Aires [in 1908], where you dominated everyone and everything—but as a result of the indecent productions and of the subsequent clamorous public protests you were shown the door and replaced after one year. With your impertinent chatter *'in the name of Art and in order to realize reforms never before conceived by anyone* (sic)' you enticed and secured [the cooperation of] many ingenuous people; you set up societies that made affiliates of Italy's most important theaters, with the goal of dominating the theatrical market and putting the brakes on the singers' growing [economic] demands, and creating at the same time your famous *'technical mechanism,'* with the deplorable results of which everyone is aware. The societies vanished, the theatrical market worsened, the singers' demands reached incredible levels as a result of the competition you had created, the technical mechanism either was not hit upon or worked poorly, there was no glory and even less money."

This is how I answered him, Duke, and this is the list of artistic merits that, in your opinion, make him worthy of the right to enter La Scala. And in the meantime we are sadly witnessing some very strange couplings: Duke Visconti di Modrone and Walter Mocchi—La Scala and the Colón of Buenos Aires—in other words, Patronage and Speculation. Illegal couplings—not long-lasting, I hope. Because if one were to lose hope that the present state of things is transitory, it would be better for La Scala to return once and for all to the impresarios, to the speculators. We would not hear, now and forever, the critics' alluring blandishments, nor would we have to witness with disgust the public's passive acquiescence—which are the chief causes of the artistic debasement that has already taken place and of the moral one that has now begun. All would awaken from the lethargic torpor into which they have sunk [as a result of] their obsequiousness toward patronage and, as used to happen in the old days, [the audience's] chairs would be sent flying onto the stage, and the conductor would be removed or thrown down from his podium.*

I have finished—I have protested and I know that I have done so in vain. I have done it, however, to carry out a compelling but sad duty.

Sincerely yours Arturo Toscanini

"Patronage and Speculation": five years later, when Toscanini was entrusted with the reorganization of La Scala, these were the two principal dangers he sought to circumvent. He succeeded, in part because, at a theater as large and as costly to run as La Scala, and under the altered economic and social conditions that dominated postwar Italy, neither noblemen-patrons nor impresario-speculators could continue to assume the financial risks alone; but his success was mainly the result of his ability to find alternative solutions—thanks to what the head of La Scala's technical staff later described as Toscanini's "extremely well-balanced and harmonious intellect."[5]

The exactitude of that description is borne out by a letter written by Giacomo Puccini to the *Corriere della Sera* at the beginning of the Ente Autonomo's second season. "I visit all the world's theaters," said the composer, "and I see and study what is done elsewhere: this seems to me the moment to say that what is being done at La Scala today is not being done at any other theater. Toscanini has achieved here not only the work of an organizer, he has created an institution that is the pride of Italian art."[6]

---

* Toscanini is describing a type of behavior that was not uncommon in Italy in the heyday of the impresario system: when audiences felt that the level of the production they had paid to see fell significantly short of their expectations, they often reacted violently. People in the gallery would heave benches over the railing and down onto the stage, and the police would be called in to clear the theater and to save impresarios and performers from being physically assaulted. In my biography of Toscanini, I described his indirect involvement in one such event, in Bergamo in 1897.

*

This is a much-expanded version of a talk, "Toscanini e l'idea dell'Ente Autonomo del Teatro alla Scala," given during one of a series of seminars held in Parma in October 1987 under the auspices of the Orchestra Sinfonica dell'Emilia-Romagna, and printed, in part, in the orchestra's magazine, *Croma*, vol. 3, no. 5, February 1988 ("Toscanini e l'idea dell'Ente Autonomo del Teatro alla Scala"). A typewritten copy of Toscanini's letter to Duke Uberto Visconti di Modrone was in the possession of Elena Cesari Silva (1896–1988), widow of the musicologist Gaetano Cesari (1870–1934); she generously gave me a photocopy of it in 1983.

CHAPTER 5

Toscanini and Mussolini

T HE maturation of Toscanini's opposition to fascism is one of the most noteworthy episodes in the history of the relationship between art and politics in our century. The political views that Toscanini had acquired in his youth were straightforward and unsophisticated. His father, an irresponsible tailor with a strong sense of adventure, had left home in his mid-twenties to join Giuseppe Garibaldi's irregular army and to help Italy's struggle for independence and reunification. Claudio Toscanini had participated in the successful northern Italian and Sicilian campaigns of 1859–60 and in the disastrous battles of Aspromonte (1862), Condino (1866), and Bezzecca (1866). The remaining forty years of his life were given over to insignificant antiroyalist and anticlerical political activities, unsteady application of his trade, scatterbrained business ventures, drink, vagabonding, and, above all, the recounting of his youthful exploits.[1] Arturo Toscanini did not inherit his father's interest in alcohol or moneymaking schemes, and he was the opposite of Claudio in his ability to concentrate on his work. What he did absorb from his father was an intense dislike of the Church and the monarchy, strong nationalistic sentiments, and the unshakable belief that the Trent and Trieste regions, which were still in Austrian hands, rightfully belonged to Italy.

At the outset of World War I, this belief led Toscanini to favor Italian intervention against the German-speaking powers. Criticism of his enthusiasm is legitimate, but he at least had the courage of his convictions: although he was forty-eight when Italy entered the war, and had been a conductor for twenty-nine years—including periods as director of La Scala and the Metropolitan Opera, he immediately gave up all his regular engagements, conducted only benefit performances for the duration of the conflict, and contributed to funds for musicians who had been reduced to penury by wartime unemployment. He eventually had to sell his home to provide for his family. In 1917, Toscanini formed a military band and took it to the front, where he conducted it during the victorious assault on Monte Santo and at the disastrous rout at Caporetto. He was decorated for bravery under fire.[2]

The government's inability to deal with postwar turmoil persuaded Toscanini that drastic changes were needed in the country's political structure. Early in 1919, he attended a political meeting held in Milan by Benito Mussolini, who was then advocating a Bolshevik-like platform that included universal suffrage, international disarmament, and the end of compulsory military service; the formation of national and international constituent assemblies; the abolition of the monarchy, all titles of nobility, and the upper house of parliament; the election of judges; the dissolution of limited liability companies; the elimination of banks and the stock exchange; the limitation of private capital and the confiscation of unproductive capital; land for the peasants and union participation in the management of industry, transport, and public services; an 80 percent tax on war profits; death duties; and the confiscation of unused private and ecclesiastical property. Never a man for compromise solutions, Toscanini was positively impressed by this program, and his impression was strengthened by the admiration expressed for Mussolini by many of the conductor's intellectual acquaintances, including the Futurist writer and propagandist Filippo Tommaso Marinetti. When, at the last moment, Mussolini decided to put forward a list of candidates in Milan for the parliamentary elections of November 1919, Toscanini's name appeared on the slate. Marinetti had persuaded him that, although there was no chance of victory, the fledgling movement needed a name as famous as Toscanini's to gain credibility. The new *fasci di combattimento* (combat groups) received fewer than 5,000 votes, in contrast to 170,000 for the Milanese socialists. Not even Mussolini was elected; his political career was considered finished, but he had merely lost his taste for elections. Toscanini's unwanted political career was indeed over, at least officially. He did, however, pay the then considerable sum of 30,000 liras that he, like the other candidates, had pledged in order to cover the party's expenses. [3]

Toscanini made his next political gesture a year later, when he took his newly formed Milanese orchestra (soon to become the orchestra of the reorganized La Scala) to perform in Fiume (Rijeka), contested between Italy and Yugoslavia; the city had been occupied by Gabriele D'Annunzio's troops. Even the horrors of the world war had left Toscanini's nationalism intact, and he appears to have been pleased by the display of military exercises, including battle cries, that the poet's men put on for the orchestra. D'Annunzio decorated Toscanini and his musicians and made a revoltingly fulsome speech in honor of the "Symphoniac" and his "Orphic Legion."[4]

By then, Mussolini and his adherents had veered sharply to the right and had adopted violence as a means of obtaining power. On the eve of the so-called march on Rome (October 1922), Toscanini told a friend of his disgust, "If I were capable of killing a man," he said, "I would kill Mussolini."[5]

The new prime minister, however, wished to be considered a cultivated man; and La Scala, for economic reasons, needed to remain in the government's good graces. When Mussolini visited Milan in April 1923, he had himself photographed with the entire company, including Toscanini. The previous December, however, during a performance of *Falstaff*, the conductor had had his first skirmish with supporters of the new regime. As he entered the pit to start the last act, a group of Fascists began shouting at him to conduct the party hymn, "Giovinezza." Toscanini signaled the orchestra to go on with the opera, but the disrupters would not be silent. He broke his baton and left the pit, shouting and cursing. After a long wait, a member of the administrative staff announced that the anthem would be played at the end of the performance; Toscanini then returned to the pit. Maria Labia, who was singing the role of Alice Ford, recalled:

When the opera ended, the manager told us, "Stay where you are, everybody, and sing the hymn with piano accompaniment." Toscanini intervened, "They're not going to sing a damned thing; the Scala artists aren't vaudeville singers. Go to your dressing rooms, all of you." And we went. The hymn was played by the piano [alone] because the orchestra, according to Toscanini, did not know it.[6]

Still more upsetting to Toscanini, however, was Giuseppe Gallignani's suicide in December 1923, after he had been abruptly fired from the directorship of the Milan Conservatory, perhaps for lack of enthusiasm for the regime.7 A few months later, the conductor declared that he would leave La Scala if the Fascists carried out their threat to take control of the theater's board of directors. In a letter of June 6, 1924, Senator Mangiagalli, the mayor of Milan, warned Mussolini of this possibility and its potential consequences:

> As I was so invited, I shall engage Your Excellency on the Scala question, which may seem small but is not so, and which could seriously damage the structure of the Municipal Administration. Allow me, first of all, to set forth a premise. La Scala now has worldwide prestige and fame, thanks to Toscanini. Astronomic distances separate him from other conductors. He may have his faults, but he also has great moral virtues. His disinterestedness is total, as a result of which he has hurt himself by remaining at La Scala to ensure its primacy. He has turned down fabulous offers [from abroad], and he would not accept the check for 100,000 liras [about $20,000, a considerable amount of money in those days] that we offered him as a bonus payment. La Scala is his passion; it is the temple of art, and he does not want it profaned by selfish interests or party passions. . . . The Fascist party wishes to have three Fascist municipal representatives [on the Scala board]; but besides disrupting the harmony among the various political groups, this would give Toscanini the impression of a political act. He won't hear of it. Can we allow Toscanini to leave and La Scala to lose its prestige? I cannot agree with the Fascist party in its [attitude of] not caring a rap. . . .8

Toscanini had his way. He might have been temporarily reconciled with the regime, but that very month the Fascist-perpetrated murder of the Socialist party's secretary, Giacomo Matteotti, enraged him. Late in 1924, when rumors that he was to be offered a senatorship were circulating, his wife confidentially asked the journalist Ugo Ojetti to help forestall such an offer. At one time, she said, her husband would have been proud of such an honor, but now he would certainly reject it, "and who knows what words he would use?" Ojetti made sure that the offer was never made.9

Toscanini's friendship with the Liberal Senator Luigi Albertini, whom the Fascists had ousted from the editorship of the *Corriere della Sera*, helped greatly to develop his awareness of the dangers of fascism. In April 1925, he turned down the senator's request that he sign Benedetto Croce's anti-Fascist manifesto; later that year, however, when the government ordered that pictures of Mussolini and the king appear in every public building, including theaters, Toscanini countermanded the order at La Scala, Italy's most important theater. As long as he remained there, the pictures were not displayed. Mussolini also decreed in 1925 that on April 21, a national holiday honoring the Birth of Rome, all places of public entertainment were to play "Giovinezza" before beginning their performances. Toscanini circumvented the command by scheduling a rehearsal, rather than a performance, for that evening. He received word from government authorities that he was not to reuse the trick the following year. A few months later, Toscanini met Mussolini—for the last time, it seems, and at the latter's command—at the Milan prefecture. It was probably this meeting that Toscanini later described as a long harangue on the Duce's part. The conductor, who was kept standing, stared at a spot on the wall over Mussolini's head, restraining his notorious temper but refusing to reply to the accusations of bad behavior and the threats of dire consequences for La Scala. The official press release stated blandly: "HIS EXCELLENCY MUSSOLINI, the Prime Minister, had a conversation with Maestro ARTURO TOSCANINI and took a lively interest in La Scala's activities and in the important concert tour the Maestro will soon begin in New York."[10]

Ignoring government orders and Mussolini's threats, Toscanini kept the theater dark on April 21, 1926. Mussolini, who arrived in Milan a day or two later for an official visit, sent for La Scala's administrators and declared that if they could not control Toscanini, they ought to replace him; otherwise, they would never again see the Head of Government in their theatre. He wished, he said, to attend the world premiere of Puccini's *Turandot*, which was scheduled for the 25th; "Giovinezza," he insisted, must be played when he entered the house.

But Toscanini *was* La Scala in the 1920s. For members of the administrative staff, which existed above all to carry out his orders, it was an unprecedented and unenviable task to convey an order to Toscanini, who was at least as irascible and, in his own field, as important as Mussolini. In the end, they simply told him what the prime minister had said. Toscanini retorted that he didn't mind having "Giovinezza" played if they would get someone else to conduct it—and *Turandot*. In 1926, Toscanini was more essential than Mussolini to La Scala's well-being: *Turandot* was performed with the Maestro and without the Duce. The next day's *Corriere della Sera*, which had been pruned of its openly anti-Fascist writers, reported:

> During the intermission, the audience awaited Mussolini's previously announced arrival. But the prime minister did not wish to attend, and explained the reason behind his sensitive gesture: he did not want his presence in any way to distract the public, whose attention had to be entirely devoted to Puccini and his last work. Mussolini will attend a later performance of *Turandot*.

Some days later, Toscanini, who was close to nervous exhaustion at the end of a particularly demanding season, had to cancel his remaining performances and go to the seaside for a rest. The Fascist press used the occasion to circulate rumors that he had left La Scala forever because he had objected to the new law instituting a national corporation of opera house managers. In effect, the Fascists were giving La Scala a chance to dump Toscanini, and Toscanini a chance to withdraw without hurting his pride.[11]

Toscanini stayed at La Scala, but the rift between the conductor and the Italian government was real and growing, and word of it became international news. The managers of the New York Philharmonic, with which Toscanini had made a phenomenally successful debut as guest conductor a few months earlier, were delighted. They hoped to wrest him away from La Scala and make him their principal conductor. Although their wish was eventually fulfilled, the process proved slower than they had hoped. Not until the summer of 1928 did he decide to leave La Scala, effective the following spring.

His last Milan season was, in many respects, the most memorable of all, especially the triumphal tour to Vienna and Berlin, with which it ended. Public and critics in Austria and Germany reacted with stupefied admiration. Mussolini, who closely followed reports on all things Italian in the foreign press, must have been thoroughly pleased to read such national pride-inducing statements as the following:

. . . Let us hope that the German artists who attended this performance [*Falstaff*, in Berlin] have learned something; in any case, the Italian opera company has given us a delightful but dangerous measuring stick for judging German art. . . . [Alfred Einstein, *Berliner Tagblatt*]
. . . La Scala's performances moved and shook the public . . . [It was] a success without precedent in the modern history of opera in Germany. . . . [Karl Holl, *Frankfurter Zeitung*]
. . . In Berlin, the excitement rose to such a fever pitch that it actually made us fear for German art, for the prestige of German musical culture. . . . [H. R. Gall, *Bayerischer Courier*][12]

Consummate propagandist that he was, Mussolini knew how to turn such material to account. On returning to Milan, Toscanini received a pompous telegram from the Duce: "La Scala's performances made known not only the great historic virtues of an artistic organization but also the new spirit of Contemporary Italy, which unites to its will to power the necessary harmonious discipline required in every field of human activity." Toscanini understood Mussolini's implication: like it or not, by contributing to the glory of La Scala he was also contributing to the glory of the new fascist society. He replied that "today, as yesterday and as always, I am serving and shall serve my Art with humility but with intense love, certain that in so doing I am serving and honoring my Country."[13] He must have thought, as he wrote that sentence, that he performed such a service wherever he was working, whether within or outside of Italy. But he could not have imagined that seventeen years were to pass before he would next perform with an Italian organization.

TOSCANINI'S departure from the Italian musical scene was not entirely voluntary, nor was it wholly politically induced. He was sixty-two years old in 1929 and had decided to concentrate on the concert repertoire, which was less taxing, physically, than the multifaceted business of rehearsing and performing opera. The growing strength of the Italian musicians' and theater workers' unions disturbed him, too—not because of their economic demands, which he considered just, but because of their desire to have more say in the running of the organization, which he believed would lead to chaos. In addition, the New York Philharmonic was at the time one of the greatest orchestras in the world, and Toscanini was being offered a salary unprecedented in his field (over $100,000, net, for fifteen weeks' work) to make it into *the* greatest. He still intended, however, to conduct in Italy when the artistic circumstances were right, and when he would not have to put up with fascist interference.

When he took the Philharmonic on its first European tour in the spring of 1930, the itinerary included four Italian cities: Milan, Turin, Rome, and Florence. The presence of Crown Prince Umberto at the Turin concert made the playing of the Royal March obligatory; Toscanini might have been willing to conduct it if regulations had not required that it be followed by "Giovinezza." Under the circumstances, he refused. A compromise was eventually reached: after the orchestra was seated and tuned, a military band came out to play the hymns. In Rome, the queen and other members of the royal family wished to attend a performance; and a possibly more serious incident was averted only when they wisely announced that their presence would be unofficial. No anthems were played.

This episode no doubt encouraged Toscanini to believe that he could continue to use the weight of his fame in order to go about his business as if the Fascists did not exist. The regime, however, was increasingly displeased with his behavior, and the chief of Mussolini's political police began to amass reports from paid informers throughout Europe. The first important notice referred to his 1930 visit to Berlin with the New York Philharmonic:

> . . . having been asked repeatedly to attend a reception that was being organized in his honor at the headquarters of the local [Italian] Fascist party organization, the Maestro always replied that he could not participate because he was tired. When pressed, and when asked whether he would authorize the sending of a telegram in his name to the Duce, in which he would state that he did not agree to the function only *because he was tired,* he replied sharply that *he was not attending because he was an anti-Fascist, because he held Mussolini to be a tyrant and oppressor of Italy, and that rather than break with these convictions, he was prepared never to return again to Italy.*[14]

A copy of this report was handed to Mussolini, who underlined the phrases here reproduced in italics and brought the information to the attention of Foreign Minister Dino Grandi. Toscanini had become someone to be watched; but he did not fully recognize the danger implicit in his position until the following year, when he found himself at the center of an incident that caused greater international embarrassment to Mussolini's government than any event since the Matteotti affair.

Toscanini had accepted an invitation to conduct two concerts (May 14 and 16, 1931) at Bologna's Teatro Comunale, with the house orchestra, to mark the seventy-fifth birthday of the composer and conductor Giuseppe Martucci (1856–1909), whom he had greatly admired. The programs were to consist entirely of Martucci's music, and Toscanini refused payment for the engagement. By chance, a Fascist party festival was also taking place in Bologna that week. On the day of the first performance, Toscanini was told by the Deputy Mayor, Giuseppe Lipparini, that the Minister of Communications, Costanzo Ciano, and the Undersecretary of the Interior, Leandro Arpinati, would be in the theater, and that he would therefore have to begin the concert with the royal march and "Giovinezza."[15] As Toscanini later described the episode:

This happened a few minutes after the last rehearsal, at which I had warmly exhorted the members of the orchestra to take their places only two minutes before the performance, with a maximum of concentration, conscious of the reverent and loving demonstration that they had been called to participate in—in order that no sounds other than Martucci's music should make contact with the public. I concluded, "Gentlemen, be democrats in life but aristocrats in art." I could not, therefore, accommodate Professor Lipparini's request—as unexpected as it was out of place—and allow the concert suddenly to take on a gala or political character, since no preliminary sign or newspaper advertisement had announced this. Instead, I very gladly accepted the conciliatory proposal later formulated by the prefect of Bologna together with the deputy mayor, which they communicated to me at five in the afternoon. The proposal was set forth in these terms: when the ministers entered the theater, a band would play the national anthems in the lobby of the Comunale. But at eight o'clock, the situation changed. The conciliatory formula did not satisfy the ministers, and we were back at the earlier order; and I remained more steadfast than ever in my conviction about maintaining the commemorative character of the evening. At nine-thirty [the scheduled starting time], Mr. Brianzi of the municipal administration telephoned me [to say] that I could go to the theater, advising me that Their Excellencies would refrain from attending the concert. And I fell right into the ambush.[16]

With Toscanini as he arrived late at the Comunale were his wife, Carla, their younger daughter, Wanda, and a family friend, the lawyer Enrico Muggiani. (The conductor's son, Walter, had been assigned to accompany Martucci's widow to the concert. He had arrived in a different car and had entered by the main door.) On getting out of his car, Toscanini found himself surrounded by Fascist youths. One of them—Leo Longanesi, a young journalist who later invented the mindless and widely used phrase, "Mussolini is always right," and who, still later, achieved celebrity as author, editor, caricaturist, and publisher—asked him whether he would play "Giovinezza."

"No."

Longanesi hit Toscanini in the face and neck and shouted insults that were echoed by others in the crowd.* Toscanini's wife, chauffeur, and friend managed to rescue him from the onslaught and to get him back into the car. When the harm had already been done, some *carabinieri* (national police), who had been standing by in their plumed ceremonial hats, came over and told the chauffeur to get going. The Toscaninis were sped back to their hotel.[18]

Rumors of the attack quickly circulated in the packed theater, where the public was already impatient as a result of the long delay. A functionary finally announced that the concert was being postponed because the Maestro was indisposed. Many members of the public began to shout, "It's not true! It's not true!" Armed black-

---

* Public revelation that Longanesi was the perpetrator of what became famous in Italy as the "Bologna slaps" came only in 1984, with the publication of his biography by Indro Montanelli and Marcello Staglieno. Longanesi was not well enough known in 1931 to have been recognized by Toscanini or by many others present, and the secret was kept in the Longanesi family for half a century. (It was, however, suspected by several journalists, and this suspicion was known to Mussolini's police informers.) The authors report that the Toscaninis were being put up at one of Bologna's best hotels at the city's expense, but fail to mention that the conductor had refused a fee or that his participation had drawn sellout crowds to concerts where ticket prices had been raised for the occasion, for the Comunale's benefit. This and other aspects of the incident, as well as the general political situation in Bologna at the time, are discussed at length in Luciano Bergonzini, *Lo schiaffo a Toscanini. Fascismo e cultura a Bologna all'inizio degli anni Trenta* (Bologna: Il Mulino, 1991).[17]

---

shirted guards, apparently panic-stricken, shut the exits but were then ordered to reopen them. The public surged into the streets, and one orchestra musician said there was so much commotion in the center of Bologna that a revolution seemed to have broken out.[19]

Respighi and his wife were in the audience that evening; they had heard of the "Giovinezza" dispute in the afternoon and realized that something untoward must have happened. "Respighi was beside himself," wrote his wife in a letter to Walter Toscanini many years later, ". . . and said it was a disgusting and shameful thing for Italy. I took Respighi and Mary Molinari [wife of the conductor Bernardino Molinari] with me, and we left by the stage [door]. . . ."[20] They drove to Toscanini's hotel, where the conductor was nursing cuts on his face and neck. He had no serious injuries, but Elsa Respighi later described his mood as that of a caged beast.[21] Two hundred Fascists were soon parading from party headquarters to the hotel, where they gathered beneath Toscanini's windows and shouted insults and obscenities; there was some fear that they might begin hurling objects as well. Mario Ghinelli, the local party secretary, asked to speak with a member of the Toscanini group. The conductor and his son were ruled out as negotiators because of their quick tempers; Carla Toscanini went instead, but the Fascists refused to deal with a woman. Respighi then volunteered to represent the family. He was told that the Toscaninis were to leave the city before sunrise; their safety could not otherwise be guaranteed. Elsa Respighi and Mary Molinari helped them to pack their bags as quickly as possible, and the Toscaninis departed at 1:20 A.M., arriving in Milan by sunrise.[22]

Arpinati phoned Mussolini immediately after the attack, and Gaetano Cesari, who was in town to report on the concerts for the *Corriere della Sera*, bribed a telephone operator to report what had been said. The operator told him that Mussolini had responded to the news with these words: "I am really happy. It will teach a good lesson to these boorish musicians." Mussolini ordered the Milan prefecture to take away the Toscaninis' passports and to place their house under surveillance.[23]

The following day, Toscanini sent a telegram to Rome:

To His Excellency Benito Mussolini,
Last evening, while going with my family to Bologna's Teatro Comunale to carry out a kind act of friendship and love in memory of Giuseppe

Martucci (having been invited there by the mayor of the city for a religious and artistic commemoration, not for a gala evening), I was attacked, injured, and repeatedly struck in the face by a contemptible gang. The undersecretary of the interior was present in Bologna. Not fully satisfied with this, the gang, its ranks swollen, stood threateningly under the windows of the Hotel Brun, where I was staying, uttering every sort of insult and threat against me. Not only that: one of its leaders enjoined me, through Maestro Respighi, to leave the city by six A.M., not being able to guarantee my safety otherwise. I am communicating this to Your Excellency so that, despite the silence of the press or false information, Your Excellency will be able to have precise news of the deed, and so that the deed be remembered.

Salutations

Arturo Toscanini[24]

Although Mussolini never replied to Toscanini's message, he did, according to the composer Vincenzo Tommasini, tell a mutual acquaintance, "He conducts an orchestra of one hundred people; I have to conduct one of forty million, and they are not all *virtuosi*."[25]

The Italian press, which was completely under Fascist control, either refrained from mentioning the incident or threw the blame for it entirely upon Toscanini. Longanesi—without, of course, mentioning his part in the affair—wrote an article for the official newspaper (appropriately named *Assalto*, assault) of the Bologna Fascist Federation; it was reprinted in several papers throughout the country:

Thursday evening, we were the protagonists of a confirmation of Bolognese Fascism that was not only political but also aesthetic.

In all the theaters of Italy, Maestro Toscanini had for some time been playing the part of the pure aesthete who soars above politics and is contemptuous of the miserable laws of governments or, rather, of his government. In the name of musical purity, of a decadent aestheticism conceived by people who had picked up the crumbs of Wagnerism, our concert performer had decided not to play the royal march at the beginning of performances attended by a member of the government or the royal family. [*N.B.*: Longanesi was equivocating; he well knew that Toscanini had not refused to perform the royal march but, rather, to follow it with "Giovinezza," as the regime required.]

"I don't want to infect the air, the atmosphere of the hall, with profane music, with political anthems," he said; "I don't want to disrupt the religiousness attendant upon the elevation of a piece of music." [*N.B.*: This was, of course, an invented "quotation."]

Defending himself with such a foolish aesthetic rule, fit for Anglo-Saxon old maids, our holy man proclaimed his sublimity before every performance, as well as his abstention, if thus we may call it, from the simple duties that no citizen refuses to carry out.

Bellini, Verdi, and Rossini, artists of much greater imagination than our concert performer, would have laughed at such pained and sublime religiousness. . . .

But our Maestro . . . had already instinctively discovered—sly and astute man that he is—that the canons of musical religiousness proved to be of assistance in building up his fame: the more his bizarre ideas took shape and were reechoed, the more the public's admiration and awe grew. It is an old trick of *fin-de-siècle* Nietzscheans, an old type of rhetoric that defines genius by its anomalies, a pose in use fifty years ago, at the time of the development of medical theories about the characteristics of genius, when it was commonly believed that artists were high-strung, that they vibrated like telegraph wires, and that they had one sole god: Art; one sole law: Art; one sole discipline: Art. . . .

True to this aesthetic, our Toscanini got himself up in an ascetic face for the ladies in the first tier of boxes, invented half-light [*sic*], interrupted performances because somebody had dropped a penny, and swore before Art not to play the royal march. Musical Italy didn't say a word; it remained openmouthed and gawking before the new orchestra chieftain. Toscanini adopted Wilde's motto, "A king may bow before an artist's brush," raised his baton as if it were Wotan's sword, and proclaimed his musical republic. With the business about "I won't pollute the religious atmosphere with the royal march," he even managed to create a political stand for himself; from holy mystic he turned into holy warrior, a Saint Expeditus of symphony concerts, in frock coat and patent leather shoes.

But in Wagnerian and Rossinian Bologna [*N.B.*: Rossini was connected with the Bologna Conservatory from 1837 to '48; Wagner's *Flying Dutchman*, *Tannhäuser*, *Lohengrin*, *Tristan*, and *Parsifal* all received their first Italian performances in the city], the illustrious lay-apostle found an audience that believed in a stronger religion than his: that of the state. The Bolognese Fascists asked Maestro Toscanini—mystic or not, but thus far an Italian citizen, thanks to his birth and civil status—to respect what every other citizen of the realm respects. The public would not have been prevented from applauding the illustrious Maestro had he conducted the royal march or allowed someone else to conduct it.

As the news reports have stated, our little musician replied to the authorities' and Fascists' invitations with a repeated, insolent No. This was followed by a few slaps, some heckling, and the end of an aesthetic.[26]

Less sarcastic but equally misleading was the report in the Fascists' national daily, *Il popolo d'Italia*:

Maestro Toscanini's inexplicable behavior met with just retaliation from the Bolognese Fascists. For some time the Maestro, like a god angry with everyone, had been showing off his attitude. Not even for the sake of propriety and courtesy could he conquer his contempt for logic and common sense. The belief that playing the national anthems would have been an offense against art is an outrage to the sensibilities of Fascists and of the Italian people. The reaction was therefore legitimate.

It only remains to be asked whether Maestro Toscanini was the best person to carry out the Martucci commemoration, when we recall that he recently traveled through Italy with exotic groups and programs [*N.B.*: the New York Philharmonic playing standard symphonic repertoire], flaunting the indignation of a misunderstood genius in his own country's face. We must conclude that it would have been much better to ignore the Maestro who, in political matters, was anti-Bolshevik in order to win a little medal [*N.B.*: presumably a reference to his First World War decoration which, however, had nothing to do with Bolshevism], and in artistic ones was angry simply over rivalries at La Scala [*N.B.*: where he had had no rivals].

In any case, however, let no one who has the sensitivity and the spirit of the race and of the country forget the signs of our faith and of our unity. Not to understand this would mean setting oneself outside art and life and exposing oneself to severe lessons from those who have a clear-cut sense of duty, pride, and Italian and Fascist logic.[27]

Finally, in *La tribuna*, the following conclusion was drawn: ". . . A slap at the right time and place can sometimes have a salutary effect—above all, that of reconfirming, and sonorously, that the old formula of art for art's sake is not very suitable *today*."[28]

But the Fascists did not know their man. Toscanini was interested in art for humanity's sake. "The lesson they wanted to teach me," he wrote, ". . . was to no avail, nor will it be to any avail in the future, for I would repeat tomorrow what I did yesterday if the same conditions prevailed in Italy or in any other part of the world."

I know perfectly well how great the moral, political, and patriotic value of a national anthem played at the right time is—and I have never refused to play that of the nation to which I belong, in any situation, so long as its moral and patriotic meaning was unmistakable.

Did I not cross Italy and North America shortly after the war, at the head of the Scala orchestra, in a long series of concerts of national propaganda, playing my country's anthem everywhere? And have I not conducted it innumerable times, in my forty-five-year career, for patriotic events . . . for gala evenings and at Exposition openings, in the presence of the monarchs? And did I not conduct it on Monte Santo under enemy fire? . . .

To conclude: Am I, then, to take newspapers like the *Resto del Carlino* [Bologna] or the *Corriere della Sera* [Milan] seriously when, overnight, they replace the Hosannas to Toscanini with the Crucifixus? When they, like the *Popolo d'Italia*, even find my person unsuitable for commemorating Giuseppe Martucci? And all the others that have actually called me unpatriotic? How tiny are these people, and of what little value is all this business, barely deserving of my compassion!

"The spine bends when the soul is bent." It is true. But the conduct of my life has been, is, and will always be the echo and reflection of my conscience, which does not know dissimulation or deviations of any type—reinforced, I admit, by a proud and scornful character, but clear as crystal and just as cutting—always and everywhere ready to shout the truth loudly—that truth which, as Emerson so rightly says, always comes into the world in a manger, but is rewarded by having to live until it is completely enslaved by mankind. [29]

Mussolini's delight over what had happened to this "boorish musician" cannot have lasted long. Artists and intellectuals throughout the country soon began to learn something of the incident; and the foreign press carried detailed, if not always accurate, accounts of it. Letters and telegrams bearing messages of solidarity reached Toscanini from all over the world: one informer for the political police estimated that the conductor had received 15,000 such messages, and stated that an extra postman had been taken on to deal with the overload.[30] Leading Italian musicians came to visit Toscanini, although they knew that their movements were being reported by the police. Serge Koussevitzky canceled his scheduled concerts at La Scala in protest over the affair, declaring that "Maestro Toscanini does not belong only to Italy but to the whole world."[31] Béla Bartók presented a protest resolution at a meeting of the UMZE (New Hungarian Music Society): "The UMZE is deeply shocked and roused to indignation by the news of the grave assault that has been made on Arturo Toscanini. The Society wishes to assure him of its most wholehearted sympathy and solidarity, and salutes him with the utmost admiration."[32] Ossip Gabrilowitsch, pianist and conductor, and his wife Clara Clemens, daughter of Mark Twain, took a train from Zurich to Milan as soon as they heard of the Bologna incident. According to Gabrilowitsch:

[Toscanini] greeted us most cordially and seemed spontaneously inclined to describe the entire Bologna experience. He did so with undisguised indignation against the Fascist factions who had set the trap for him. In the expression of his feelings the great artist before us also divulged the great man. . . . His declaration of dislike for the present state of affairs in Italy was expressed in bold, round phrases. And this declaration he has repeatedly given outside the privacy of his home, so that no one can mistake his attitude. "Truth," he said, "truth we must have at any price, and freedom of speech, even if that price should be death. I have said to our Fascists time and again: You can kill me if you wish; but as long as I am living, I shall say what I think."[33]

All this negative publicity caused Mussolini to order that Toscanini be closely observed—that his mail be opened, his telephone line tapped, and the comings and goings at his home reported—and that all potentially useful information be passed on to the Duce's office. Five days after the Bologna incident, a telegram typical of the dossier's contents was sent from Milan to Rome:

Ministry of the Interior
CIPHER OFFICE   Telegram/24583 (6) EAS
FROM MILAN 19.5.31 8:20 O'CLOCK RECEIVED 10:30 O'CLOCK

MINISTRY INTERIOR GEN. ADMIN. [illegible code letters and numbers follow]

No. 019228 Yesterday Maestro *Toscanini* did not leave own home stop During day telegrams and letters brought to him among which one sender Esposito and a visiting card from Lawyer Cuciniello stop Following people went to visit Maestro Toscanini Dr. Ravagio family doctor, Maestro [Vittorio] Vanzo [conductor], Maestro Mario Castelnuovo Tedesco, Signor [Raffaele] Calzini [journalist], Maestro [Umberto] Giordano, Maestro Polli, Signor Gonnelle, and Signora Vercelli stop Inform that [the following] have been identified and have confessed having taken part in group that shouted "Viva Toscanini" the other evening in front of the same's residence Giovanni Bodrone, Ernesto; Missiroli, Roberto; Gilli, Carlo; Ferticucci, Carlo; Giovanardi, Eugenio; Arienti, Lodovico; and Valcarenghi, Aldo, all students [at the] Liceo Berchet except Gilli [who is] first-year student jurisprudence stop Aforementioned Valcarenghi confessed he was instigator yesterday evening's demonstration and distributor of the famous libels of "Giustizia e Libertà" among schoolmates stop* All students except Gilli confess having received said libels stop Yesterday evening during symphony concert Teatro alla Scala at end of the first part several youths in top Gallery shouted "Viva Toscanini" greeted by long applause noteworthy part of public filling theater stop Through prearranged [police] forces nine individuals were quickly stopped [and] identified as those responsible stop These for the most part confessed [and] are being held pending further checks stop Meanwhile several hundred Fascists gathered before said theater [and] with singing of "Giovinezza" headed toward [Toscanini's house in] Via Durini where they put on demonstration hostile toward Maestro Toscanini stop Prearranged forces [of] public order were able to avert attempted invasion building stop Fascist column then went Galleria

---

* Valcarenghi was the son of the codirector of the Ricordi Company. The conductor Gino Marinuzzi, his wife, and daughter happened to be visiting the Valcarenghis when agents arrived to arrest the young man. "My father rushed to the prefect, Fornaciari," wrote Lia Pierotti Cei Marinuzzi many years later, "to try to convince him to minimize the incident. But Fornaciari was furious. 'I'll send him into internal exile,' he thundered. 'I'll show him, and others like him!' We feared for the fate of our dear friend. He was given a three-year prison sentence, but fortunately he was released a few months later, because he was so young."[34] Giustizia e Libertà was a major underground anti-Fascist organization.

Vittorio Emanuele [*N.B.*: center of Milanese popular social life] where broke up orderly fashion after having sung Fascist anthems stop Public order normal stop

Prefect FORNACIARI[35]

The contents of Mussolini's file on Toscanini have long been known. A recently rediscovered classified dossier, however, held by the chief of the political police (Ministero dell'Interno, Direzione Generale di Pubblica Sicurezza, Divisione Polizia Politica, fascicoli personali), demonstrates the extent of the government's worry over the Bologna incident's domestic and foreign repercussions. The file preserves over 100 reports, all unsigned, from informers in ten Italian cities and in France, Germany, and Switzerland, as well as requests from the Ministry to local prefects for information on individuals known to have been politically sympathetic toward Toscanini. A sampling of the material shows the level of concern and confusion:

Rome, May 15: "This morning a rumor has been spread . . . , especially in foreign press circles, that Maestro Toscanini has been manhandled by the Fascists. The wildest conjectures have been made. . . ."[36]

Milan, May 16: "[Toscanini] has always had everything from his country: awards, honors, celebrations, offerings, praise from the press. If Toscanini acts this way, what should those people do who have suffered injustice, sorrow, slander, never an act of recognition? . . . Those responsible will do what is necessary, so that the Maestro will talk about us [Fascists] as little as possible."[37]

Milan, May 16: "Nothing is spoken of in Milan except the Toscanini episode in Bologna. . . . I made the rounds of all the main newsstands . . . to find a copy of 'Resto del Carlino,' but was unable to find a copy. Sold out! . . . His Excellency Gen. Sen. Carlo Porro . . . said that the Maestro has so boundlessly high an opinion of himself that he thinks he is on a level with the sovereigns. . . . [Toscanini's] deed in Bologna, according to Porro, is more the cowardly deed of a thoroughly cowardly person than a political action. But that's not how it is seen in the city's cafés. . . . At the Campari, [one man] told me that we need 100 Toscaninis in Italy, or rather in Milan, and that there are thousands and thousands who see things Toscanini's way but don't have the courage to say so. . . . [Another man] told me that, for many people, Toscanini's action in Bologna was an occasion for great jubilation, because it is interpreted as a big-gun intellectual's show of contempt toward the Regime. In reality, [he said,] the intellectuals are all against the Regime . . . but they are fearful, like the bourgeoisie. The fact that Toscanini actually said NO to Ciano and Arpinati emboldens vast numbers of people who hope that others will repeat the gesture."38

Rome, May 17: "In the Transatlantico [press room of the Chamber of Deputies], the most interesting subject was the slap given Toscanini. [Fascist leaders] Balbo, Manaresi, Riccardi, Bacci, Ferretti Lando, Diaz, Rossoni, Pierazzi, and other lesser people gathered around Arpinati, who was joined by Ciano. Arpinati recounted the story. He wanted to have Toscanini arrested; but he said that the Duce, reached by telephone, replied that the matter should be dropped. . . . Meanwhile, the Rome correspondents of foreign newspapers have received urgent telegrams requesting details. . . ."39

Naples, May 17: "The Toscanini incident . . . has aroused unanimous disdain and disapproval in all circles, even in the most markedly Fascist circles. The slap given the great, elderly conductor by an anonymous, third-rate hero is considered a mad, reprehensible gesture, and the solidarity of *Popolo d'Italia* with so vulgar an act of hooliganism is spoken of with unanimous harshness."40

Florence, May 17: "Many . . . think that [the incident] can severely damage our country, since Maestro Toscanini is well known for his obstinacy, and since he spends much of his life abroad. He will therefore not fail to carry out anti-Italian propaganda."41

Milan, May 17: ". . . for years . . . every editor at *Popolo d'Italia* has known of Toscanini's anti-Fascist beliefs."42

Milan, May 20: ". . . People are saying that if some poor devil had done less, much less, than Toscanini, he would have been sent into internal exile. . . . Everyone is now reading newspapers in the hope of seeing that a strong action has been taken against Toscanini. It is feared that if he is given the option of leaving the country, he could be used as an emblem . . . against us. . . ."43

Zurich, May 20: "The anti-Fascist press is, of course, taking advantage of the incident; but what is making an enormous impression everywhere, even on the friends of Fascism, is the fact that the celebrated Maestro Toscanini was attacked in Bologna by Fascists. . . ."44

Milan, May 20: "Monday evening May 18, at the Teatro alla Scala, which was filled with an elegant audience for a great symphony concert, at a certain moment—as if obeying a silent order—cries of *Viva* were addressed to Maestro Toscanini from the orchestra seats, the galleries, and the boxes. The demonstration was nearly unanimous and lasted several minutes. Alone among the public that was applauding the Maestro (who was not even present), old man [Tito] Ricordi, a good patriot (of the well-known Music Publishing House), stood up austerely and shouted, 'Viva l'Italia,' for God's sake! And from the galleries, jammed with students from the Polytechnic and the University, there came an even more heated reply, 'Yes, viva l'Italia! But viva, viva Toscanini, Italy's glory!' There was no violence. It was noted that the Milanese aristocracy filling the boxes joined the demonstration for Toscanini with obvious enthusiasm. . . ."45

Milan, May 21: ". . . From now on, the cries of Viva Toscanini! will have to be understood as Down with Fascism! This is absolutely not the moment for either slaps or beatings. It is urgent that many leaders in Milan be changed in order to attempt a Fascist reconstruction; otherwise (in Milan) there may be some nasty surprises. . . ."46

Paris, May 23: ". . . Newspapers of every political leaning have given . . . prominence to the act of the Bolognese Fascists. There have been many comments in Parisian artistic circles, which, of course, side with the musician. . . ."47

Milan, May 27: ". . . a demonstration [at La Scala] of solidarity with Maestro Toscanini . . . provoked a certain reaction in the souls of many Fascists, especially the students who belong to the GUF [Fascist University Groups]. Thus, on the evening of Friday, May 22, seventy of them trickled in [to La Scala]. Their admission was paid by the [Fascist] Federation and the GUF. The students occupied the [Scala] gallery. That evening, the concert was conducted by the German [*sic*] Fritz Reiner. There was a nice patriotic demonstration to the tune of the national anthems. . . . The students, however, were watchful, and noticed people who made unkind comments regarding the demonstration and fascism. These incautious people got what they deserved. One with a short beard, later identified as a professor at the Liceo di Milano—although he denied it—was slapped by a few students and then led to police headquarters . . . ; three other youths, . . . who said the Maestro might as well have been asked to play the anthems of every country, including Russia and Spain, . . . were followed by a group of five students from the GUF. . . . following explanations and arguments, [the five] handed out a good dose of punches. . . . A taxi driver expressed his poor opinion of the Fascist students and made insulting statements against the regime . . . ; one athletic student . . . grabbed the driver and gave him a good, hard lesson. . . . I have just learned that the GUF's Directorate has met to discuss initiating a series of punitive expeditions, because the spread of anti-Fascist propaganda, which is carried out especially in the bosom of certain intellectual circles, can no longer be tolerated."48

Milan, May 27: "There is a great deal of electricity in the air, and in so stating, I am not overdramatizing. . . . Anti-Fascists are indignant toward the perpetrators who manhandled Toscanini and friends in Bologna, and toward Prof. Bruno [of the Milanese police headquarters] for having caused terror and despair in many Milanese families as a result of the arrests he ordered for students from the Liceo Berchet [who demonstrated in Toscanini's favor . . .]; and most of the old Fascists, devoted to the Duce, are indignant because . . . Bruno is creating an atmosphere of victimization that will work entirely negatively for . . . Fascism. Those of our young people who committed the grave crime of applauding Arturo Toscanini on his return from Bologna, in a moment of fanatical enthusiasm for him, ought at most to have been given a spanking . . . ; but to have . . . turned our houses upside down, searching for documents attesting to a criminal organization against the Fascist State and the Duce, and then to have taken these young people away from us, and even to have sent some of them to prison—believe me, this is the best system for creating real antifascism and for creating martyrs cheaply. [. . . Regarding the counterdemonstration against Toscanini:] When the demonstration had moved into Piazza della Scala, the most hotheaded participants shouted, 'What does Toscanini do? He makes us sick! What is Toscanini? A pederast! What is Toscanini's wife? A whore! What is Toscanini's daughter? A whore!' This dialogue caused real indignation among those present. Many asked themselves whether this is the Fascist style of the new generations. . . ."49

Berlin, June 4: "My attention has been drawn to the following telegraphic dispatch, sent . . . from Milan today to Berlin's democratic *Vossische Zeitung*, published in this evening's edition under the headline, 'Will Toscanini be able to conduct at Bayereuth [*sic*]?': 'The Bayereuth Festival's director, Mrs. Winnifried [*sic*] Wagner, has asked Toscanini when at the earliest he will be able to be in Bayereuth for the new production of *Parsifal*, for which his speedy arrival is desired. Toscanini has passed the question on to Italian government authorities, with a request to have his passport returned so that he may leave with his family by the end of this week, if possible. . . . The Italian government's reply is still being awaited. Meanwhile, the Deputy, Hon. Scorza, president of the Fascist Students' Association, in a speech to Milanese Fascist students, branded as anti-Fascists all those who have shown their adoration for Toscanini, and emphasized that for the Italian people it is superfluous to be judged abroad by its conductors and singers. Foreign crowds have always gone into ecstasy over them, while the talents and work of [other] Italians abroad have been repaid by contempt and whippings. Today, Italy's good name depends exclusively upon Mussolini's genius. . . .' "50

St. Moritz, June 21: ". . . since the evening of the 10th of this month, Maestro Toscanini, together with his wife and daughter, has been staying in the Villa Chantarella in St. Moritz-Dorf. Almost every day, he receives the hotel manager, Emil Thoma-Badrutt, a well-known anti-Fascist, and the piano teacher Robert Gruner. Yesterday, a commission made up of various leaders of anti-Fascist parties came to congratulate him on having escaped from danger and for his decisive stand against Fascism. . . ."51

How strange, in the midst of all this, and how typical of Mussolini's ability to turn everything to account, was his comment to Emil Ludwig, probably made very shortly after the Bologna incident:

"Music seems to me the profoundest means of expression for any race of men. This applies to executants as well as to composers. If we Italians play Verdi better than do Frenchmen or Germans, it is because we have Verdi in our blood. You should hear how Toscanini, the greatest conductor in the world, interprets him."

"The very mention of the man is an argument against what you have just been saying," [Ludwig] replied. . . . "You could not find any German to conduct Beethoven so well as this remarkable Italian; and yet I have heard Verdi better produced in Germany than anywhere in Italy. . . ."

"You are only right in respect of exceptions," said Mussolini. . . .52

And when, a dozen years later, the deposed and ailing dictator—now ruling the infamous Salò Republic as a German puppet—was queried by Nino D'Aroma about his musical preferences, he remarked, "Among conductors, Toscanini. The man is contemptible for his behavior; as an artist, however, he is immense. I, for my part, shall never deny the extraordinary emotion that he gave me with his Beethoven concerts, nor the friendship that he offered at his peril to our *fasci [di combattimento]* in 1919."[53]

Mussolini had certainly demonstrated his gratitude in odd ways; for although the Fascists never again dared to assault Toscanini physically, they kept close tabs on him throughout the 1930s and occasionally attacked him in the press. And the conductor did have a way of provoking the Duce. Late in 1931, for instance, spies informed the chief of the political police that Toscanini had been welcomed as a conquering hero by anti-Fascist Italians in New York,[54] and that he had given a large sum to the Giustizia e Libertà organization in Paris.[55] Another report revealed that the French Prime Minister, Edouard Herriot, had made Toscanini a Commander of the Legion of Honor in 1932, and that when the two men happened to meet during an Atlantic crossing some months later, Herriot told Toscanini "that His Excellency Manzoni, who was then the [Italian] ambassador to Paris, had let it be known that the granting of such an honor to Maestro Toscanini would not be much appreciated by the Duce. . . . Herriot is said to have been greatly astonished by Manzoni's out-of-place and politically ill-advised observation."[56] Several documents indicate that Mussolini attempted to bring Toscanini back into the fold in the summer of 1934. For instance:

> The Duce is said to have personally offered Toscanini the direction of the Royal Opera Theater [Rome] and, at the same time, the general directorship of all Italian theaters; but Toscanini is said to have contemptuously refused. When friends pressed the Maestro . . . to consider the offer, pointing out that it had come from the Duce himself, Toscanini is said to have answered with these words, "I don't give a damn."[57]

In October 1935, shortly after the government had banned the sale of foreign newspapers within Italy, agents intercepted a subversive telephone conversation between Toscanini and a woman identified only as Signora Ada. (This was almost certainly Ada Mainardi

Colleoni, wife of the cellist Enrico Mainardi; she is reputed to have been one of Toscanini's lovers during that period.)

TOSCANINI: It's a really dirty piece of work to put a country in this situation! It's unheard of that a person can't read the paper he wants and has to believe everything that they print! It's unbelievable stuff! And it isn't even clever, because it will generate still more doubts. To force a people this way . . . with a slipknot at its throat! . . . You have to read and know only what they want. . . . There must be only one mind! This is no longer living!

ADA: It's frightful! Worse than Russia! For the previous few days the news vendors had already had orders not to display foreign papers. . . . You can see that they're plotting something.

T: No, it's only this: the people must be kept in complete ignorance . . .

A: It gives you a feeling of suffocation.

T: I can't wait to leave, because I can't stand it any longer! These things shock me . . . To see people enslaved this way! . . . They grab you by the throat here, they choke you! You have to believe what that mind [i.e. Mussolini's] believes . . . And I'll never believe what he believes . . . I never have believed it! I was weak only for a moment [*N.B.*: clearly referring to his support for Mussolini in 1919], and now I'm ashamed of myself! . . . We've reached the bottom of the barrel . . . Yet there are people who feel nothing, who live like this . . . But for me it's a kind of suffering that annihilates me.[58]

A notation on the transcript reads, "Which proves what we already knew, that Toscanini is indomitable."

For Toscanini, Italy had been reduced to a holiday site, a place where he could spend periods of rest between engagements elsewhere. He continued to receive many invitations to conduct major ensembles throughout his country, and he gave serious consideration to some of them. In the end, however, he realized that some degree of personal compromise would always have been required, had he accepted; and he resisted all temptations. When in Italy, Toscanini occasionally attended other people's performances—police informers duly noted the names of people who greeted him—and was as outspoken both in public and in private as Gabrilowitsch's statement indicated. His rented summer villa on the Isolino San Giovanni, a tiny island in Lake Maggiore, became a meeting place for anti-Fascist artists and intellectuals. Family movies from the mid-1930s show assemblages of writers and musicians (Erich Maria Remarque, Rudolf Serkin, and Adolf, Fritz, and Hermann Busch) who had fled Hitler's Germany, as well as such improvised entertainments as a burlesque of the Fascist Youth Corps' marches choreographed by Cia Fornaroli, Toscanini's daughter-in-law, who had been prima ballerina and head of the ballet school at La Scala until her family connections cost her her job.

Toscanini eventually extended his anti-Fascist protest to Germany and Austria (see subsequent chapters) and accepted invitations to conduct in countries in which he had not previously appeared (except, in some cases, on tour with American or Italian ensembles): France, Holland, Sweden, Switzerland, and especially England, where he gave extraordinarily successful concerts with the BBC Symphony Orchestra from 1935 to 1939. In a sense, he was dancing a circle around the fascist-controlled countries. His withdrawal from the Salzburg Festival in 1938 caused the mayor of Lucerne to ask him to conduct there that summer; Toscanini's acceptance was the cornerstone on which the Swiss city built itself an enduring European music festival of major proportions. Fascist party bosses in Italy were not pleased with Toscanini's openly contemptuous behavior. What truly incensed them, however, was the frenetic rush of Italian music lovers and of the cream of Italian society to attend his concerts across the border. The political police went into paroxysms of activity not seen since the weeks following the Bologna incident, and informers' reports again began to flow:

Rome, August 4, 1938: ". . . The 'key' to these [musical events] is a Wagner concert to be conducted by Toscanini on the 25th of this month at 4 P.M. in the park opposite the villa at Tribschen, . . . where Wagner lived from 1866 to 1872. . . . The thousand seats are already completely sold out, 350 of them to Italians from Milan, Genoa, Turin, and Rome. I don't believe that the purchase of these tickets on the part of some of them has been made only out of great love of art. It is surprising that among those who have reserved a place we find Signora Alfieri, wife of the Minister of Popular Culture. . . . Our Ambassador in Berne, His Excellency Attilio Tamaro, . . . has assured me that he has given instruc-

tions that no official Italian representative in Switzerland attend the
concert. . . ."59

When Toscanini applied to Milan police headquarters to have his
passport renewed so that he could leave for Switzerland, the local
chief telephoned the Interior Ministry in Rome for permission to
grant the request; the matter was referred to Mussolini, who gave his
authorization.60 At the same time, however, he ordered that Italians
returning from the concert in cars be stopped; but he later decided
merely to have their license plates noted.61

One of the informers dispatched to Lucerne reported that, in
addition to Mrs. Alfieri, the concert was attended by such notables
as Countess Volpi di Misurata, wife of a leading Fascist financier and
government minister; Remigio Paone, director of Italian theaters;
Marchioness Marconi, widow of the physicist and inventor; the
composers Italo Montemezzi and Vincenzo Tommasini; Senator
Giacomo De Martino; the wife of Senator Borletti; members of the
Puccini family; the well-known Milanese lawyer Luigi Ansbacher;
possibly the former Prime Minister Ivanoe Bonomi; Count Giovanni
Ascanio Cicogna; the publisher Leo Olschki; and dozens of other
artists, intellectuals, and aristocrats. What most irritated Mussolini
was the presence of Maria José, consort of Crown Prince Umberto.
By attending the concert, the princess was making a small but
significant protest gesture—by the standards of the day. Toscanini
undoubtedly knew this; but he also knew that however admirable
she may have been as an individual, Maria José represented the royal
family, which was in thrall to Mussolini. When she went backstage
to greet the conductor after the performance, hoping that he would
autograph her vocal score of the Verdi *Requiem*, he refused to see her.
Carla Toscanini, greatly embarrassed, ran back and forth between
her husband in his dressing room and the princess just outside the
door, trying to persuade one or the other to back down. Both were
adamant. But Toscanini, as usual, had his way. Maria José left
without meeting him.62

The Lucerne episode led to dozens of telegrams and telephone
calls and hundreds of pages of reports to and from the political police regarding all Italians whose license plates had been noted
by informers. The government seems to have gained no useful

information from these efforts; but party boss Roberto Farinacci's newspaper, *Il regime fascista* of Cremona, published a libelous article against the conductor and those who admired him:

THE HONORARY JEW

Toscanini has conducted a concert in Wagner's honor at the Tribschen museum. Even the Swiss press reproved this gentleman who, merely because he knows how to conduct an orchestra, thinks he has the right to act basely.

Indeed, when two non-Jewish young ladies presented him with a bouquet of flowers at the end of the first part, he threw down his baton and abandoned the podium. But the most interesting fact is that the "great democrat" declared himself willing to give a concert for the people without earning a penny—except that ticket prices were stupefying: 22.55 Swiss francs. Thus, no plebeian could attend. It is true that he was not paid, but he asked for 100 seats in the theater, hotel rooms for himself and his family, and the same for the numerous Jews who accompanied him.

Toscanini's disinterestedness cost the concert organizers 6,000 Swiss francs; if one adds to that the gifts presented to him, the figure rises to 40,000 Italian liras. . . .

Since Toscanini is doing all this in a purely anti-Fascist spirit, we would like to know who those Italians were who went there. . . . This should not be difficult, because we know the numbers of the Italian cars' license plates.

Well, then—so that people won't say that we take shots in the dark— we invite our comrades in Milan to look up the owners of the automobiles bearing the following plates: MI 1-4505, MI 4215; comrades in Florence, the car FI 1-4395; and comrades in Rome, the cars 6288 and 4-1857.[63]

The Milanese and Florentine papers hastily found and printed the names of the car owners,[64] but there is no record of reprisals. Some of the calumnies in the article are gratuitous; some accusations contain a small portion of truth. The concert organizers probably did put up Toscanini and his immediate family at hotels and provide tickets—but certainly not a hundred of them—to the event. These are customary practices. The prices were raised—quadrupled—for

Toscanini's concert, a sure sellout, in order to subsidize the rest of the newborn festival. The article conveniently does not mention that as the demand for tickets had been so overwhelming, Toscanini agreed to conduct a second concert two days later, again without drawing a fee, and with the tickets at normal prices. He did run away from the floral presentation, as he had been known to do on other occasions: he superstitiously associated such doings with mortuary rites.

On returning to Italy for a holiday later that summer, Toscanini and his wife had their passports taken away by the Fascist authorities. Galeazzo Ciano, who was then foreign minister, wrote in his diary: "The Duce is annoyed because many Italians, and above all the Princess of Piedmont [Maria José], went to Lucerne for [Toscanini's] Wagner concert. But the withdrawal of the passport is related to a wiretap, from which it seems that Toscanini attacked the Duce for his [new] anti-Semitic policy, terming it 'medieval stuff.' "* Ciano also warned Fulvio De Suvich, Italy's ambassador to the United States, not to become involved in the affair: "The Duce flies into a rage if you talk to him about Toscanini."[66] De Suvich, however, was worried about what the American reaction to the incident would be if Toscanini did not reach New York in time for his October engagement. He broached the matter with Mussolini, who agreed to

---

* The transcript of this conversation—again between Toscanini and "Signora Ada"—reads, in part:

T: Who knows where it will all end. Anything is possible!

A: What makes you see red is the lying, the bad faith . . .

T: . . . They don't even have the sense to say, "Let's disguise things." They want people to be stupid.

A: In fact, they're reducing them to that, little by little!

T: . . . I'm going to the Isolino within the next few days, and I'm going to do everything to have things moved out . . . because I don't know what could happen next.

A: Yes, it's for the best. But I don't think they can push things too far . . .

T: There's no limit now. Tomorrow they'll say, "Give me your money, do this . . ." They're capable of anything. Promises no longer exist; they don't remember today what they said yesterday. It's shameful! When it was a matter of [the laws regulating] foreigners, okay; but now, there are people who have worked for years, who have done so much! [Jewish] children can't go to school . . . this is medieval stuff!

A: Yes, exactly.

The bottom of the transcript bears the words "by order *of the Duce* take away Toscanini's passport."[65]

give back the passport if the conductor would request it of him. Toscanini would not bend even to that degree—although his wife wrote (September 16) to the chief of the political police to warn that there could be "unpleasant interpretations and comments on the part of the foreign press" if the passport were not forthcoming.[67] Toscanini considered escaping in a hydroplane that would take him from the Italian to the Swiss part of Lake Maggiore; this appealed to his sense of adventure, but he feared that there might be reprisals against family and friends. A Swiss journalist, friendly with Walter Toscanini, threatened to make an uproar in the world press; and Mussolini realized that he had created unnecessary problems for himself.[68] In a brief note (August 6, 1938), the Duce's office chief informed him that Toscanini "insists on having his passport renewed as soon as possible. Bocchini [chief of the political police] asks whether he may grant it." At the top of the page, the exasperated Duce scrawled "Sì";[69] and in a note to the chief of police he ordered, "Return the passport."[70]

Toscanini spent the war years in New York. He joined the Mazzini Society, a group of liberal and socialist Italian expatriates who favored the establishment of an Italian republic following the downfall of fascism, for which they all fervently hoped. Their leaders included the historian Gaetano Salvemini, the art critic Lionello Venturi, church historian Giorgio La Piana, author and literary historian Giuseppe Antonio Borgese, Colonel Randolfo Pacciardi, Alberto Tarchiani (later Italy's ambassador to the United States), and Count Carlo Sforza, who was a cabinet minister both before and after the Fascist period. Toscanini was asked to accept the presidency of the society; he refused the office but offered his continuing support.[71] Salvemini later wrote that "our most effective argument in our criticism of fascism was Arturo Toscanini. . . . He did not write or give lectures, but his very existence was a formidable accusation against a political regime that could have chased such a man out of his country."[72] Early in 1943, Salvemini and La Piana published their booklet, *What to Do with Italy*, and dedicated it "To Maestro Arturo Toscanini who, in the darkest days of fascist crimes, of Italy's dishonor, of the world's madness, remained intransigently faithful to the ideals of Mazzini and Garibaldi and, with tenacious faith, anticipated the dawn of the second Italian *Risorgimento*."[73]

The Toscanini family assisted large numbers of refugees from

Europe in securing American entry visas, jobs, and homes. Once the United States had entered the war, Toscanini added numerous benefit concerts to his regular performance schedule. The proceeds from most of these went to the Red Cross, but some performances raised money for government war bonds. The Fascists made the most of this: they claimed that Toscanini was paying for bombs that were destroying his country. And when Toscanini conducted the American premiere (July 19, 1942) of Shostakovich's Seventh ("Leningrad") Symphony, which was said to symbolize Russian resistance to the German invasion, the Roman daily, *Il messaggero*, apostrophized:

> O you good Bolognese fascist who, in days that have now been forgotten by too many people, gave him those sonorous slaps when he refused to play the national anthems, stirring up an enormous international clamor—why didn't you increase the dose that he so deserved, so as to render him permanently unable to work? You would have made it impossible for this Italian to debase Italy before the enemy today.[74]

The article was signed by "Tito Silvio Mursino"—the anagrammatized name of the Duce's journalist son, Vittorio Mussolini.

On July 25, 1943, Toscanini conducted a live radio program of Verdi excerpts with his NBC Symphony Orchestra in New York. He had just left the stage with soprano Gertrude Ribla after a performance of the aria "Pace, pace, mio Dio," from *La Forza del Destino*, when an announcement was broadcast into the hall and over the air: Mussolini had been deposed. Toscanini rushed back onstage, clasped his hands and gazed heavenward, in a sign of thanksgiving; while the audience, equally beside itself, applauded, cheered, screamed, and all but tore the studio to pieces. That same day, printed posters were pasted all over La Scala's signboards: "*Evviva Toscanini, Ritorni Toscanini.*"[75] The lawyer who had paid to have those placards printed and had then put them up with his own hands was arrested and beaten when the Fascists resumed control of the city a few weeks later. His enthusiasm for Toscanini cost him seven teeth.

The Mazzini Society broke up soon after September 8, 1943, when the Allies concluded an armistice with the king and Badoglio. Sforza, Tarchiani, and their faction accepted the compromise, but Salvemini and the others insisted that any dealings with anyone who had been tainted through collaboration with the Fascists—above all, the king and Badoglio—were immoral and politically unwise. Toscanini decidedly favored the latter opinion; and when Salvemini asked him to make a public statement, in print, to represent their point of view to the Allies, he accepted. This was the only significant, individual public statement Toscanini ever made on any subject, and the editors of *Life* magazine gave him the editorial page of their issue of September 13, 1943. He wrote directly in English and with great care; but a member of his family claims that a critical reference that the conductor made to the Church's position on fascism was removed by the editors before publication.[76]

In his declaration ("To the People of America"), Toscanini said he felt that he could act as interpreter of the wishes of the Italian people, who had been "choked for more than twenty years." He asserted—and this was his main point—that the king and Badoglio "cannot be dissociated in any way from the Fascist and military clique. They cannot be the representatives of the Italian people: they cannot in any way conclude peace with the Allies in the name of Italy, so betrayed by them." He predicted that there would be a revolution in Italy, and that for this to "result in orderly democratic government, as we hope, it will be necessary for the Allies to support all democratic elements currently arrayed against the King and Badoglio." These "elements," however, included the long-suppressed socialists and communists, and the idea of dealing with them instead of supporting the king and Badoglio was unlikely to be greeted with enthusiasm by Roosevelt and Churchill.

Toscanini also suggested that Italy's frontiers be left as established before Mussolini's accession, that economic assistance be given to the new government, and that "the Allies permit our volunteers to fight against the hated Nazis under the Italian flag with conditions substantially similar to those of the Free French," in order to facilitate an unconditional surrender of the Italian armed forces. Citing Shakespeare's *Henry VI*, he said:

> Do not forget that we Italians have been the first to endure the oppression of a tyrannical gang of criminals, supported by that "fainthearted and degenerate King" of Italy—but that we have never willingly submitted to them. Countless thousands of men and women in Italy shed blood, met imprisonment and death, striving fiercely against that horde

of criminals, enduring also the apathy and indifference of the world then full of admiration for Mussolini.[77]

When Sforza wrote Toscanini to explain why, in his opinion, the Allies were right to continue to accept the king as titular head of Italy, Toscanini replied in typically unequivocal fashion:

> From this moment on you may consider me a *traitor to my Country*! Not even to save Italy could I come to terms with those who have shamefully betrayed her for more than twenty years! I would not even be able to speak to or look at those two wretches. I feel sorry for you. . . . Our tastes are very different. . . . Your politics may be intelligent and shrewd, but I condemn them and despise them—and I declare myself against you and the Allied government that has fully demonstrated its complete ignorance and ineptitude in understanding the honest and simple Italian soul. Their policy toward Italy has been a shameful fiasco—and, as Dorothy Thompson says, a complete disaster. Their *"unconditional surrender"* is ridiculous. . . . And now they want to put the anti-Fascist forces in the hands of those who have betrayed them for long and, alas! sorrowful years![78]

On June 12, 1944, *Life* magazine carried a lengthy article entitled "An Italian Manifesto," co-signed by Salvemini, Toscanini, Borgese, La Piana, Pacciardi, and Venturi. Once again, they urged the British and Americans to stop supporting the king's government, but this time they went further in their condemnation of Allied policy. The plea—desperate, heartfelt, and impassioned—was largely disregarded.[79]

Some months earlier Toscanini, who had previously turned down several lucrative offers to appear in commercial films, contributed his services to the making of a propaganda short for the Office of War Information. He conducted the NBC Symphony in the overture to *La forza del destino* and another Verdi work, the *Hymn of the Nations*—a cantata written for London's International Exposition of 1862. The piece makes use of the themes of "God Save the Queen," the "Marseillaise," and Italy's "Mameli Hymn," whose first line Toscanini changed from *"O Italia, patria mia"* (O Italy, my country) to *"O Italia, patria mia tradita"* (my betrayed country); and he wrote a bridge passage at the end and added the Socialist "International" and

"The Star-Spangled Banner" in tribute to the other two major allies. The film was distributed in the liberated portions of Europe.[80]

As the war dragged on and Italy's situation became increasingly desperate, Toscanini grew more and more restive. "I think of my poor, dear Italy," he wrote to his daughter Wally in November 1944, "mishandled and torn asunder by enemies and friends alike, and I don't know why I'm not there to do more than what I can do here."[81] He found some consolation in the visits of other Italian exiles whose anti-Fascist convictions he shared; and one of these, Armando Borghi, a well-known anarchist whom Toscanini and Salvemini had helped to free from detention by American immigration authorities, wrote of their acquaintanceship in *Il mondo* a few months after the conductor's death. Borghi pointed out that until the United States entered the war, the anti-Fascists were a small minority among influential Italo-Americans:

> ... As far as the roughnecks of the colony were concerned, Toscanini had betrayed Italy and the Duce, and, as Don Basilio says, calumny always leaves its mark. ... Let's reflect upon the fact that Toscanini was the only world celebrity [of Catholic origin] who never went to visit the Pope, never surrounded himself with priests and friars and nuns, never conducted music in church [*N.B.*: he did so on three or four occasions, but never for religious functions], never gave benefit concerts for religious organizations, either in Italy or in America.
>
> Toscanini had shouted his no to fascism right in its historic capital: Bologna, in the heart of the Po Valley ... whose agrarian Don Rodrigos [*N.B.*: reference to the villain in Manzoni's *I promessi sposi*] had provided fascism with its first scoundrels and financiers. Toscanini's no in Arpinati's home territory was a bomb blast. Mussolini understood this. ...
>
> [... Toscanini] was a thousand times stronger than the rest of us, who acted with "political" preparation and premeditation. He was *defenseless* at the time of fascism's rise; he was not furnished with the armor of suspicion that we had, and that came of our political convictions. Toscanini was ... absorbed by the majesty of his art. But his interior world predestined him to be what he was. ...
>
> ... Had it not been for the "now you see me, now you don't" attitude towards the rescue, not of poor devils, but of [Fascist] big guns like Farinacci and Starace ..., the dissensions among the anti-Fascist leaders [in New York] would have remained in the background. This

necessity *not to soften*, in what was then the conclusive hour of the war, showed everyone and everything in its true light. In that hour Toscanini openly ranked himself against compromise and against the compromise brokers. As a result, he broke with the Mazzini Society, at the moment in which it was about to become a Noah's ark for saving the blackshirt big guns of the entire colony. . . .

We were often in touch at that time. We discussed politics and post-Fascist society. We also discussed anarchy, which he found a "reasonable" ideal. He laughed at those who called him a future Paderewski. In fact, he had never accepted, nor did he later accept, honors or decorations that he could have had for the asking in Italy, in America, in the whole world. . . .[82]

At war's end, Toscanini contributed one million liras toward the reconstruction of La Scala, which had been semidestroyed by Allied bombs in 1943, and gave a special concert in New York that raised $30,000 for Italian welfare societies, especially the War Orphans Committee. At the end of that performance, New York's Mayor Fiorello La Guardia and the new Italian ambassador, Tarchiani, went to greet him in his dressing room. They found themselves turned away: Tarchiani was one of those who had compromised with the so-called demo-fascists; Toscanini would not see him.[83]

In February 1946, when the Italian government announced that a referendum on the abolition of the monarchy would be held in June, Toscanini made up his mind to go home, to conduct a concert for the reinauguration of La Scala. Seventy-five percent of Milan's historic center had been destroyed or seriously damaged during the last twenty months of the war, but—typical of the Milanese mentality—the first important building to be put back in shape was La Scala. Antonio Greppi, the city's first postwar mayor, stood staunchly behind the popular slogan "bread and theater." With permission from the Allied occupation forces, financial support from a variety of Italian sources and painstaking work on the part of La Scala's chief engineer, Luigi Lorenzo Secchi, and his staff, the 168-year-old house was nearly ready for use on April 25, the first anniversary of the liberation.

Toscanini had arrived in Italy two days earlier and had begun to lay down the law. Jewish musicians who lost their positions at La Scala in 1938 and who managed to survive the German occupation were to be reengaged—first among them, Vittore Veneziani, the chorus director. Others who had fallen into political disfavor under fascism were also given back their jobs.

On May 11, La Scala, still smelling of fresh paint, was filled to nearly twice its normal capacity, and the audience included government officials and the leaders of the major political parties. Even Ferruccio Parri, legendary Resistance leader and head of the postwar government of national unity, was present. Greppi, whose son died as a partisan fighter, had wanted to make a brief speech before the concert, but Toscanini had vetoed the idea: there had already been plenty of talk; concerts were for music. Although the concerts that Toscanini conducted later in that brief season included a good deal of American, Soviet, and other "Allied" music that had not been performed in Italy during the war years (accompanied, naturally, by a substantial dose of German classics), for the first program he chose music by Italian composers only: Rossini, Verdi, Boito, and Puccini. Outside the theater, tens of thousands gathered in Piazza della Scala and in Piazza del Duomo—both closed to traffic—and in the arcaded Galleria that connects them, to listen to the performance on loudspeakers. The concert was broadcast throughout Italy and via shortwave to much of the rest of the world. At precisely 9 P.M., as the nearly octogenarian Toscanini walked onto "his" stage for the first time in sixteen years, the people in the theater leaped to their feet, applauding frenetically, shouting "Toscanini! Toscanini!" and weeping. The dictatorship, the war, and the prolonged mass sufferings were things of the past. At the end of the last piece, the applause and cheering went on for thirty-seven minutes. Backstage, the orchestra gave Toscanini a commemorative gold medallion bearing the inscription: "To the Maestro who was never absent—his Orchestra."[84]

The press coverage given to Toscanini's return would be inconceivable in other countries and under other conditions. As usual, he granted no interviews and made no comments to journalists, but his views on contemporary Italian events were known. Several political commentators affirmed that Toscanini's baton did more for the antimonarchic cause than the combined orations of the Christian Democratic, Communist, and Socialist party secretaries, De Gasperi, Togliatti, and Nenni.[85] Toscanini's influence cannot be evaluated, but certainly the conductor was pleased with the results of the

referendum (held three weeks after the Scala inaugural), which led to
the establishment of a republic. Although he could have resumed the
direction of La Scala, by then Toscanini's activities were largely
confined to New York, where working conditions satisfied him. He
conducted occasionally at La Scala until 1952 and spent long holiday
periods in Italy until 1955, a year after his retirement. What he
himself had referred to as his "proud and scornful character, but
clear as crystal and just as cutting," had saved him from the shame
that touched most other musicians in Fascist Italy:

> You are too poisoned by the atmosphere that surrounds you to be able to
> value people like me, who have remained and will remain above the mud
> (not to give it a worse name) that is drowning the Italians!!! You are all
> living, now, in the midst of shame and dishonor, without giving any sign
> of rebellion. . . . I can only believe that you've never understood me,
> never valued me at my *real* and *true worth*! I was too far above you, and
> your vantage point deceived you. . . . I am disgusted at belonging to the
> family of artists . . . who, with a few exceptions, are not men, but poor
> beings, full of vanity. . . . Life no longer holds any interest for me, and I
> would pray God to take it away from me immediately if it weren't for my
> firm, *never diminished hope* to see the *criminals* swept off the face of the
> earth before I go. . . . Live happily and healthily if you can. . . .
>
> Arturo Toscanini,
> letter to a lady in Rome,
> New York, May 16, 1941[86]

This chapter, in a slightly different form, appeared under the title "The
Toscanini Case" in my book *Music in Fascist Italy* (London: Weidenfeld and
Nicolson, 1987; New York: Norton, 1988); it is now out of print.

The book was generously received in most quarters but was violently
attacked in the *New Republic* (September 5, 1988), by an American aca-
demic, Richard Taruskin, whose areas of expertise, I have been told, are
early music and Russian opera. Since Taruskin built his entire review on
the assumption that my main motive in writing the book was to be able to
measure "every other Italian musician [of the Fascist period] against
Toscanini's [political] example" so that I could find all the others "wanting,"
and since the question of artists' responses to political nefariousness has
interested me for many years, for personal as well as scholarly reasons, I
want to answer a few of his charges.

The first paragraph of my book contains a question about Italian musicians under Mussolini's regime: "Did any of them protest, and if so, with what consequences?" Taruskin, in his review, quoted it thus: "Did they not protest, and if so [*sic*], with what consequences?" He inserted the grammatical error so that he could then insert the [*sic*], with a knowing wink at the reader. Thus he launched his assault, not only on my work but also on my "skewed and ruinously simplified perspective." (I think he meant simple or simplistic rather than simplified, but let's not get bogged down in *sics*.) But my investigation did not end with that first question. It led me to ask many others, and they in turn led me to decide to research and write my book.

Taruskin declares outright that twentieth-century Italy has been a musical backwater, "rather a poor place to observe music," and that "perhaps the larger problem is that Italian fascism was not worse." Since he finds neither music in Italy nor the history of Italian fascism particularly worth studying, he ought to have disqualified himself from reviewing a book called *Music in Fascist Italy*. Instead, he turns his review into a catchall discussion of the relationship between fascism and "modernism." The names Pound, Eliot, Heidegger, Berg, Webern, and, of course, Paul de Man flash before our eyes and disappear, and we are left none the wiser about any of them, although we now know that the reviewer has heard of all of them. Mainly, however, Taruskin harps on the political attitudes of Schoenberg and Stravinsky, who play minuscule roles in my book, and of Heinrich Schenker, who plays no role at all in it—or, so far as I can see, in the story of "modernism."

Taruskin berates me for being "stern enough when dealing with the Mascagnis and the Pizzettis"—minor composers, in other words—whereas I merely use the term "bamboozled" to describe Stravinsky's fascination with Mussolini. He has missed the point. Marguerite Yourcenar, who lived in Fascist Italy, wrote that "fascism's bloated façade" hid a "hollow reality" that fooled many foreign artists "who rejoiced at seeing the trains run on time (at least in theory), without dreaming of asking themselves toward which station the trains were running." This nicely describes Stravinsky's relationship to Fascist Italy during his occasional, brief visits there: his revolting yet superficial enthusiasm for Mussolini demonstrates that he was indeed "bamboozled," that he believed that fascism's repressive tactics were leading to desirable goals. The "Mascagnis and Pizzettis," on the other hand, lived in Italy; they knew perfectly well that fascism was not achieving the wonderful transformation of society, which, fascists claimed, would more than compensate for the death of "decadent" democracy. Documents prove that the Mascagnis and Pizzettis were not, in their hearts, enthusiastic about fascism but merely wished to reap benefits from the regime, as they would have wished to do under any other form of government,

democratic or otherwise. My point is that the opportunism of large numbers of well-known Italians, from the king on down, was the key to fascism's two-decade grip on power—a far more important factor, in the long
run, than the criminality or self-delusion of fascist potentates. This opinion
earned me a brilliant comeuppance from Taruskin: "What could be more
fascist, ultimately, than to prefer a grand crime to a petty one?" (It seems
that *everything* is grist for the mill in musical academia. Professor Taruskin
could more properly have applied his rhetorical question to his own, earlier
statement: "perhaps the larger problem is that Italian fascism was not
worse.")

Notwithstanding Stravinsky's antidemocratic tendencies and Schoenberg's despotic behavior and pre-Hitlerian German supremacist statements, I do not hear the "aesthetic fascism" that Taruskin claims to hear—if
I have understood him correctly—in their music, any more than I hear
Bismarckian aesthetic qualities in the music of Brahms, who admired the
Iron Chancellor. And if all major artists who behave despotically are to be
defined as fascists, few major artists will qualify as nonfascists.

Toscanini, like most other Italian conductors of his generation, was
sometimes guilty of despotic behavior toward the people who worked
with him; and if Taruskin had taken the trouble to read eyewitness
accounts of Italy's anarchic orchestras and opera companies at the turn of
the century, he would have understood why. Instead, he uses the fact to
support his nonsensical theory that "Toscanini's resistance to Mussolini"
was nothing more than a tale of "two Duci engaged in a protracted battle
of wills." He sees a sinister parallel between a conductor who lost his
temper over lackluster playing, liked to dress well, and insisted on high
fees from organizations that could afford to pay them (when they could
not—and this Taruskin does not mention—Toscanini conducted for nothing) and a dictator who abolished freedom of speech and of the press for
forty million people, imprisoned or executed his opponents, conquered
defenseless Ethiopia, helped Francisco Franco to win the Spanish Civil
War, and led his militarily unprepared country into the most devastating
war in history.

Taruskin's assumption that I wrote my book in order to make other
Italian musicians look bad next to Toscanini is absolutely off the mark, for
Music in Fascist Italy was planned without a section on Toscanini. Although
the sixty-page dossier on him in Mussolini's files was more substantial than
that on any other musician, I had already had access to it a decade earlier,
when I was writing my biography of the conductor. (Until I found that
dossier, I had assumed that the story of Toscanini's antifascism was greatly
overblown, and I had intended to say so in the biography.) In the new book,
I meant to confine mention of Toscanini to unavoidable passing references.

When work on the book was two-thirds done, however, authorities at the Central State Archive in Rome gave me permission to examine the secret files of the Fascist political police's General Administration of Public Safety. The dossier on Toscanini is nearly 500 pages long, greater than the combined length of all the other dossiers in all the Italian government files on all the musicians and musical institutions of the Fascist period. It is one of the basic, documented examples of fascist paranoia regarding subversives. This evidence, added to the material I had found in the New York Public Library a few months earlier concerning Toscanini's withdrawal from the Salzburg Festival in 1938 (see Chapter 7), made me reconsider the "political" Toscanini in an extra chapter appended to *Music in Fascist Italy*.

Taruskin does not take Toscanini's antifascism seriously; but Mussolini, his subordinates, and the hundreds of people employed at various times to follow the conductor, tap his telephone conversations, open his mail and telegrams, and prepare detailed reports on the people who visited him took it very seriously indeed. Toscanini was not a profound student of international politics; I make that clear in my book. He was, however, the most famous Italian antifascist and therefore, as far as Mussolini's propaganda was concerned, the most dangerous one. According to Taruskin, "Sachs gives no evidence that Toscanini was regarded in Italy as a political resister." Anyone who has read this chapter will know that that is false: see, for instance, the informers' reports on pages 77–81. Mussolini received reports on Toscanini's antifascist opinions at least as early as 1924; and the assault on the conductor in Bologna in 1931, and the subsequent demonstrations for and against him in Bologna and Milan, prove that Toscanini's resistance was known to anyone who read the newspapers. The recently published diaries of Yvon de Begnac (*Taccuini mussoliniani*. Bologna, 1990), one of Mussolini's closest confidants, reveal yet again that Toscanini was considered a serious political resister. Mussolini named him along with only three other Italian artists and intellectuals—Giuseppe Antonio Borgese, Gaetano Salvemini, and Ignazio Silone—as one of the real anti-Fascists who "don't keep themselves covered"; and he compared them, with a certain grudging admiration, to the "tepid, obscurantist" antifascist intellectuals in Milan and Florence who tried to stay in both camps simultaneously.

One weekend in 1938, following a serious scare involving the confiscation of their passports, Toscanini and his family hurriedly packed their essential belongings and departed for the United States; they did not return to Italy until after World War II. (One of Toscanini's daughters, Wally, Countess Castelbarco, remained in Italy at first but, when the Germans occupied the country, had to escape to Switzerland with her young daughter, Emanuela. Wally had learned that the Germans intended to arrest her—which meant almost certain deportation to a concentration camp—

merely because she was Toscanini's daughter.) Yet Taruskin says that Toscanini "allowed himself to be portrayed—inaccurately—as an exile." Perhaps he believes that only people who are officially expelled from their country of origin qualify as exiles. If this is true, there were almost no exiles from fascist Europe.

In my opinion, the most remarkable anti-Fascist discussed in my *Music in Fascist Italy* was not Toscanini but Massimo Mila (1910–88), the outstanding musicologist and critic, whose convictions landed him in prison for the first time—briefly—when he was nineteen. Later, he was involved in the important center-left underground group, Giustizia e Libertà; he was caught in 1935 and spent five years in prison, after which, undaunted, he became an important figure in the Resistance movement in northern Italy. Mila was little known at the time and enjoyed no special privileges, whereas Toscanini was an international celebrity who did not have to pay the full price for his opposition. On the other hand, most of Italy's international celebrities chose not to act as Toscanini acted. I agree with the unsuspecting Milanese "man on the street" who, in 1931, told one of Mussolini's informers that Milan needed a hundred Toscaninis, and that there were thousands and thousands of people who saw things Toscanini's way but didn't have the courage to say so. Toscanini's political behavior was consistent, honorable, and honest. Of how many public figures has this ever been true when the going was rough?

CHAPTER 6

"Come Back, Thou Bold Singer!": Toscanini and Bayreuth

Berlin, 18 January 1901

Sir,

My son has described to me the performance of *Tristan* that he attended in Milan, and he has had so many good things to say about it that I am taking upon myself the duty of expressing to you the contentment I feel in knowing that a work of such great difficulty was performed with care on a foreign stage.

My son has stressed the meticulous zeal that you brought to the orchestral preparations and the excellent results obtained through that zeal, together with your ability as a conductor. He has also told me that the singers were in perfect command of their roles and delivered them with warmth and enthusiasm.

Lastly, he has spoken to me with great pleasure about the sets owing to Mr. Fortuny's* talent. And—to crown it all—he has praised the audience's rapt attention and perceptive liveliness.

All these indications of your respect for and intuitive understanding of the incomparable work to which you have dedicated yourself, Sir, with so much ardor, have made my son very happy to have been a witness, and from afar I join in his satisfaction.

---

* Mariano Fortuny (Granada, 1871–Venice, 1949) was a well-known set designer and inventor of technical innovations in the theater.

Please be so kind, Sir, as to communicate my feelings to all the interpreters of *Tristan und Isolde* and accept for yourself my congratulations and my sincerest regards.

C. Wagner[1]

WHEN Richard Wagner's widow, Cosima Liszt von Bülow Wagner, sent this letter to Arturo Toscanini, the thirty-three-year-old conductor was in the midst of his third season as conductor of Milan's Teatro alla Scala. The production of *Tristan* to which she referred had opened on December 29, 1900; it was the opera's Milanese premiere and only its fourth production in Italy. (Toscanini attended the first one, conducted by Giuseppe Martucci at Bologna in 1888, and conducted the second one at Turin in 1897.) In 1899, when he attended the Bayreuth Festival for the first time—to hear the *Ring* conducted by Richard and Cosima's son, Siegfried, *Die Meistersinger* conducted by Hans Richter, and *Parsifal* conducted by Franz von Fischer—he sent a picture postcard of Wagner's grave to his brother-in-law, the violinist Enrico Polo; next to the photo he had written, "Here is the tomb of the greatest composer of the century!"[2]

Siegfried Wagner had gone to Milan in 1901 mainly to have a look at La Scala's new lighting system, but, as Cosima's letter indicates, he had indeed been impressed—albeit with reservations—by the *Tristan* production. "I have good things to report from Milan," he wrote to his half sister, Daniela Thode–von Bülow, on January 15, "since the Tristan performance was truly, movingly outstanding":

Charming sets designed by the young Fortuni [*sic*], especially the first act. [Giuseppe] Borgatti [the Tristan] indescribably *Italian-ish*,* a mime-like Isotta [Italian for Isolde; sung by Amelia Pinto], who, with moving innocence, got all of her positions wrong in the first act. Gratifying, on the whole—and finally, it was not entirely without value to see that the house, filled to overflowing—this was the seventh performance— listened very quietly and shushed energetically whenever there was

---

* In translating this letter, I have used the word "Italian" and its variants to translate Siegfried's word *Honol* and its variants. They are not to be found in standard German dictionaries and are unknown to all the native German-speakers I know, including Siegfried's daughter, Friedelind. Given the context in which Siegfried uses it, *Honol* seems to have been a private or code word for "Italian"; it may have been mildly derogatory.

---

any chattering in the galleries. The work grips with such elemental force that even the most frivolous idiots shut their traps. . . . Toscanini [is] an excellent conductor. After the first act I was taken onstage and presented to the board of directors, among whom a splendid-looking Duke [Guido] Visconti [di Modrone] (almost like a Barbarossa)—they gave me champagne and drank to the trionfo dell'arte tedesca [triumph of German art]. The whole made a beautiful and valuable impression. The poor *Italian* operas by Puccini and Mascagni fail beside it. Toscanini was very nice— Dettelchen, if you have a moment's peace, it would be very good of you to send him a line. It would be a beautiful reward for his sincere efforts (the house was even kept dark during the acts). The letter will of course find its way into the newspapers, but in the end that doesn't matter. Coming from you it would have special value. Toscanini and the other *Italians* spoke very humorously and wittily about Mascagni and his colleagues and said with pride that in Milan their operas have never been successful; ma in Germania [but in Germany]![3]

The suggested letter was quickly written, but by Cosima herself, as we have seen, rather than Daniela. It did not find its way into the newspapers; it was first published fifteen years after Toscanini's death, in a scholarly book.

There were almost certainly other occasions on which Toscanini's work was observed by Siegfried and his siblings. From the early years of this century the Wagner family considered Toscanini the greatest conductor in the world; but they could not invite him to Bayreuth because he was non-Germanic, and even before World War I the festival was a center of nationalistic conservatism. The first postwar festival season took place in 1924; Siegfried would have liked to invite Toscanini to conduct a new production of *Tannhäuser* at Bayreuth shortly thereafter, but the festival's conservative supporters would have denied him the necessary funds. He and his English-born wife, Winifred Williams, initiated a fund-raising campaign, so that they could distance themselves from the ultraconservatives. By 1929 they had raised 200,000 marks, a large sum at the time. A new production of *Tannhäuser* was duly scheduled for the 1930 festival and was offered, along with an older *Tristan* production, to Toscanini, who accepted the invitation.

In 1930, the senior conductor at Bayreuth was the seventy-one-year-old Carl Muck, a fine artist (and a former conductor of the

Boston Symphony Orchestra), who had been responsible for the festival's *Parsifal* performances since 1901. Muck was the rallying point of the festival's most conservative supporters, and for professional as well as nationalistic reasons he was not pleased that Toscanini had been invited to Bayreuth. Since the festival orchestra was really two orchestras, each of which played approximately half of the works scheduled, Muck saw to it that Toscanini was given the weaker group to work with. Toscanini battled with the orchestra until the handicap was overcome; understandably, however, he was not pleased with Muck's behavior.

The impression that Toscanini made on the Wagners is summed up in a letter of Blandine Gravina, one of Cosima's daughters by her first husband, the conductor Hans von Bülow. "For eight days," she wrote, "we have been totally caught up in Toscanini's orchestra rehearsals for *Tannhäuser* and *Tristan*. It is the most incredible thing we have ever experienced. Eva [Chamberlain-Wagner, Blandine's half sister], usually impassive, is completely overwhelmed by his greatness." Eva and the others were overwhelmed, in the first place, by Toscanini's purely conductorial talents, the technique and powers of persuasion with which he elicited the best possible results from all concerned; and they were amazed when, rehearsing entirely from memory, he corrected numerous errors that had gone unnoticed for decades by Bayreuth's other celebrated conductors. They were equally impressed by his fanatical attention to detail: Daniela Thode treasured, for instance, a two-page, handwritten note, cordial but insistent in tone, that Toscanini had sent her regarding a single lighting detail in the first act of *Tannhäuser*. And they were incredulous at his refusal to accept payment for his work at Bayreuth; he even turned down a gift of 10,000 marks that the family offered him at the end of the season. He viewed his participation in the festival as an offering at a shrine.

Above all, the Wagners and their adjuncts fell under the spell of the Italian conductor's Wagner interpretations. The only instance of international interpretive incompatibility seems to have been the one described by Kurt Söhnlein, Bayreuth's set designer:

> First ensemble rehearsal on stage of *Tannhäuser*, second act with chorus and orchestra, entrance of the guests: Toscanini takes the famous march (tempo indication: Allegro) unusually fast and increases it still more in

the second half, almost to a Presto. Result: the chorus members stumble over each other. Interruptions, repetitions, two, three times—five, six times! Toscanini rages and shouts all his renowned Italian invective. The chorus members look for help from their longtime conductor, the incomparable Prof. Hugo Rüdel, who is standing at the right front of the proscenium. He shrugs his shoulders in resignation, makes a small backward movement with his head in the direction of the conductor's podium. Embarrassed silence for several long seconds.

Then Siegfried, who is standing at the left of the proscenium, walks slowly to the center of the stage, until he is right out on the apron. He raises his hand a little and says very calmly, in a gentle, muted tone of voice [and in Italian], "Dear Maestro, a little slower, please! There's a difference between singing in the flexible Italian language and in rough German! And we Germans feel this music in another way—than you!" He pauses briefly and lowers his voice still more before the two words "than you.". . .

The angry man stares in silence, his arms folded, for three, five, ten, fifteen, maybe twenty seconds. Deathly silence. Finally, without saying a word, he picks up the baton, raises it, and begins at a slightly slower tempo. Siegfried bows his head a little in thanks, gives an obliging little smile, and goes back to his place. Now all the entrances click perfectly.[4]

Siegfried Wagner, with his fundamentally sunny character, was one of the few people who knew how to deal with Toscanini at such potentially explosive moments, and Toscanini appreciated his talent. Friedelind Wagner, Siegfried's daughter, has said that years later Toscanini told her, "You're just like your father. No matter what happens, you always laugh."[5]

The *Tannhäuser* production opened on July 22, 1930; Sigismund Pilinszky sang the title role, Maria Müller was Elisabeth, Herbert Janssen was Wolfram von Eschenbach, Ruth Jost-Arden was Venus, and Erna Berger was the Shepherdess. The next night Toscanini conducted *Tristan und Isolde*, with Lauritz Melchior and Nanny Larsén-Todsen as the protagonists, Alexander Kipnis as Marke, Rudolf Bockelmann as Kurwenal, and Anny Helm as Brangäne. The profound impression that Toscanini had made on the Wagners during the rehearsals was repeated at the performances. "When I saw [the conductor] Fritz Busch leave the theater," wrote Blandine to Toscanini's wife, Carla, "his eyes full of tears (he who has never had

faith in *Tannhäuser*, nor in the profound *meaning* of Bayreuth)—
I felt drawn toward him by a real impulse, for the first time since
I've known him. . . . Only an artist who, along with his Genius,
possesses a soul of marvelous *human goodness* can stir such a heav-
enly breeze in the souls of others."* The future was to bring even
more overblown statements from Wagner's daughters and step-
daughters. It is useful to remember, however, that they had heard
Wagner's music conducted by Wagner himself, as well as by his
celebrated disciples Bülow, Hermann Levi, Hans Richter, Felix
Mottl, and Anton Seidl. Their measuring stick was an extraordinary one.

SIEGFRIED Wagner, whose already weak heart was aggravated
by the contentiousness of the Bayreuth factions in 1930, died
two weeks after the opening of the festival. His widow, Winifred,
immediately took charge, and in so doing greatly angered her sister-
in-law, Eva Chamberlain, and half sister-in-law, Daniela Thode,
who were a generation older than their brother's wife. They were
pleased, however, by one of Winifred's first important acts: she
informed Muck that his services would not be required for the 1931
festival. *Parsifal* was to be conducted by Toscanini.

Nineteen thirty-one proved to be one of the most difficult years
in the festival's history. In the hope of strengthening her position,
Winifred had engaged Heinz Tietjen, a powerful German theater
administrator, as Bayreuth's artistic director and Wilhelm Furtwängler, principal conductor of the Berlin Philharmonic, as musical
director. Tietjen was not happy about sharing power with Furtwängler and did everything he could to create dissension between
the conductor and Frau Wagner. At the same time, the entire Wagner

---

* The letters of Cosima Wagner's daughters to Toscanini were written in Italian,
with occasional lapses into French and English, both of which he read fluently and
spoke passably, and into German, which he read considerably less easily and rarely
attempted to speak. Blandine Gravina's Italian was excellent—she had lived most of
her life in Italy—whereas Daniela Thode's and Eva Chamberlain's was stiff and
often ungrammatical. In translating parts of their letters, I have not attempted to
reproduce their mistakes or to indicate where they switched from one language to
another. All of the women addressed Toscanini with the formal *Lei* for "you," even
in their friendliest or most hysterically worshipful letters. Cosima's letter to
Toscanini, published at the beginning of this chapter, was written in French.

family—as well as Tietjen and, to some extent, Furtwängler—had to concern themselves with Toscanini's humors, as he had become the festival's star. His naturally volatile temperament was even more unpredictable than usual in the summer of 1931. In May he had been assaulted in Bologna by Fascist thugs for his well-known anti-Fascist beliefs and for refusing to begin a concert with the party's hymn, and he had subsequently decided not to conduct again in his country until democracy was restored; the Fascist government had confiscated his and his family's passports and did not return them until two weeks before he was due to leave for Bayreuth. In addition, he was suffering terribly from a worsening bursitis condition in his right shoulder. And he objected to Winifred's close connections with Adolf Hitler and the rising Nazi movement in Germany.

Furtwängler arrived in Bayreuth before Toscanini. By mid-June he had begun to rehearse for his festival debut with *Tristan*, one of the works Toscanini had conducted the previous year and one of the works in which he admired his younger colleague. "Furtwängler is *immeasurable*," wrote Liselotte Schmidt, Winifred's young secretary; her letters to her family are a good source of information:

[June 18] I would not have expected it. There is a temperament and an urgency in the playing, so that every bar is an experience. The critical aunts [Mmes. Gravina, Thode, and Chamberlain], struck dumb with astonishment at first, now express themselves very enthusiastically. They would never have thought that after Toscanini's *Tristan* such a performance was at all possible. . . . Toscanini will be happy, too, that there are better people [in the orchestra] this year. By the way, he sent a very beautiful and heartfelt telegram to Furtwängler, on [Furtwängler's] first rehearsal day, for the start of his Bayreuth appointment [as musical director]. Really nobly felt. Wini is happy that the first days have been so promising and are proceeding so harmoniously!

[June 26] I really must continue to say: you poor, poor, poor things, who can't experience at first hand, even a little bit, these many, great sensations. Of course I mean "Tosca" first and foremost. [Tosca was the nickname that Carla Toscanini used for her husband; the Wagners used it, too, but not when he was around.] Early yesterday, Thursday, he began his *Parsifal* rehearsals, and thus I was also there at the moment when he entered the rehearsal room and was festively greeted and applauded by the orchestra. He cannot be compared with any other musician at Bayreuth, so high does he stand above the others, despite their masterly performances. One can only say he is a saint, or as Frau Chamberlain nicely put it, "a priest of art." Frau [Winifred] Wagner, who got home [from a trip] at ten o'clock, dedicated yesterday evening to him, as he sat motionless for twenty minutes at the grand piano in Siegfried's study, buried in the *Parsifal* score. Moreover, he knows every note as exactly as perhaps only the Master himself knew it (he always conducts from memory), he also sings many passages, in German for the most part and very expressively, although he otherwise speaks no German. Yesterday I saw a German transcript of *Parsifal* lying on his night table; he had made it for himself and it must have been his bedtime prayer. [*N.B.*: he had presumably written out the text in German to help himself memorize it; his previous performances of *Parsifal* had all been in Italian.] So far he hasn't played [the piano] at night. He has breakfast at 7:30. He is very satisfied with the orchestra (so far he hasn't broken any batons), and things are generally going well. Of course, I cannot talk with him [because of the language barrier], the aunts look after that, so I gave him a very hearty handshake and experienced his unforgettable glance. . . .

[July 1] Things are going well with Tosca; he is a love, a real angel, but is making a lot of difficulties over the cast. Unfortunately, the pains in his arm are very great, but yesterday he heroically rehearsed the whole third act of *Parsifal*; it was unrepeatably beautiful and solemn. In the performance itself it will certainly not be possible to get *so very much* from it!

[July 7] The very pleasant evening had an unexpectedly exciting conclusion for me: as the space in [Winifred's] car was somewhat tight, I had to ride home all alone with Tosca [in the car provided for him], which made him as happy as a lark. We could communicate at best only by our eyes, and every time he looked at me he said, "Belli occi" [*sic.: begli occhi*]— beautiful eyes, whereupon I said the same to him and he caressed me very gently. Yesterday he held the ensemble rehearsal for the third act of *Parsifal*; today come the first and second acts. God knows that there can be no nostalgia for Muck, only *the* Maestro perhaps could do it more beautifully; it was simply unearthly.

[July 18] At the next table [at the festival restaurant] sat Toscanini with his numerous family. The Maestro and I again frequently "made eyes" at each other!! [*N.B.*: that this is Fräulein Schmidt's last reference to her flirtation with the Maestro leads one to suppose that it either ended abruptly, which is unlikely, or became a matter that she chose not to write home about, which would be more in keeping with the sixty-four-year-old Toscanini's previous and subsequent history.]

[July 23] On August 4 a concert in memory of Cosima and Siegfried Wagner will take place in the Festspielhaus. Richard Wagner's Faust Overture (Toscanini), Prelude to Siegfried Wagner's [opera] Heilige Linde and Liszt's Orpheus ([Karl] Elmendorff [who conducted the *Ring* at Bayreuth during both of Toscanini's seasons there]), and Beethoven's Eroica (Furtwängler). This last is of course a concession to the great man [Furtwängler], who originally wanted to conduct everything himself and proposed an all-Beethoven evening, neither of which was feasible, of course. He explained very simply that he was not going to conduct any "Dynasty Program," as if *he* would have any idea!!!!! If things go on like this, one will never emerge from this horrible situation with him, and you can imagine that dear Frau [Winifred] Wagner is much vexed as a result of this; on the other hand, however, she cannot even have true and necessary confidence in him.

[August 5] Yesterday there was, unfortunately, a great disappointment, since Tosca did *not* conduct [at the memorial concert]. I'll tell you more by word of mouth!

What had happened? Daniela Thode, in an addendum to her manuscript, "Bayreuth since 1930," accused "them"—Winifred, Tietjen, and Furtwängler—of having

neglected to invite [Toscanini], the foreign guest and greatest conductor, to take the first rehearsal. . . . There remained only Tuesday, August 4, for his rehearsal of the Faust Overture. . . . Furthermore, the Maestro, whose work on it was not yet ready, did not expect to find himself in front of a sold-out house and paying public—money [was changing hands] for the memorial celebration! He began, was not satisfied, rapped twice; suddenly, while still in the Introduction, he calmly put down his baton and, just as calmly, quickly and quietly walked out. There was great consternation among all who were present and a great uproar in the orchestra. The Maestro had disappeared. They hunted for him through the whole town—in vain. Only later did we hear that he had gone into the nearby mountains. In the evening, while the memorial celebration was going on up in the Festspielhaus, he had been to the cemetery and had laid flowers on Siegfried's grave.

Ten months later, Furtwängler, who by then had broken with Winifred and resigned from the festival, sent Eva Chamberlain a fuller account of the memorial concert incident:

> Berlin W. 10   June 22, 1932
> Hohenzollernstrasse 9
> Most honored and respected lady,
>   Since my relations with Bayreuth and the work at Bayreuth have come to such a sad and unexpected close, and since I have never had the opportunity to discuss all these things with you face to face, I am sending you herewith my correspondence with Frau Winifred Wagner and am attaching a report of the events relating to Toscanini in the summer of 1931 on the occasion of the memorial concert. This has been distorted by certain parties and used propagandistically against me. I think that you will recognize, after having read this correspondence, that I had Bayreuth's interests at heart to the very end but, in this case, could not have acted otherwise. The reasons for Frau Wagner's secrecy, considered purely objectively, are still completely unclear to me today, and she alone must bear the responsibility for all that has occurred.
>
>   I remain, with best greetings,
>   Your very devoted
>   Dr. Wilhelm Furtwängler
>
> *Enclosures*
>   The following report of the affair of the memorial concert for Siegfried and Cosima Wagner in Bayreuth in the summer of 1932 [*sic*; read 1931] is intended to deal with the misunderstandings that have intentionally been circulated about the relations between Toscanini and Furtwängler. This concert was the basis for irresponsible antagonism.
>   The program was decided upon four weeks prior to the concert by Toscanini and General Manager Tietjen, and it was agreed that Elmendorf[f] would conduct pieces by Liszt and Siegfried Wagner, Furtwängler the Eroica, and Toscanini the Faust Overture by Wagner. Since the rehearsal schedule had to be established, *Toscanini was first of all* asked by Furtwängler at which time he preferred to rehearse. Friday, July 31, a day without a performance [of an opera], was scheduled as the

first rehearsal day. On the day before the rehearsal Mr. [Max] Smith [an American journalist who spoke Italian and who had been a friend of Toscanini's since his Metropolitan Opera days], at Toscanini's behest, stated that the latter wanted to drive to Marienbad on Thursday evening and could only come to the rehearsal late in the morning; therefore, he asked to be allowed to rehearse *after* Furtwängler and Elmendorf[f], without having settled on a precise time. It was therefore decided that Furtwängler would begin to rehearse on Friday morning at nine o'clock. Unexpectedly, however, Toscanini—who, contrary to his intentions, had not gone to Marienbad—came to the Festspielhaus early in the morning, stayed awhile to listen to the rehearsal, but then left. His reason was that it seemed senseless to him to have to rehearse, since the orchestra would already be tired from rehearsing with the other conductors. Although the orchestra was extremely busy with the performances, it was agreed upon that he would hold his rehearsal—which, he declared would not be longer than 1¼ hours—the next day, before the beginning of the final rehearsal. The next day, the parts for the Faust Overture, which he was to conduct, could not be found; and, typical of the prevailing atmosphere, two highly agitated répétiteurs appeared at Furtwängler's apartment, with the singular contention that he must have the parts. Only later were the parts found, in a cupboard in Toscanini's Bayreuth apartment, where his servant had stowed them. For this reason, Toscanini's rehearsal could only begin 35 minutes later than scheduled. After Toscanini had rehearsed the Faust Overture for 5/4 [*sic*] of an hour, Furtwängler spoke with him again and emphasized that both he and Elmendorf[f] would gladly schedule all their pieces after him, and that above all he should not feel that he had to rush his rehearsal in any way. At the final rehearsal, too—to which only the artists' friends and relatives were admitted—he would be able to stop and to rehearse as much as he liked. Shortly after the beginning of the final rehearsal, the regrettable incident occurred: Toscanini lost his temper because of a small error in the celli, who declared that he had been beating in eight at the previous rehearsal but was now beating in four. He broke his baton and left the podium in a huff. All the pains that Furtwängler took thereafter to persuade him to continue the rehearsal were fruitless; and in the evening, too, he did not appear on the podium.

The result of this incident was a serious rebellion on the orchestra's part, and only with great difficulty did Furtwängler then manage, in the end, to induce the orchestra to play the rest of Toscanini's performances. Personal relations between Furtwängler and Toscanini were always as good as they could imaginably have been. The selection of the orchestra, which was Furtwängler's work, was fully satisfactory to Toscanini, as he indicated to Furtwängler several times. Even the unfortunate incident of the memorial concert did not disturb relations between Furtwängler and Toscanini, as it did, however, between Toscanini and Bayreuth and between Frau [Winifred] Wagner and Toscanini. Furtwängler, who wanted above all to retain Toscanini for Bayreuth, made repeated attempts to mediate to that end (at the close of the festival and still later in Switzerland), unfortunately to no avail.

There are many discrepancies between Frau Thode's account and Furtwängler's. He had been closer than she to the events described, and his account has a more realistic ring than hers. Furtwängler was certainly correct in saying that his relations with Toscanini were excellent at the time. The summer of 1931 was a difficult period in Toscanini's life, and the series of minor irritations that led up to the memorial concert incident were merely a cumulative last straw; the incident had little or nothing to do with his relations with Furtwängler.

Nor did it adversely affect Toscanini's other work at Bayreuth that summer. The *Tannhäuser* performances (with Melchior in the title role, Gerhard Hüsch as Wolfram von Eschenbach, Maria Müller as Elisabeth, Anny Helm as Venus, and Erna Berger as the Shepherdess) and those of *Parsifal* (with Fritz Wolff and Gunnar Graarud alternating in the title role, Herbert Janssen as Amfortas, Ivar Andrésen as Gurnemanz, Elisabeth Ohms as Kundry, Gotthold Ditter as Klingsor, and Dezsö Ernster as Titurel) were magnificent by virtually all reports. The music critics of Germany's right-wing newspapers had to excogitate addenda to claptrap Nazi racial theories in order to explain how an Italian could conduct Wagner so well. According to Paul Pretzsch, for instance, in the *Chemnitzer Tageblatt und Anzeiger*, Toscanini's conducting was "*echt wagnerisch*," authentically Wagnerian, to such a degree that an unsuspecting listener would never have realized that the conductor was not German. "No one has ever surpassed Toscanini in depth of respect for Richard

Wagner's work and in the accuracy and beauty of the performance of these scores." Pretzsch pointed out that Toscanini had studied not only the composer's instructions printed in the orchestra scores but also those contained in Wagner's collected writings and letters, in the written and oral testimony of his contemporaries, and in Felix Mottl's piano reductions of the operas:

> This is how thoroughly the Latin Toscanini knows the whole creative output of the German master. Are all the famous German conductors able to say the same? Unfortunately not! . . .
>
> Such immersion and such ideally fulfilled performances of German music cannot, however, be within the capabilities of a pure Latin; such a thing could be understood only if there were some basic racial connection in Toscanini, through which purely external political boundaries would lose their significance. Toscanini is a northern Italian. The great intermixing of Nordic blood in northern Italy has often been stressed even in our own day by race researchers. The Nordic influence in the background and especially in the creations of the great Italian painters and sculptors of the Renaissance is unmistakable. . . . By labeling [Toscanini] a "Latin," one is not really examining this man's essence thoroughly; and one must be careful not to judge his participation at Bayreuth with this oversimplified categorization.
>
> . . . Anyone who experienced this year's third and fifth *Parsifal* performances, with the Norwegian and yet so truly "Bayreuthian" Gunnar Graarud as Parsifal, knows that they were the incomparable high point of this year's festival and, moreover, that Richard Wagner's Bayreuth must thank these two magnificent artists—neither of whom was born within Germany's borders, but both of whom are essentially Nordic blood-relations—for these rays of the purest brilliance.
>
> What strikes us Germans as foreign in Toscanini, and where we cannot agree with him, is in his judgment of the human voice. In this respect the Germans feel differently than the Italians: we agree with Richard Wagner, who wanted no vocal ostentation in his works but, rather, authentic, expressive human performers with well-trained, healthy voices. The Italian in Toscanini often places the singer before the actor, which is in keeping with his Italian nationality, but which meant that the selection of certain roles for this year's festival was insufficient for German sensitivity.

Pretzsch's last paragraph is even more absurd than the rest of his article: nearly all of Toscanini's singers at Bayreuth were German and/or German-trained—trained specifically to appeal to "German sensitivity."

TOSCANINI was by no means unhappy with his Bayreuth performances in 1931, but he was disgusted by the infighting and political intrigue that characterized the festival. He departed on August 20, the day after his last performance; in taking leave of Daniela and Eva he told them that he had sent back, unread, a letter that Winifred had had delivered to him, as well as her gift of a Wagner manuscript—the draft of the Flower Maiden scene from *Parsifal*. He had written to thank her for her hospitality, he said, but had added that he was deeply disillusioned with Bayreuth and would not return for the 1933 festival. (None was scheduled for 1932.) He had come to Bayreuth as if it were a temple, he said, but had found himself in an ordinary theater.

But Bayreuth was a temple *and* an ordinary theater: a temple to Wagner's family and disciples, who believed that the composer's work had a world-historical significance similar to that of a major religion; and an ordinary theater insofar as its day-to-day artistic, financial, and organizational difficulties resembled those of other opera houses. The combination had always been potentially explosive, but the explosion had been postponed as long as Richard, Cosima, and Siegfried Wagner had reigned. With all three gone, the Festspielhaus no longer possessed a safety valve. Frau Thode and Frau Chamberlain could not forgive Winifred for excluding them completely from the festival's administration at the time of Siegfried's death, and they saw Toscanini's withdrawal not only as a disaster in itself but also as a direct result of their sister-in-law's newfangled, sacrilegious methods. The day after Toscanini's departure, Frau Chamberlain sent Tietjen a list of complaints that she claimed to have heard the conductor make during the festival—a list that, to her way of thinking, was nothing less than a *J'accuse* against Winifred and Tietjen himself; in her attempt to discredit their management, she blurred the line between Toscanini's reasonable demands and his whims:

1) The Festival administration did not consult with [Toscanini] regarding the choice of new conductors to be brought in.

---

2) The [timing of the] public announcement that Furtwängler was to be made "musical director."

3) No notification of Frau Leyder's [probably Frieda Leider] cancellation. . . .

4) Without Toscanini's knowing it, Ullstein's photographer was given entry to a private rehearsal at the house where Toscanini was staying.

5) Toscanini's remarks to [the stage manager, Alexander] Spring about mistakes in the staging (for instance, the missing shrubbery for Gurnemanz at Kundry's awakening in the third act) *went unheeded.*

6) After a few preliminary queries regarding his participation in the [memorial] concert, a long silence followed, and the program was communicated to him without further discussion, as a fait accompli. [*N.B.*: this differs considerably from Furtwängler's account.]

7) The first and only rehearsal for this concert took place on the very day [of the concert] and was held *before a full house.* Toscanini declared that the Faust Overture is a very hard and little-played work, and is not one of the orchestra's "repertoire pieces." To satisfy his artistic conscience, painstaking *private* work had to be undertaken. He took it badly that in regard to the [subsequent] slanderous press attacks [on him], no objective clarifications were forthcoming from the Festival administration.

8) Toscanini was profoundly hurt that my sister-in-law *never* said a word to him during an intermission or after a performance, [and] he especially and most crucially regretted the lack of this personal touch after the last performance of *Parsifal.* He said bitterly, "Even if there was no spontaneous impulse to do so, courtesy at least demanded it."

Tietjen replied that everything possible had to be done to win back the "God-given Maestro," and he admitted that mistakes had been made on everyone's part. He added, however, that "despite my boundless admiration for the Maestro, I cannot declare him to be guiltless, since even you, highly honored and respected lady, probably do not know about the things that happened during the last five hours of his stay in Bayreuth." In a later letter to Frau Thode, Tietjen specified that by sending back Winifred's letter and gift, Toscanini had "unequivocally made it known that his annoyance was greater than the common courtesy one shows a lady, even had she not been his hostess. I was a witness to this more than painful scene during the last hours of Toscanini's sojourn in Bayreuth, and I was a witness to the collapse of a woman who must have felt her honor deeply wounded by this affront." Frau Thode answered that she already knew perfectly well what had happened to Winifred on the last day of Toscanini's stay, and implied that she didn't care a rap.

But Winifred was just as determined as her sisters-in-law to bring Toscanini back to Bayreuth, especially since Furtwängler, the festival's other star, was also on the verge of withdrawing and did, in the end, withdraw. Even Tietjen had a great deal of prestige to gain by persuading Toscanini to return—and nothing to lose, because Toscanini, unlike Furtwängler, was not interested in participating in the festival's administration and therefore represented no threat to Tietjen's potential sovereignty. The Winifred-Tietjen and Thode-Chamberlain factions jointly decided to leave Toscanini alone until he returned to Europe after his winter season with the New York Philharmonic.

In October, however, before Toscanini left for America, the Bayreuthers found themselves locked in public combat with him. First, Max Smith, with Toscanini's approval, made public the conductor's remark to Winifred Wagner about leaving an "ordinary theater." Then the German newspapers picked up a report in the English-language press, according to which Toscanini had declared that he would never again conduct at Bayreuth, where "Wagner was degraded by Hitler's propagandists." This was an extremely controversial statement in Germany fifteen months before Hitler assumed control of the government. "Toscanini's two published remarks, interpreted by the whole German press as authentic statements by the Maestro, have produced such a devastating impression and influence both at home and abroad," wrote Tietjen to Frau Thode on October 27,

> that unfortunately I must now talk about the last and greatest danger, namely, that I see our work imperilled in the most serious way. I have believed just as little as you, honored and respected lady, that the Maestro could have said such infamous things to the press, because if he had done so, the whole thing would have gone entirely against Siegfried's memory and against Siegfried himself, and this I cannot believe. I believe, honored and respected lady, that for you the great moment has come (since you enjoy the Maestro's full confidence) to put yourself

forward in order to protect the work. *The whole Wagner family* must stand together in complete solidarity in this infamous affair. Existing differences must be cleared up through totally frank discussions and clarifications, which I am entirely ready to arrange. Please, honored and respected lady, induce the Maestro as quickly as possible to make absolutely clear, in a letter to you or to me, that he has had nothing to do with any interviews or press publications in his name. I see this as the last possibility of winning him quickly back to Bayreuth, because the German press, in this time of confusion, is already trying to politicize Bayreuth, and if it succeeds our work is lost.

Toscanini had indeed made the remarks that the press had picked up, although the political comment had been leaked without his approval. He was firmly opposed to the Wagners' political opinions—most family members had been Nazis or at least pro-Nazi virtually from the party's inception—but he shared the older Wagners' principle of keeping art and politics separate. (Not until 1933 would he discover that even the older Wagners were willing to make exceptions to that principle in order to contribute to the luster of a political movement that claimed Richard Wagner as one of its precursors and inspirers.) He therefore made, through Max Smith, another press statement, in which he said he was sorry that his remark had been published; but he did not deny having made it:

> I must stress that I never tie art to politics, which don't concern me at all, either in my own country or in foreign countries; for I feel that every person has the freedom to believe as he will. When I left Bayreuth, I only expressed to Frau Wagner, in a letter, my deep bitterness over the artistic disillusionment I experienced in the theater that I had believed to be a temple of art.

This may have mollified the unobservant, but Tietjen, for one, was not satisfied. He dispatched Frau Thode to Milan, in the hope that the conductor would provide a written retraction of his earlier statements. On November 1 she sent Tietjen a report on her visit:

> You can imagine my serious, wide-ranging conversations, in the course of which I read your letter, or rather translated it, to the dear Maestro, with the omission of a few words. He listened to it intently. He will *not*

write a letter such as you wished either to you or to me. (His telegram to his advisor, Smith, has stated everything clearly and cleanly, in regard to the lying attacks on the part of the press.) But in response to my earnest and repeated pleas, he explained to me again and again in the most unequivocal and forceful way "that he had never granted an interview in his artistic career, nor had he done so in this case, and that by no means had he or would he have relations with the press at all." Most of the articles he hasn't seen at all, except the ones that overzealous friends had brought to his attention—thus I hope that he will not be told about the infamous piece in the *Deutsche Zeitung* and will never be forced into a position in which he will have to break his silence. . . . He knows nothing of the "*two* publications"—his telegram [about the "ordinary theater"] is the first and, God willing, the only authentic (published) declaration in this sad affair. He gladly gives you . . . permission to make his words to me public, and I, too, willingly allow you to use my name. . . .

Concerning the misunderstood term "ordinary theater" I have written you already. As to my reproach to our great friend in this regard—he repeated that this expression did not refer to the *artistry* of our per-formances—he would rather have hit himself in the face [than said such a thing]—but to totally different things that I could only get out of him face to face [*i.e.*, not in writing]. . . .

I did what I could—I did not achieve what you so much wanted, . . . so please treat me indulgently.

All through the winter of 1931–32 and on into the spring, correspondence continued to flow between the two Wagner factions, and Daniela and Eva maintained their friendly contacts with Tos-canini. For his sixty-fifth birthday (March 25), Eva wrote him that her soul was "filled with an ardent prayer: 'Oh kehr' zurück Du kühner Sänger'" ("O come back, thou bold singer"; quote from *Tannhäuser*).[6] On May 19, Winifred visited Toscanini at the vacation home he rented on Lake Maggiore. While she was flying back to Germany that evening, Toscanini wired Daniela: "Winifred come and gone the sky is beautifully clear again agreed I will conduct five [performances of] *Parsifal* eight *Meistersinger* I hope that Wagner's divine spirit will protect me I embrace my dear friends Eva Daniela with immense emotion have a good trip Toscanini." Winifred's point of view is presumably represented in Ms. Schmidt's letter of May 20:

A victory!!! Fu[rtwängler] has [in the meantime] definitely canceled, during the next few days an ugly battle will be enacted in the press—staged by [Berta] Geissmar [Furtwängler's secretary-manager]. Fu. does not yet have any idea about Tosca[nini], and it must not yet be made public, thus no one should feel betrayed! But the thought of having a dear person back again and that the other one—the desecrator of the temple—has been gotten rid of is too blissful for me to be able to keep it from you. The beloved mistress [Winifred] came home with this news yesterday evening, beside herself with happiness.*

WINIFRED Wagner must have been beside herself with happiness again eight months later—on January 30, 1933, to be precise—when Adolf Hitler became chancellor of Germany. In the weeks that followed, Toscanini, who was then in New York, learned that many German musicians he knew and respected—Bruno Walter, Otto Klemperer, the Busch family, and others—were fleeing their country for "racial" or purely political reasons. On April 1, he became the first signatory of a protest message cabled to Hitler by a group of American and American-based musicians. Two days later, Hitler sent him a letter in which he expressed the hope that he would be able to greet him personally at Bayreuth that summer, "to thank you, the great representative of art and of a people friendly to Germany, for your participation in the great Master's work";7 but the next day, Toscanini's recordings and broadcasts, and those of the other signatories of the cable, were banned by the German state radio network. On April 29, Toscanini replied (in English) to Hitler that "it would be a bitter disappointment to me if any circumstances should interfere with my purpose to take part in the coming Festival Plays." By mid-May, Toscanini had realized that "circumstances" in Germany were becoming increasingly sinister and that a return to Bayreuth would mean compromising his human principles. Daniela Thode was again dispatched to Italy, with the blessing of all the Bayreuth factions, to try to persuade Toscanini to change his mind;

* I assume that the drastic change in Schmidt's attitude toward Furtwängler reflected the change in Furtwängler's relations with Winifred Wagner. Hardly more than a year earlier (April 17, 1931), Schmidt had written that Furtwängler "is very simple, natural, without pose and presumption (one can only hold against him that he brought along the loathsome Geissmar, a devilishly shrewd and clever 100 percent Jewess!)." This last remark gives an idea of prevailing attitudes at Wahnfried.

in the end, however, all she could do was communicate his message to the rest of the Wagner clan:

> The sorrowful events that have wounded my feelings as a man and as an artist have not yet undergone any change, contrary to my every hope. It is therefore my duty today to break the silence I had imposed upon myself for two months and to inform you that for my peace of mind, for yours, and for everyone's, it is better not to think any longer about my coming to Bayreuth.

His decision wounded him as deeply as it wounded the festival. In 1937, in a note to Friedelind Wagner—the family rebel, whom he would help to immigrate to the United States at the beginning of the war—Toscanini summed up his feelings: "Bayreuth! The deepest sorrow of my life."

The basic facts of this story were set forth in my biography of Toscanini, but the documents (most of them unpublished) on which this chapter is based came to my attention later. Brief excerpts from a few of the documents appeared in the Italian edition of my *Toscanini* (Turin, 1981) and in my article "Arturo Toscanini: Some New Discoveries," in the January 1982 issue of *Ovation* (New York). Most of the chapter, however, was written for this book. My thanks to Dr. Manfred Eger, director of the Richard Wagner Museum in Bayreuth, and to Elisabeth Furtwängler, the conductor's widow, for permission to quote from the material.

Friedelind Wagner, the "family rebel" mentioned in the last sentence of this chapter, died at the age of seventy-three on May 8, 1991, while this book was in production. She was a generous, outgoing friend and at the same time a solitary human being. Friedelind considered herself an honorary stepdaughter of Toscanini, who helped her immigrate to and survive in the United States during World War II; by a somewhat macabre coincidence, she died only one hour after Wally Toscanini, the older of the conductor's two real daughters, passed away in Rome at the age of ninety-one.

CHAPTER *7*

Toscanini, Hitler, and Salzburg

ARTURO Toscanini's professional relationship with Austria be-gan fairly late in his life, flowered for four years, and ended abruptly when the Nazis came to power. Until he was past fifty, he regarded the Austro-Hungarian Empire as his country's enemy. His father had taken part in Garibaldi's campaigns of the 1850s and '6os to free the Austrian-occupied portions of the Italian peninsula. In 1915, when the Italian government was considering entering the Great War—and deciding on which side to fight—Toscanini strongly supported intervention against Germany and Austria. Not until 1929, when the breach between Italy and Austria seemed permanently mended, did he first perform in Vienna; he was then sixty-two and at the height of his international fame. His initial Viennese performances, at the head of the entire La Scala ensemble, were extraordinarily successful; and he drew similar enthusiasm from public, press, and musicians when he returned to the city the following year with the New York Philharmonic. Galvanized and perhaps a bit alarmed by Toscanini's triumphs, the members of the self-governing Vienna Philharmonic repeated, ever more fervently, their long-standing invitation to him, to appear as their guest con-ductor. The deteriorating European political situation soon helped them to realize their goal.

In 1931 Toscanini had come to realize that he would not be able to conduct again in Italy as long as the Fascist regime was in power, and in the spring of 1933, following Hitler's accession to the German chancellery, he made up his mind not to return to the Bayreuth Festival, where his appearances in 1930 and 1931 had been phenomenally successful. This decision attracted worldwide attention. The celebrated violinist Bronisław Huberman, a Polish Jew, pointed out to him that by performing in neighboring, non-Nazi Austria, Toscanini could make a still stronger protest against Hitler. The Vienna Philharmonic, alerted to Toscanini's interest by its half-Italian president and principal bassoonist, Hugo Burghauser, and encouraged by the Austrian government, once again renewed its invitation. This time Toscanini accepted.

His first performances, in October 1933, were a high point in the orchestra's history. Apparently happy with the Philharmonic and pleased by the unparalleled reception he had received in Vienna, Toscanini returned repeatedly during the following seasons, conducting programs that ranged from Bach to Shostakovich. In 1934 he led the orchestra in concerts at its summer home in Salzburg and was so delighted with the festival and with the beauty of Mozart's native town that he agreed to return the following year to conduct two operas, *Fidelio* and *Falstaff*. In 1936 he added *Die Meistersinger* and, in 1937, *The Magic Flute*. He was to have repeated all four works and to have added *Tannhäuser* in 1938, in a reconstructed theater to which he was contributing financially. Because of Hitler, however, the 1937 series—the culmination of a lifetime's theatrical experience—turned out to be Toscanini's last performances of complete staged operas.

Early in the 1980s, material providing the background to Toscanini's dramatic, politically motivated break with the Vienna Philharmonic and the Salzburg Festival at the time of the Nazi Anschluss became available to scholars at the New York Public Library's Performing Arts Research Center at Lincoln Center. The evidence is contained in a file of forty letters and telegrams, written for the most part by Toscanini and his colleagues, and beginning with a cable, dated December 16, 1937, from Erwin Kerber, director of the Vienna State Opera and the Salzburg Festival Society. Kerber told Toscanini, who was in New York then and throughout the period covered by this correspondence, that existing plans for the following summer's programming had been confirmed. He followed this message with a long letter regarding rehearsal schedules and details of casting, from which we learn that the German government was trying to prevent members of its artists' unions from appearing at Salzburg because the festival had in part taken on an anti-Nazi appearance. Kerber emphasized that "the situation between Austria and Germany will become more difficult week by week"—a statement intended to prepare Toscanini for inevitable casting changes. The usually wily State Opera director had failed to realize that the political implications of his words would alert Toscanini to far deeper problems.

The conductor was rapidly becoming a symbol of nonpartisan resistance to fascist tyranny and an example of committed solidarity with the victims of racism. Late in 1936, Toscanini, a nonpracticing Catholic, had gone to Palestine at his own expense to conduct the first concerts of what later became the Israel Philharmonic, an orchestra formed primarily of Jewish refugees from Germany. Jewish communities throughout the world were grateful to him for his deed, and on February 3, 1938, the governor of New York sent him a telegram: "My heartiest congratulations to you on the award of the American Hebrew Medal for the promotion of better understanding between Christian and Jew in America. Herbert H. Lehman."

The next item in the library's file seems, in retrospect, to have come from a never-never land in which politico-historical cataclysms merely provided a backdrop for backstage squabbles. Bruno Walter, who had been conducting at Salzburg for many years, wrote from St. Moritz on February 4 to inform Toscanini that their colleague, Wilhelm Furtwängler, was exerting pressure to be allowed to conduct at Salzburg during the 1938 season.

Toscanini had invited Furtwängler to conduct at La Scala in 1923; and thirteen years later, as retiring musical director of the New York Philharmonic, he had recommended that the orchestra's board select Furtwängler to succeed him. The announcement of the appointment caused a political uproar. Furtwängler had compromised himself by conducting for Nazi officials, including Hitler, and by accepting honors from the regime. Unlike his younger colleagues Karl Böhm and Herbert von Karajan, he never joined the Nazi party, and he eventually helped to save many Jewish musicians, often at considerable personal risk. Yet he certainly had not taken an unequivocal stand against fascism. Toscanini's recommendation to the Philharmonic was most likely made not only because he respected Furtwängler as a musician but also to give the German conductor an opportunity to take such a stand. Furtwängler, however, was unwilling to give up working in his native country, and the New York position was therefore out of the question.

Toscanini now believed that what he had previously seen as mere indecisiveness on Furtwängler's part was really unpardonable weakness; when Furtwängler was engaged to conduct the Beethoven Ninth at Salzburg in 1937, Toscanini communicated his disapproval to the administration. The two men met for the last time at that summer's festival, and Furtwängler told Toscanini that he would like to conduct opera there the following year. Toscanini knew, however, that the time for political fence-straddling was past. He replied, "You conduct at Bayreuth, I conduct at Salzburg." Each had made his choice and now had to accept the consequences.

But in his letter, written in an awkward Italian (which I have tried to preserve in the translation) that was nevertheless better than Toscanini's German, Walter suggests that Furtwängler had chosen to take Toscanini's words literally rather than to accept their political implication:

Dearest friend Toscanini!

Remembering the events of last year and to avoid new difficulties I believe I must prepare you in good time that once again Furtwängler is doing everything he can to conduct in Salzburg. When he was in Vienna he spoke with the Minister, Dr. Pernter, he told him that he had given up Bayreuth and wants to conduct in Salzburg. (Remember, that you had told him: "You conduct in Bayreuth and I in Salzburg"; so he has now eliminated this reason.) Furtwängler insisted with great energy, and after the answer of the Minister who had promised you, that Furtwängler would not be invited to Salzburg, he has demanded that Pernter beg you once again to consent to Furtwängler's participation.

I would be very grateful if you would write me in a few words your opinion and if the fact, that Furtwängler is no longer going to Bayreuth could change your attitude in this affair.

I hope not. Because Furtwängler's atmosphere is—at least for me—politically, personally, and artistically—intolerable; and particularly at Salzburg. You want nothing but art, and you know, that I too have nothing in my heart but the same; thus the pure spirit of artistic work reigns until now in Salzburg. But Furtwängler has one sole idea: himself, his glory, his success; he is a man of talent, of personal weight but bad-hearted, which expresses itself even in his music-making. I have now in Vienna had new proofs of how bad he is because of his "intrigues" against me—once I will tell you of them. If Furtwängler conducts philharmonic concerts in Vienna and in combination with these one or another performance at the Vienna Opera, I don't want, I cannot make opposition. But if it would be a matter of regular activity at the Opera (which he desires) or in the brief Salzburg season of even one single concert or one [opera] performance I would find it intolerable for me and I would have to say good-bye. [*N.B.*: Furtwängler had of course already conducted at Salzburg the previous summer.]

It seemed to me necessary to inform you of the situation but I have written this letter with the painful feeling that it may give the impression of an "intrigue" on my part. Truly, there exist more noble and more important subjects tying me to you of which I would much prefer to speak than this impure affair; but in fact it is a matter here of "intrigues" on Furtwängler's part against you, against me, against the spirit of Salzburg and it is necessary to know of them and possibly to act in the higher interest. I would therefore like to know your opinion upon which my "modus procedendi" depends to a certain degree. Naturally I promise to keep your answer confidential as I beg you to treat discreetly this letter of mine too.

I hope that you are in very good health and that you feel satisfied and happy with your work in New York. In April I hope to see you again and to look at the new house in Salzburg together with you.

Very affectionate greetings, also to your family and also from mine, in true friendship your faithful

Bruno Walter

Furtwängler must have been so desperate to keep his career afloat outside as well as inside Germany that he was willing to sacrifice Bayreuth in the attempt; and Walter was equally desperate to protect his own position in Vienna. Toscanini had no official power at the festival; but since his presence was its biggest drawing card, the administration was reluctant to make any decision on musical policy without his consent. (All of Toscanini's Salzburg appearances were completely sold out excepting a single *Falstaff* evening in 1937 with 98 percent attendance. His performances brought seat sales for the whole festival up to an unprecedented average of 88 percent.) One wonders what Walter's *modus procedendi* would have been had Toscanini said, "If Furtwängler has really given up Bayreuth, let him come to Salzburg."

TOSCANINI never had to deal with the matter: by the time Walter's letter reached him, political events had made it obsolete. On February 12, Austrian Chancellor Kurt von Schuschnigg met Hitler and bowed to some of his demands: he accepted Artur Seyss-Inquart, a leading Austrian Nazi, as minister of the interior and head of the national police force, and he aligned Austria's foreign and economic policies with Germany's. Schuschnigg hoped that these concessions would allow his country to maintain its independence.

Two days after that meeting, Toscanini's daughter Wally, who spoke German well, received a cable from Max Reinhardt, the celebrated Austrian Jewish director and impresario. Reinhardt had spent much of his working life in Germany but had immigrated to California after the Nazi takeover. During the intervening years he had returned annually to the Salzburg Festival, which he and Hugo von Hofmannsthal had founded in 1920, and where their celebrated production, *Jedermann* (Everyman), was always a major event. Reinhardt had become a great admirer of Toscanini's work. (The two also had a mistress in common, the actress Eleonora von Mendelssohn, great-grandniece of the composer and goddaughter of Eleonora Duse.) In his cable, Reinhardt told Wally: "The latest developments in Austria are still unclear as seen from here but in the opinion of many competent people are in any case serious stop May I beg you in most cordial friendship to inform me promptly of your esteemed father's possible intentions and resolutions as I would like to make my own arrangements in accordance Greetings of high esteem from your Max Reinhardt." And two days after the Reinhardt cable, a similar request for word of Toscanini's plans was sent by the German soprano Lotte Lehmann, who had sung in Toscanini's Salzburg productions of *Fidelio* and *Meistersinger*, to Margherita De Vecchi, a close friend of the Toscanini family: "Please dear Margherita wire me what Maestro thinks about Salzburg Will he come there now or shall he cancel Am very excited and worried Please give him my love Answer collect by Western Union Mark Hopkins Hotel yours Lotte."

Walter, Reinhardt, and Lehmann—all outstanding figures in the musical-theatrical world—were hanging back. If Toscanini were going to take a principled stand, they could not very well do otherwise; if he were not, they could afford to wait and see what would happen next.

The file does not contain answers to their inquiries. But on February 16, the date of Lehmann's telegram, this cable was sent to Kerber: "The current political events in Austria oblige me to renounce my Salzburg Festival participation Greetings Toscanini." And Toscanini sent a similar message on the same day to the governor of Salzburg Province.

BOTH panic-stricken recipients of this news cabled Toscanini the very next day. They told him, and they probably even believed, that the situation was not as bad as he thought, that false rumors must have been circulating in New York, and that he should await clarification, which would be forthcoming through the Austrian Foreign Office. They must have known, however, that Toscanini rarely changed his mind on matters of principle; when the contents of his cable to the Governor were published the next day in newspapers throughout the world, they were accompanied by the rumor that the festival's directors were already trying to replace Toscanini with Leopold Stokowski. If this is true, their attempts were unsuccessful. Furtwängler, however, immediately applied to the Reich's Chancellery in Berlin for permission to replace Toscanini. Hitler turned down the request but changed his mind after the Anschluss.

Toscanini began to receive letters and telegrams of congratulations and thanks for his uncompromising stand against fascism as soon as his cables became public. Richard Benda (secretary of the Society of Professional Musicians), all thirty members of the orchestra at New York's radio station WOR, *New York Times* music critic Olin Downes, and many others wrote to express their admiration. From exile in London, Luigi Sturzo, the priest who had founded Italy's Popular Party, which had been banned by the Fascists, sent Toscanini a laudatory article he had written, along with a note:

February 23, 1938
Dear Illustrious Maestro,
    Having read the news of your refusal to continue to conduct operas and concerts at Salzburg following the nazification of Austria, I wrote

an article for three daily newspapers; one in Paris (*L'Aube*), the second in Brussels (*La Cité Nouvelle*), the third in Bellinzona (*Popolo e Libertà*).

I take the liberty of sending you the Italian original, along with my most cordial and devoted homage.

Luigi Sturzo

Most moving was a letter from Gaetano Salvemini, one of Italy's finest historians. An exile from his native country, Salvemini was at that time on the faculty of Harvard University. The handwritten letter is on Viking Press stationery:

February 18, 1938
Dear Maestro,

I have been repeating to myself for two days that it would be absurd on my part to inflict one more letter on you, amid who knows how many other letters and telegrams that you will be receiving these days. But so be it. Whether it is absurd or not absurd, I have to write to you, to tell you of my emotion, admiration, recognition, and enthusiasm for the new proof of generosity and character that you have given by refusing to go to Salzburg.

In these Borgia-like years, you are the only person whose moral light remains steady amid the universal baseness. Among those who speak to the future, you are the only one who has always remained faithful to the pure and beautiful tradition of the Italian soul. You are the only one who, at those important moments when we were lost in the darkness of despair, shouted words of faith, duty, and hope at us.

In its three-thousand-year history, Italy has produced the most unheard-of contrasts: Marcus Aurelius and Romulus Augustulus, St. Francis and Alexander VI, Dante and Stenterello, Leonardo da Vinci and Bertoldino.* Fate has not been so adverse today as may seem, at first glance, to be the case, to those of us who have been scattered through the world by the tempest. To those cowards who bow down before the Great Beast, taking it to be Italy, we can teach that Italy is today represented not by Mussolini but by Toscanini.

---

* As Salvemini well knew, Italy was the victim rather than the progenitor of the Spanish Pope Alexander VI Borgia. Stenterello was a good-natured simpleton in late eighteenth-century Florentine popular theater. Bertoldino was a similar figure in early seventeenth-century comedy.

Thank you, dear Maestro, for the good you do us, for the strength you give us—not to speak of the pure happiness for which we are indebted to your art.

May our Italy live forever—the Italy of Mazzini, which still continues, through you, dear Maestro, to speak to the world in terms worthy of its history and its nobility.

G. Salvemini

The file also contains letters that urged Toscanini to reconsider his stand in order to help save Austria. None of the writers of these letters specified, however, what other course a musician ought to take to influence Hitler's policies. Others rushed to persuade Toscanini to start festivals in the United States, Holland, and elsewhere. The only one of these pleas to which he appears to have replied directly was a cablegram from Reinhardt, who had followed the conductor's lead and had publicly given up Salzburg:

Hollywood March 4 1938
On my initiative a group of influential people intends to found in California a new Salzburg[:] to organize[,] that is[,] productions in better climatic and political circumstances and probably with vaster means stop In beautiful countryside a theater for operas concerts and dramas would be built responding to all the requirements and furnished with the most recent refinements which could perhaps already be opened in the fall stop If it were possible to interest you illustrious Maestro in the idea of transferring your incomparable art here for a part of the year spring summer or fall provided that your conditions were completely met you would be promoting this effort to create a new and free artistic center far from the artistic areas politically profaned[.] You would add a historic labor as pioneer to the sublime work of your life since along with the friends of art throughout the whole world crowds from the surrounding places would also attend[.] They heretofore have barely been brushed by art but their calm receptivity and capacity for enthusiasm is certainly greater than that which the feverishly restless New York can give stop If therefore you do not in principle exclude this certainly fecund possibility I beg you to give me telegraphically permission to send you a representative of that group before your departure [for Europe.] In any case please attribute the urgency of this call not only to the situation of the moment but above all to my devoted affection and to my long-

standing aspiration for an artistic collaboration with you With profound
homage Max Reinhardt

An undated handwritten draft of Toscanini's telegraphic reply states:

Dear Max Reinhart [*sic*] Thank you for your high esteem which honors
me[.] I have reflected on your proposal but my age no longer allows me to
embark upon a new theatrical undertaking stop The contract drawn up
the other day with the N.B.C. [Symphony Orchestra] eliminates any
possibility of accepting other commitments. Very sorry[.] I greet you
cordially. A.T.

Age and existing responsibilities were the excuses that Toscanini
most readily used when he did not want to do something. We can
only regret that he did not undertake to conduct opera in collaboration with Reinhardt during the last years of the director's life.

The most extraordinary of the communications that Toscanini
received following his Salzburg decision came from friends and
colleagues in or directly connected with Austria. A former lover,
Elsa Kurzbauer, who had since been befriended by Toscanini's wife,
Carla, cabled to Signora Toscanini:

Vienna, February 18, 1938
Everyone very desperate because of Maestro's renunciation which is
unfounded regarding conditions Chancellor and Governor Rehrl remain
here thus giving better guarantees You probably heard greatly exaggerated newspaper reports Salzburg Festspielhaus and season would be
ruined Very worried long silence Please telegraph me news Affection   Elsa

At the bottom of Elsa's cable, someone—probably Toscanini—drew
three bold exclamation points.

Lotte Lehmann's telegram to Toscanini reveals her fear:

San Francisco February 19, 1938
Dear Maestro Do not be angry with me I do not believe everything that
is said in the newspapers I do not think that the situation is clear enough
I do not want to lose my second country unless it is absolutely necessary
but I would sing there only if art remains free stop It is very unfair to

have asked artists their opinions of so uncertain a situation I beg you not
to be unfair toward your very devoted   Lotte

Burghauser hoped that Schuschnigg's latest reassuring speech
would bring Toscanini back to Salzburg. And Cosima Wagner's aged
daughter, Daniela Thode, torn between her irreconcilable idols,
Toscanini and Hitler, cabled the conductor from Bayreuth: "Deso-
late I beg you not to abandon us Daniela." This appeal had no greater
effect than the one she had made five years earlier, urging Toscanini
to return to the nazified Wagner festival.

From Vienna, Bruno Walter, who still refused to understand
what was happening, bombarded Toscanini with cablegrams like
this one (February 19):

Continuation Austrian cultural program convincingly and unequivocally assured to me by very authoritative source I have signed new
contract with Staatsoper stop Please support from your side as well
contribution to Salzburg In friendship Walter

These messages were followed by a letter in clumsy Italian:

Vienna, February 20, 1938
Dearest friend,
    You have known me for some time and I am sure that you have
confidence in my conscience and my truthfulness. Please believe me that
I would be the first to leave if there would be a change in the principles
necessary to the life of an artist who needs freedom in his spiritual life.
Up to now Austria's cultural course has not changed. I have the government's assurance that nothing will change. All I want to ask you is to
await how things develop in Austria. If Austria either becomes united
with Germany or accepts German orders for her policies, please do not
doubt that I too would leave here immediately. But up to now the
chancellor defends Austria like a true Knight of the Holy Spirit, making
concessions in the least important areas to save independence in everything that counts. Therefore the government needs to be supported and
it would be a fatal blow to lose your friendship which [it] needs more
than ever and which up to now it deserves more than ever. I only want to
ask this: wait, dearest friend, until the development of events can prove
in clarity where Austria's course is going. If this course adapts

itself to the German course, your attitude was just and it will also be mine. But if developments should prove that Austria is not changing important principles, please return to Salzburg which can no longer live without you and don't leave me there alone, because your absence would mean Furtwängler's activity, intolerable for me and I too would therefore leave Salzburg, in order not to be taken for a colleague of Furtwängler. The reasons for your resolution have been influenced by the news in the papers; this news has been false or exaggerated. I live here, I am in touch with the events themselves and I would like to assure once again that up to now nothing has happened, that could offend humanity. The publication of my new contract with the Staatsoper was necessary to calm those souls who were agitated by rumors. Once again: please wait and don't leave Austria in case it goes its own independent road and don't leave me. And once again believe me that I too would leave Austria if developments become unworthy for an artist to work or to live here.

Best wishes and most cordial greetings from your faithful friend

Bruno Walter

Walter apparently believed that, in the event of a complete Nazi takeover in Austria, Hitler would offer him a choice as to whether or not he would continue his activities there! But by the time his letter arrived in New York, Toscanini had already answered him. His handwritten draft (February 21) of the cable he sent is typical of him:

Futile to await your letter my decision however painful is final stop. I have only one way of thinking and acting. I hate compromise. I walk and I shall always walk on the straight path that I have traced for myself in life. Cordial greetings.

Two cable messages bring the file to an abrupt end. The first, sent to Toscanini on March 2 by the festival's administration, expresses the hope that clarifications had by then been made (the Austrian consul general had sought a meeting with him, but we do not know whether he had granted it) and that he would change his mind. "[. . .] Please as soon as possible not later tenth March communicate this regard Otherwise we are forced to consider your renunciation final."

The reply: "I am surprised by your insulting telegram and I am surprised that the finality of my decision was not already understood from my first cable. A. Toscanini"

A few days later, Hitler entered Austria, and in the following month an overwhelming majority of the Austrian people voted in favor of unification with the German Reich. That summer, Furt-wängler, Hans Knappertsbusch, and Vittorio Gui conducted what had been Toscanini's Salzburg productions, in the newly recon-structed theater for which he had helped to pay. Bruno Walter, Lotte Lehmann, Hugo Burghauser, and Elsa Kurzbauer all found refuge in the United States, the last two with the assistance of Toscanini and his family. Like Toscanini, they all lived to see the fascist powers defeated.

This chapter first appeared in the quarterly literary journal *Grand Street* (Autumn 1986), under the title "Salzburg, Hitler and Toscanini." It was later published, in whole or in part, in *La Stampa* (Turin, October 30 and 31, 1986) under the titles "No a Salisburgo nazista" and "Una bacchetta simbolo di libertà"; in *Nuova rivista musicale italiana* (Rome, April–June 1987) as "Toscanini, Hitler e Salisburgo"; in *Le Monde de la musique* (Paris, May 1987) as "L'Homme revolté: Toscanini, Hitler et Salzbourg"; and in the *Neue Zeitschrift für Musik* (Mainz, July–August 1987) as "Salzburg, Hitler und Toscanini." About 15 percent of the *Grand Street* version has been eliminated here to avoid, as much as possible, overlap with Chapters 5 and 6.

CHAPTER *8*

The Toscanini Legacy

IN December 1986, Arturo Toscanini's heirs and the New York Public Library signed an agreement that settled the fate of one of the most important musical archives of the century, after seventeen years of frustrating uncertainty.

For a substantial portion of the musicians and other artists and intellectuals of his day, as well as for millions of casual listeners, Toscanini represented the highest level of artistic responsibility on the part of an interpreter toward the works of art being interpreted. Throughout much of his long life, and especially during the 1920s and '30s, when his career was at its apogee, he found himself at the center of a cultural world that had never before accorded so much respect to an orchestra conductor.

Thus, the Toscanini archive—the Toscanini Legacy, as it is officially known, within the library's structure—has a significance that is broadly cultural and historical as well as musical. Its contents are probably more varied and extensive than are the archives of any other performing musician of Toscanini's day, thanks, above all, to the efforts of the conductor's son. Walter Toscanini (1898–1971) was a born collector, whereas his father rarely saved letters, contracts, programs, photographs, newspaper clippings, or any of the other mementos that most performers treasure. He even hated making phonograph records—at least until his last years—not only because the acoustical results were often unsatisfactory, but also because he was usually dissatisfied with his own work. During the 1920s, Walter had run an antiquarian bookshop and small publishing house in Milan, together with his future brother-in-law, Count Emanuele di

Castelbarco. Later, he developed an outstanding collection of historic material relating to the ballet, influenced, no doubt, by his wife, Cia Fornaroli (1888–1954), prima ballerina at La Scala during the 1920s; that collection, too, now belongs to the New York Public Library. After he and his family moved to the United States in 1938 for political reasons—Walter was even more rabidly anti-Fascist than his father—he dedicated himself increasingly to assisting his aging father. Simultaneously, almost automatically, he collected everything that had to do with his father's career.

In 1967, ten years after his father's death, Walter became gravely ill. The family's mansion in Riverdale (Bronx) was sold in 1970, a year before Walter's death, and its contents were packed up and taken away in twenty-three moving-van loads. Most of the material was deposited in the vast basement of the Library and Museum of the Performing Arts, the New York Public Library's Lincoln Center branch; but when Walter died, the archive's fate had not yet been decided. The University of Texas made a bid, but not all of the conductor's heirs—who included his daughters, Wally (later represented by her daughter, Countess Emanuela di Castelbarco) and Wanda (Mrs. Vladimir Horowitz), and Walter's son, Walfredo, a graduate of the Yale School of Architecture—believed that Texas was an ideal location for Toscanini's archives: apart from a few performances the conductor had given there in 1950, the state had no connection with Toscanini. Offers came from other sources, too, but difficulties always arose. By the twentieth anniversary of Toscanini's death, the salability of his name had begun to decline, and so had the resources of many American cultural institutions. In 1979, there was an offer from McMaster University in Hamilton, Ontario, which had recently acquired Bertrand Russell's papers; but this proposal, too, fell wide of the mark.

Once in a while, the New York Public Library would make its collective voice heard. In 1984, serious negotiations between library representatives and the Toscanini family began—slowly, at first—and an inventory was prepared, thanks to nine months of intensive work under the supervision of Arthur Fierro, who had been Walter Toscanini's assistant in the 1960s. By the time the agreement was signed, the material had reportedly been valued at between $1.5 and $2 million, but the family was said to have received only about $350,000 from the library; the rest of the collection was given as a donation.

The archive includes approximately 1,700 hours of recordings of Toscanini, dating from the period 1920–54. About 90 percent of this material is unpublished; it is made up of live recordings of concerts, opera performances, and rehearsals. There are, for instance, many New York Philharmonic radio broadcasts recorded between 1931 and 1936 and all of the more than 200 NBC Symphony broadcasts, recorded between 1937 and 1954. The estimated 500 hours of rehearsal tapes constitute, in themselves, one of the most important legacies in the history of recorded sound.

Thousands of orchestra and opera scores, many of them annotated by Toscanini, in addition to a large number of orchestra parts containing his indications, make up another of the fundamental sections of the collection and are another source of enormous interest for musicians. There are also rare scores and scores of works studied but never conducted by Toscanini, whose musical interests extended from Frescobaldi and Monteverdi to Bartók and Stravinsky.

Of interest to historians is the biographical archive, which contains documents and other relevant material that Walter Toscanini managed to collect from all the countries in which his father had conducted, as well as correspondence with Giacomo Puccini, Claude Debussy, Richard Strauss, Richard Wagner's family, Zoltán Kodály, Victor De Sabata, Serge Koussevitzky, Felix Weingartner, Leopold Stokowski, Bruno Walter, Erich Kleiber, Enrico Caruso, and dozens of other musicians. There are also letters from other artists and intellectuals—Stefan Zweig, Paul Valéry, and Albert Einstein, for example—and from political figures, including Franklin D. Roosevelt, Benito Mussolini, and Adolf Hitler.

As soon as the agreement was announced, laments were heard in Italy. Why, people asked, had Toscanini's archives found a home in the United States rather than in his native country? But Toscanini did much of his work in New York, his principal home for the last two decades of his life, and there he ended his days. Walter Toscanini created the archive there, and he and other family members assumed that it would remain there. Some of them feared that in Italy the material would be less accessible than in America, because of the severely limited hours during which many Italian libraries are open to the public and the tendency of some Italian librarians to treat archives as private treasures to be defended from the people for whom they were intended—although such types exist in other countries, too. Before the library's acquisition of the archive, however, the idea of sending the collection to Italy was not ruled out. In 1982, when negotiations in America were at a halt, I participated in an appeal, launched in the *Corriere della Sera* and aimed at interesting Italian public or private institutions in acquiring the archives. To the best of my knowledge, there was not a single significant response, positive or negative; so the complaints, although not unexpected, are hardly justified.

In any case, the battle seems to have been won by all concerned. Four months before the official announcement of the acquisition, library administrators responsible for the Toscanini Legacy demonstrated their willingness to cooperate with Italian organizations by agreeing to loan valuable autograph letters and other material to a Toscanini exhibition being organized in his hometown, Parma, and expressed great interest in a continuing cooperative effort with a permanent Toscanini documentation center that the authorities in Parma were planning to set up under the aegis of the Parma-based regional orchestra of Emilia-Romagna.

This is a revised version of an article that originally appeared in *La Stampa* (Turin) on April 1, 1987. During the intervening period, the most important development in the Toscanini Legacy has been the restoration, under the supervision of Seth Winner, of recordings of three of the four operas that Toscanini conducted at the Salzburg Festival in 1937—*Falstaff, Die Meistersinger*, and *The Magic Flute*—as well as recordings of *The Marriage of Figaro* and *Don Giovanni* conducted there by Bruno Walter; the singers in the five performances include Mariano Stabile, Alexander Kipnis, Ezio Pinza, Helge Roswaenge, Jarmila Novotná, Willi Domgraf-Fassbaender, Maria Reining, Kerstin Thorborg, and Anton Dermota. These remarkable recordings had previously circulated only among specialists and collectors and in reproductions of extremely poor quality; they are now as listenable as other reasonably good recordings of the period, and they ought to be issued.

Most of Toscanini's marked scores are now available for examination; and the rest of the material, including the bulk of the documents, ought to be accessible by the mid-1990s. Bureaucratic delays have prevented the Arturo Toscanini Documentation Center in Parma, intended to be a far-reaching archive of material regarding all the important conductors of the past, from being formed; a similar project is pending at La Scala.

CHAPTER 9

Misunderstanding Toscanini

M OST of Arturo Toscanini's long life was spent in Italy. It was there, especially at La Scala, that he fought, and generally won, his great battles to update and internationalize the operatic and symphonic repertoires, and to improve performance standards in the theater and concert hall. The conductor's principal North American engagements were with the Metropolitan Opera (1908–15), the New York Philharmonic (1926–36), and the NBC Symphony Orchestra (1937–54). His popularity in the United States was at its greatest during the Philharmonic and NBC periods, and he made most of his recordings at NBC.

Joseph Horowitz, a music critic, has listened to some of those recordings, and he dislikes most of what he has heard. He is convinced, too, that Toscanini's conservative repertoire during those years had a bad influence on contemporary musical life in the United States, and that the exceptional degree of attention that Toscanini received in the press gave the public a mistaken notion of a performer's proper place in the musical hierarchy. In Horowitz's account, Toscanini and the American music industry enjoyed a mutually profitable relationship at the expense of "Music." Their alliance, he believes, paved the way for such current phenomena as television's "Great Performances" series (music for the eye) and Luciano Pavarotti's chats with Johnny Carson.

Review of *Understanding Toscanini: How He Became an American Culture-God and Helped Create a New Audience for Old Music,* by Joseph Horowitz; New York: Knopf, 1987.

Horowitz's disorganized, ponderous, and repetitive study would be eminently ignorable if it weren't dressed up as something other than the book of opinion that it is. Instead, Horowitz purveys it as a work of scholarship, at least in part. Its conclusions are extremely questionable, and Horowitz sets them up in the first pages of the book: he calls Toscanini the "high priest of the music appreciation movement of the '30s and '40s" and condemns "the Toscanini movement's infectious cultural populism," as if the conductor and his admirers—knowledgeable and ignorant, rational and fanatical, celebrated and anonymous—had banded together for seditious purposes. "No book-of-the-month club had a salesman to rival Toscanini," declares Horowitz.

Dwight Macdonald, in his essay, "Masscult and Midcult," proposed that mass culture and high culture were merging into a flavorless "midcult" that waters down and vulgarizes the standards of the high culture that it pretends to represent. Horowitz refers to Macdonald (who admired Toscanini—a fact Horowitz fails to mention) when he writes that "propagated by *Time* and *The New York Times*, Toscanini's cult was the definitive midcult phenomenon for music in this century." Never mind Stokowski and *Fantasia*, Arthur Fiedler and the Boston Pops, the apotheosis of Leonard Bernstein, the Karajan–Deutsche Grammophon–Unitel triumvirate, and whatever horrors await us in the 1990s; Toscanini's "cult" was "definitive." And later, in the possibly midcultish and certainly offensive style in which much of the book is written, Horowitz returns to this theme: "Toscanini's redundant Beethoven and Weber, Dvořák and Elgar, were as instantly and effortlessly preoccupying as a drawn six-shooter at the movies or a three-and-two count, bases loaded, at the ballpark."

For Horowitz, in short, whatever Toscanini did, or did not do, was wrong and harmful. He never granted interviews or made a public spectacle of himself—but, Horowitz says, this only contributed to the mystique that surrounded him. He was able to raise the technical standards of orchestras and operatic ensembles—but, Horowitz says, this was because he considered technique more important than substance. Toscanini's controlled yet intense way of conducting and his magnetic personality usually elicited excellence and devotion from singers and players—an extramusical and therefore, by implication, reprehensible cause of his fame. (Horowitz's pseudoanalyses of Toscanini's conducting and the NBC Symphony Orchestra's reactions to it betray his embarrassing ignorance of how conductors and orchestras function.) He had spent forty years, in Italy and elsewhere, struggling to disseminate the works of Wagner, Brahms, Mussorgsky, Tchaikovsky, Dvořák, Puccini, Debussy, Richard Strauss, Sibelius, and many other composers, before he decided to dedicate his last years to getting closer to the masters he loved best; but this concession to personal taste on the part of a man who had crusaded for the modern music of his day is described as a betrayal of artistic responsibilities. Even the expressiveness of his face is made to seem an unfair weapon used by Toscanini against "Art."

Horowitz takes us, bizarrely, back to the days of P. T. Barnum's sponsorship of Jenny Lind, and to the pages of Mark Twain's *Innocents Abroad*, to show that nineteenth-century Americans—whose major concerns, he says, were efficiency and progress—mistrusted European culture while standing guiltily in awe of it. Assimilating sophisticated culture, like reading the Bible, was considered good for the soul but boring. Barnum realized that by offering musical performances of great virtuosity, by persuading people that virtuosity and culture are synonymous, by publicizing his artists' spirituality and humanity, he could combine moral uplift with entertainment—for his own immense profit. Reasonable, so far, but Horowitz traces a long, crooked, impassable path from Barnum to Toscanini. The conductor's prodigious memory, his insistence on correct playing, and his credo of faithfulness to the composers' intentions especially appealed to Americans, says Horowitz, because Americans, more than Europeans, admire prowess, know-how, and uncomplicated moral behavior. Similarly, Toscanini's humble origins and his courageous stand against fascism are said to have appealed to Americans because Americans believe in the self-made man and have a strong, if naive, sense of justice. Toscanini was exotic and irascible enough to satisfy preconceived notions about artistic temperament, but simple and humble enough to qualify as a real person. This mattered because, says Horowitz, "more than Europeans, Americans abhor elitism and apply democratic values with broad strokes." Broad strokes, indeed!

To support these and other astonishingly simplistic ideas about Toscanini's American popularity, Horowitz quotes at sleep-inducing length from the writings of the conductor's most gushing American admirers of the period, notably the newspaper critics Lawrence Gilman and Olin Downes, whose fulsome praise was indeed revolting. But is there any reason to believe that intelligent musicians and members of the public in those days paid more attention to Gilman, Downes and Company than today's acute listeners pay to today's loudest critics? And why does Horowitz think that praise for Toscanini was more vociferous and less rational in the United States than elsewhere? "La Scala's performances moved and shook the public and sent it into ecstasy," wrote the *Frankfurter Zeitung's* critic, Karl Holl, about Toscanini's Berlin appearances in 1929, when the city's opera conductors regularly included Bruno Walter, Wilhelm Furtwängler, Erich Kleiber, and Otto Klemperer. "It remains a success without precedent in the modern history of German opera." And of the same series of performances, the musicologist Alfred Einstein, not normally given to sensationalism, wrote in the *Berliner Tagblatt*, "For us, it has been much more than an extraordinary operatic event. It has been an example; it has been the discovery of an infinitely simple secret: that the exceptional can be reached only by means of the absolute will of a man possessed by music, fanatically dedicated only to music and to nothing else, and that the basis for achieving the extraordinary consists in working, in serving the cause, and nothing else." This remark was made not by an American, or even by an Italian, but by one of the most celebrated German musicologists of the twentieth century, and at the moment when the cultural life of Berlin under the Weimar Republic was at its richest.

Likewise, when Toscanini first conducted the Vienna Philharmonic, in works of Mozart, Beethoven, Wagner, and Brahms, the music historian Ernst Decsey observed in the *Neues Wiener Tagblatt*, "It was the great Italian artist who honored our German masters and brought the Philharmonic to a hitherto unachieved triumph. . . . But it will be rather hard for those who follow Toscanini on the Philharmonic's podium, since everyone will be measured against his vastness, everyone will be compared to what is incomparable." European musicians, even those who greatly differed from him stylistically, lauded him, too. Klemperer dubbed Toscanini "the king of conductors," Monteux called him "the greatest of all," and Paderewski described him as "a transcendent genius"—hyperbole, perhaps, but certainly not American hyperbole. Comments like these, from the great majority of musicians and critics, appeared wherever Toscanini did.

No less grating than even the most uninformed fans' hosannas were Theodor W. Adorno's convoluted, dogmatic accusations, of which Horowitz approves, with reservations. Adorno was a Schoenbergian and a Marxist; thus Toscanini—who was deaf to the music of the Second Viennese School, and who received astronomical fees from an American corporation (RCA)—represented, in Adorno's estimation, poor musical judgment and crass capitalism at its worst. For a "ruined farmer," Horowitz quotes Adorno, "an order of things that allows him to hear Toscanini compensates for low market prices for farm products; even though he is ploughing cotton under, radio is giving him culture." Adorno presumably had inside information that revealed how many ruined farmers or otherwise exploited Americans counted themselves among Toscanini's fans and considered his broadcasts adequate consolation for their economic woes. And Horowitz presumably finds the premise reasonable enough to use in support of his own specious argumentation.

Horowitz speculates that Toscanini bears a significant degree of responsibility for the petrifaction of the repertoire, and that this congelation was a typically twentieth-century American phenomenon. He confutes his own argument, however, in reporting that as early as 1855, 76 percent of the Leipzig Gewandhaus Orchestra's repertoire was by dead composers, and that the programs of Vienna's Gesellschaft der Musikfreunde, London's Philharmonic Society, and Paris's Société des Concerts were similarly balanced—or unbalanced—by that time. One of the flaws in his theory of repertorial stagnation is its failure to distinguish between the operatic repertoire, which, in much of Europe throughout the nineteenth century, constantly shed old works in favor of new ones, and the symphonic repertoire, which, from the 1830s on, turned over at a much slower rate; and operas were generally aimed at a much larger public than instrumental works. Today, the apparently unbridgeable gap between most contemporary composers of music for either the stage or the concert hall and most people who listen to the classics is generally considered the result of highly complicated international social and artistic conditions that have been germinating for well over a century. Toscanini's later symphonic repertoire was a manifestation, not a cause, of these developments; and his career as an opera conductor (excepting occasional appearances at festivals) ended shortly after the premiere, which he conducted, of the last opera to enter the popular Italian repertoire, Puccini's *Turandot*.

In Toscanini's day, as before and after, there have been performers who have believed themselves duty-bound to play pieces for which they feel no particular sympathy, and there is much to be said in favor of their attitude. But Toscanini was not one of them. He began his career when Brahms and Verdi were still active; he was comfortably grounded in the music of that period. From what is known of his distaste for post-tonal music and of his unease in dealing with complicated rhythms, surely he did well not to touch this century's most adventurous works. And as the head of the New York Philharmonic and, later, the NBC Symphony, he saw to it that conductors younger than himself—conductors of the stature of Kleiber, Klemperer, Ernest Ansermet, Fritz Busch, and Guido Cantelli—were brought in to conduct the music that he himself could not or would not do, along with their share of the classics. It is understandable that some younger composers grumbled when Toscanini showed no interest in their music, but nobody suggested that he close up shop merely because his repertoire was not keeping up with the times when he was in his sixties, seventies, and eighties.

If Horowitz really believes that Toscanini, had he been willing and able during those years to perform avant-garde works, would have altered the subsequent course of American music, he is attributing much greater powers to Toscanini than even the conductor's most fanatical admirers attributed to him. And if Horowitz thinks that musical life was better in the days when concerts did consist largely of contemporary music, he ought to reflect on the contents of typical programs in the Vienna of Beethoven and Schubert: violinists playing virtuoso pieces on one string, sixteen pianists banging out Czerny's arrangement of Rossini's *Semiramide* Overture, families of eight singing popular arias in several languages, hordes of child prodigies showing off their brilliant techniques. (Alice M. Hanson has documented this repertoire in *Musical Life in Biedermeier Vienna*, Cambridge: Cambridge University Press, 1985.) Horowitz, with his antimidcult fixation, would hardly have approved of these Old World kitsch concerts. But they, not Toscanini's appearances, were the real ancestors of television's music for the eye. Toscanini's absolutely straightforward American symphonic programming had its share of flaws, but it cannot legitimately be cited in the paternity suit. Making Toscanini responsible for the tinsel of televised music in the 1980s is like making Cézanne responsible for Peter Max, Dostoyevsky for Judith Krantz, Solon for Ronald Reagan.

According to Horowitz, Toscanini ought to have conducted contemporary music, for which he was not well suited, but ought not to have conducted the Austro-German repertoire, in which he was widely appreciated. Horowitz finds Toscanini's approach to that repertoire essentially unidiomatic: "He did not so much discard tradition as disdain ever acquiring it." But Toscanini had heard such German or German-school conductors as Hans Richter, Felix Mottl, Carl Muck, Artur Nikisch, Ernst von Schuch, Fritz Steinbach, Gustav Mahler, Felix Weingartner, Richard Strauss, and, later, Willem Mengelberg, Walter, Furtwängler, Busch, Klemperer, and Kleiber, each of whom differed nearly as much from the others as Toscanini did from any of them, and most of whom admired him. (Walter's attitude was typical; John T. McClure, who produced the recordings of the German conductor's last years, reported that Toscanini, even after his death, remained "a household deity" for Walter. "I once created a brief frost by making a negative remark about him.") Recordings demonstrate that, as interpreters of German repertoire, Furtwängler and Mengelberg had less in common with, for instance, Weingartner, Strauss, Busch, and Kleiber, than did Toscanini. Julius Korngold, veteran critic of Vienna's *Neue freie Presse* and an exact contemporary (and friend) of Mahler, praised Toscanini's "wonderful grasp, highly developed understanding of the Germanic, for Wagner's art and, astonishingly enough, equally for Brahms's." Perhaps unaware that he was doing so, Korngold went on to demolish the myth of a tradition of subjectivity on the part of imaginative German conductors and of a new, cold objectivity on the part of the unimaginative Toscanini. "Like Mahler," said Korngold, "Toscanini is an 'old-fashioned' conductor who wants to present the work and nothing but the work, which emerges sacrosanct through his individuality, through his subjectivity, through his temperament, although often as if newly discovered, newly thought out."

Like everyone else, Toscanini accepted or rejected elements of others' work in accordance with his artistic metabolism and his critical faculties. He was perfectly aware that his approach often went against mainstream opinion, as is clear from the question he wryly put to the English composer Arthur Bliss: "Tell me, Mr. Bliss, do *you*, as an English musician, think that I, as an Italian, take the slow movements of Beethoven rather fast?" But Horowitz chooses to ignore all such evidence. His approach is that of the Toscanini "cultists" he berates: he wants everyone to believe that his own musical preferences are quantitatively, historically, and morally correct. Fact, logic, and the need to appear objective occasionally slow down but never quite block his strangely insistent attack.

Through most of the book, Horowitz keeps his hero, Furt-wängler, in the background; occasionally, however, he trots out some of the more nonsensical claims made by the German conductor's fanatical partisans, who have shown themselves, during the last thirty years, to be nearly as irrational as, and frequently more vicious than, Toscanini's. Both musicians were interested primarily in realizing the expressive character of the music they conducted; nearly everyone who has described working with either of them has testified to this. The two conductors heard and felt music and communicated their musical concepts in vastly divergent ways, and the differences are important to people who care about how music is performed. Listeners who are convinced and moved by Furt-wängler's recording of the second movement of Brahms's First Symphony, for instance, are likely to find Toscanini's nearly unlistenable, and vice versa. This does not mean, however, that either Furtwängler or Toscanini was musically deficient. Both were brilliant and knowledgeable, and each believed that he was serving music in accordance with his best judgment. Horowitz complains, however, that Toscanini "took his tempo from the composer's markings at the head of a movement," whereas Furtwängler said that "the quest of tempo is one which cannot be separated from the interpretation of the piece as a whole, its spiritual image." Horowitz fails to mention that all musicians, including Furtwängler, take a composer's tempo markings as one of the primary indications of a piece's essence, of its "spiritual image." Those indications are sometimes ambiguous; when they are clear—especially when metronome marks are provided—performers who stray far from them or ignore them altogether are likely to give a work a different "spiritual image" than that intended by its composer. Is this legitimate? The answer depends not only on aesthetic and historic points of view, which are subject to interesting debate, but also on instinctive and visceral responses to music, which are not subject to anything of the sort.

Toscanini believed, and said, that his task was to "come as close as possible to expressing the composer's ideas." This principle goes far beyond the infantile literalism that Horowitz infers from it when he writes that "the power of Toscanini's textual fidelity creed lay in its innocence, which bypassed moderation and worldly doubt." If that is the case, how is it possible that Toscanini's concept of so many works changed so radically over the years? In the first half of his career, Toscanini usually applied Wagnerian performance practices retroactively to late eighteenth- and early nineteenth-century works, as did most of his contemporaries. Gradually, consciously, he came to consider that approach antihistorical. He spoke often, after about 1920, of "finally" having had the "courage" to make radical choices: to take the first bars of Beethoven's Fifth, for instance, in essentially the same tempo as the body of the movement; to eliminate big, flexed rubatos from pre-Wagnerian works; to opt for unorthodox tempi when he believed they worked best. Horowitz has every right to disagree with these and any other decisions made by Toscanini; he has no right, however, to impute ignorance to the man with whom he disagrees. Even Furtwängler, in commenting on a Toscanini performance of the "Eroica" Symphony—a performance he detested—pointed out that "in Germany we have had much more literal renderings of the 'Eroica' (which is, in my opinion, not to say anything against Toscanini, as literal rendering, the true ideal of the pedant, is actually neither new nor an ideal)." It is Horowitz, not Toscanini, who has bypassed moderation and worldly doubt.

Horowitz is justified in taking issue with those Toscaninians who wanted everyone to believe that their man had cornered the musical morality market, but he is not justified in setting himself up as a moral arbiter in the same tradition. Again and again, he hammers at Toscanini's supposed artistic naiveté, merely because the conductor's artistic point of view differed from his own. According to Horowitz, Toscanini was nothing more than an "inspired technocrat," a "manager with a vision, and a genius for making the team sweat to achieve it." But the hundreds of hours of Toscanini's rehearsals that were recorded testify unanimously to his overwhelming, even monomaniacal preoccupation with musical expression. When he had to deal, as all conductors do, with wrong notes, bad attacks, bowings that didn't "sound," and wind balances that needed adjusting, he did so as quickly as possible; and he became exasperated when positive results were not immediately forthcoming. Good playing was a point of departure; rehearsals existed so that good music-making could be achieved.

A less arrogant critic could write a useful dissenting study of the Toscanini recordings. A social historian could produce a book about the impact of the public relations industry on American musical life, a book in which the Toscanini story might occupy a page or two. But the attempt to shoehorn the two subjects into a single volume was ill-judged. Joseph Horowitz has helped to obscure them both.

Most of this essay appeared in the *New Republic*, June 1, 1987, under the title "The Maestro Maligned," and in *Tuttolibri—La Stampa* (Turin), June 20, 1987, as "Difendo Toscanini: non era solo un manager della musica." For the present book, some of the material cut from the article for lack of space has been reinstated, a few details have been added, and a few changes have been made.

A year after this article was published, I read a book review by Norman Gash in *The Times Literary Supplement* (May 27–June 2, 1988), in which *Churchill's War* (Volume I), by David Irving, was described as "a study in sustained depreciation. The method soon becomes familiar. An apparatus of scholarship creates a sense of reliability; an occasional condescending compliment is offered as a proof of fairmindedness; the select quotation and malicious choice of words produce an atmosphere of general cynicism; the large generalizations floating above and detached from the narrative convey the required conclusions." I haven't read the book to which Gash refers and can't offer an opinion on the specific case, nor am I a Churchill enthusiast; but I understand Gash's point. To amass evidence on a historical or biographical subject over a long period, and *then* try to make sense of it, requires a great deal of patience and concentration. It is much easier to develop a theory and then select the evidence that substantiates it; and this, I believe, was Joseph Horowitz's technique in *Understanding Toscanini*.

Sir Ernst Gombrich, the art historian, who knew Toscanini during the 1930s, was among those who reacted with dismay to Horowitz's book and to some of the enthusiastic reviews it received. "I am both puzzled and annoyed by the campaign of slander and incomprehension that we must now endure," he said, in a letter to this writer; and in a letter to another correspondent he quoted Schiller's *Das Mädchen von Orleans*: "Es liebt die Welt das Strahlende zu schwärzen, / und das Erhabne in den Staub zu ziehen." (The world loves to blacken what is radiant, and to drag the sublime through the mire.)

One of the people who did understand Toscanini's significance was an outstanding twentieth-century Italian composer—and a Schoenbergian at that—who, by Horowitz's lights, ought to have objected to Toscanini's total lack of interest in his music. "The example that Toscanini has set us is as alive today as it was yesterday," wrote Luigi Dallapiccola, ten years after the conductor's death; "indeed, it becomes more gigantic with the passage of time. I wish that such an example would bear fruit, although I am convinced that certain phenomena cannot be repeated. Perhaps this will be possible when there is a return to 'culture' (replaced, today, by 'information'); when people will recognize that, as far as art is concerned, the moral problem is the basis of everything—that is to say, the problem of honesty toward oneself."

Just before this book was to go to press, I received a copy of Kurt Weill's recently published letters to Ferruccio Busoni (printed in *Musik und Gesellschaft*, Berlin, 3/90). One of them, written in Bologna on March 6, 1924, during the twenty-four-year-old composer's trip through parts of Italy, contains the following passage about his impressions of La Scala and Toscanini. "Of all the theatrical [situations] that I have seen," writes Weill, "this one comes closest to Mahler's ideal of an 'uncompromising' [musical theater]. Charpentier's *Louise* was performed, Toscanini conducted, and that in itself was an event that made this whole trip worth the effort. I never knew that one could play 'on' an orchestra with such freedom, with such willful rubati. It was splendidly sung [the cast included Gilda Dalla Rizza, Elvira Casazza, and Marcel Journet], the chorus was flabbergasting in the way it brought off its musical and dramatic tasks. I don't know whether the piece was so winning [only] as a result of the performance—I found it beautiful in places (such as the beginning of Act 4). You can imagine with what verve the great spectacular scene in Act 3 was brought off. I will remember this evening for a long time." For this book's purposes, the most interesting aspect of the letter is Weill's astonishment over Toscanini's freedom and rubati, since the young musician was accustomed to hearing Berlin orchestras and opera ensembles under the likes of Nikisch, Walter, Furtwängler, and Kleiber.

CHAPTER 10

Watching Toscanini

DURING a performance of *Pictures at an Exhibition* with the Vienna Philharmonic in Budapest in 1937, Toscanini—conducting from memory, as always—accidentally skipped one of the piece's episodes and began to conduct another. According to Hugo Burghauser, who was the orchestra's president and principal bassoon,

> *not one musician started to play!* It was ghost-like, a little like a nightmare: Toscanini conducted in the air, and not one sound occurred! Toscanini, for a tenth of a second, was flabbergasted and stony-faced: how come nobody plays? But in another tenth of a second he realized that instead of *Tuileries* he had conducted the beginning of *Bydlo*, which was very different in dynamic character. And with an almost undiscernible nod, he gave the right dynamic sign for the beginning of *Tuileries*, and then the orchestra, most harmoniously, as if nothing had happened, started to play. Afterwards he said: "This is the greatest compliment an orchestra can pay me: *I* make a mistake, and the orchestra at once realizes I am wrong." Why? Because his *Zeichengebung*, his gesture for communication and conducting, is so unmistakable in its one possible meaning that you cannot take it as meaning anything else; and you say: "Sorry; he's mistaken; I don't play." But that a *hundred people* should have this immediate mental contact—this happened with no other conductor in my fifty years of playing.[1]

For decades, many musicians and others interested in Toscanini's work have wished they could observe the Toscanini Phenomenon as it was described by Burghauser and many dozens of other instrumentalists and singers who worked with the conductor. Thanks to the diffusion of video cassettes, their wish is now easily fulfilled. In 1989, the Library of Congress issued a cassette that contains *The Hymn of the Nations*, a film in which Toscanini and the NBC Symphony Orchestra perform music by Verdi; and in 1990, RCA Victor Gold Seal (BMG) published video cassettes and laser disks that contain all ten of the Toscanini–NBC Symphony televised concerts.

To a public accustomed to watching what Stravinsky aptly called "a performance of a performance," in which certain contemporary conductors demonstrate to a live audience or before the television cameras the full extent of their emotional involvement in the music, these video transfers may come as a shock. Toscanini never mimicked the music's content with his face or gestures, and the intensity of the orchestra's performances is all the greater for his restraint. He apparently believed that his task at concerts was to help the orchestra project the music, essentially as they had prepared it together at rehearsals. His gestures during rehearsals were sometimes large and wild, but they were completely controlled during performances. Many conductors adopt the opposite procedure: they relax physically at rehearsals and put on choreographic displays at performances.

Physicists and mathematicians use the word "elegant" to describe simple, direct solutions to complicated technical problems. In this sense Toscanini's solutions to the technical problems of conducting were elegant, although his baton technique, according to Sir Adrian Boult,

was poor compared with Nikisch's. It didn't matter, because he had everything else. . . . The point of the stick said nothing special; it was simply that it swung along in an irresistible way, naturally, with that tremendous mind and concentration behind it. But it did not swing along in an expressive way or a way that in itself could have contributed a great deal to the performance. . . . Toscanini's movement came largely from his elbow and forearm and the expression in it came from behind the stick: it was in his mind all the time. His left hand was expressive, not used a great deal, but when it was there it was far more expressive than the right, because it was a natural limb while the stick that Toscanini used was a pretty heavy one.[2]

Boult's description is correct, as far as it goes, but George Szell came closer to the mark when he described Toscanini's technique as "deceptively simple." When one observes the videos closely, one realizes, for instance, that Toscanini, to a greater extent than most other conductors, made a distinction between the responsibilities of the right and left arms. His right arm generally moved in broad, clear, compelling strokes, not merely beating time but drawing the musicians into the music and helping them to progress through it, persuading them to bring it to life; it activated and shaped the music. His left hand was responsible for the fine tuning: from a position directly in front of him, where it was invisible to much of the audience, it cautioned and exhorted. Like many other conductors of his generation, Toscanini used a longer baton than do most of today's conductors; but unlike many other conductors of his own or later generations, he rarely used the baton for flicking cues or ticking beats. Some conductors make the straightforward job of giving cues to individual players or whole sections of the orchestra the occasion for a public display of their thorough knowledge of the score or their Jovian power to release thunderbolts of sound. Toscanini gave cues, often well in advance of difficult entrances, with a small gesture of his left index finger, or with a glance, or merely by raising his eyebrows; simultaneously, the right arm and baton continued to shape the music's progress. And only at particularly difficult mo-ments for one or more sections of the orchestra did he make tiny subdivisions with the stick. His technique would not have adapted itself well to the rhythmic and metric complexities of many impor-tant twentieth-century works, but it worked beautifully in his repertoire—essentially Haydn through Richard Strauss and De-bussy, with occasional forays backward and forward.

The audience saw virtually nothing of Toscanini's communica-tions to the orchestra, but the videos often show what the orchestra saw. The earliest of them, the *Hymn of the Nations*,* which consists of Verdi's infrequently played cantata of that name and the Overture to *La Forza del Destino*, is on the whole less valuable, visually, than the televised concerts. For the close-ups, Toscanini was obliged to con-duct the playback of a prerecorded soundtrack. He had never done such a thing before, nor did he ever do it again; and at first the

---

* See also pages 91–92.

procedure confused and frustrated him. He persisted with the project only because he cared intensely about the war effort. (Toscanini and the orchestra contributed their services gratis; previously, he had turned down offers of up to $250,000 to appear in commercial films.) The camerawork, however, is generally better in the film than in the televised concerts, the first of which was broadcast live from Studio 8H in the RCA Building, Rockefeller Center, New York, on March 20, 1948, five days before Toscanini's eighty-first birthday. He had begun his formal musical studies in 1876, the year of the first Bayreuth Festival, and he entered the television era by conducting a program of Wagner's music for a continentwide audience. Nine more Toscanini concerts were televised during the following four years (the last four took place in Carnegie Hall), and all ten events were preserved.

There are remarkable details in the film and in every one of the televised concerts, but some items reveal more than others about Toscanini's conducting. There is, for instance, a highly interesting performance (April 3, 1948) of Beethoven's Ninth Symphony. This was Toscanini's next-to-last encounter with the Ninth, which he had first conducted in 1902, and it is one of the most severe of the ten or more of his performances of the work that have been preserved. Although my object here is to discuss Toscanini's technique, not his interpretations, this performance is at times so harsh, especially in the first movement, that it demands preliminary comment. Some commentators have described the beginning of the first movement as a symbol of the creation of the universe, a bringing together of elements. The idea is interesting, but it has tended to serve as an excuse for conductors who want to adopt a tempo only one-half to two-thirds as fast as the one indicated by the composer (*Allegro, ma non troppo, un poco maestoso*; $\bm{\downarrow}$ = 88). An adagio tempo results in the transformation of one of Beethoven's greatest dramas into a Brucknerian epic. And what if the music has nothing at all to do with the creation of the universe? What if it just "means itself," as Stravinsky said of music in general? Or what if the word *Verzweiflung* (despair), which Beethoven wrote on some of his sketches for this movement, were to be taken seriously as a key to the music's subtext? Toscanini seems to have read the score in that light: as a representation of crushing terror, perpetrated by cold, pitiless, inhuman forces—a terror resolved, little by little, in the following movements, which could represent, successively, struggle, resignation, and affirmation. This rough-hewn, nervous performance of the first movement is disturbing even today, because most listeners are still accustomed to slower, smoother readings. In my opinion, Toscanini came closer to achieving a comprehensive vision of the movement in his 1952 recording. This 1948 version is more violently articulated and more drastic in its tempo changes (they vary between ♩ = 70 and 96); the vision it offers is almost unremittingly bleak.

Toscanini beats two to the bar through most of the first movement, as is normally the case. He subdivides bars 16 and 50, which immediately precede the two fortissimo outbursts, and he subdivides the strings' thirty-second-note passages in bars 130–37 and 399–406. Surprisingly, however, he does not subdivide the ritardando bars 195 and 213 in the development section or their counterparts in the coda (bars 506 and 510); instead, he curves and elongates the second beat in each of those bars, thus slowing the orchestra down without interrupting the flow of the musical discourse. Before and during the climactic passage that begins the recapitulation (from bar 297 on), he frequently beats four to the bar. He conducts this shattering passage with maximum intensity but barely moves his left hand. There are, after all, no cues to be given here, and nothing was upsetting the balance that had been worked out at rehearsals; thus, there was no need for him to rend the air violently, and he did not do so. Toscanini also controlled the extended crescendo passages, especially the one that leads to the cataclysmic fortissimo at bar 453, almost entirely through the watchful look on his face and the simple, holding gesture of his left hand.

Even in the lightest passages near the beginning of the second movement (Scherzo: *Molto vivace*; ♩. = 116, but the tempo in this performance is 124–28), Toscanini's wrist flexes very little: the work is done by the whole right arm. He beats all the bars of rest (*e.g.*, 148–50), conducts, sometimes, in perpetual-motion circles, and signals fermata cutoffs with a surprisingly slow left-hand gesture. The Trio (*Presto*; ○ or ♩ = 116, depending on the edition, but Toscanini's tempo is ♩ = 144–48) is also conducted very lightly, always in two; in this case, he cuts off the last fermata with a small right-arm movement that also serves as an upbeat for the return to the Scherzo. After the final statement of the *ritmo di quattro battute* section, Toscanini visually rebukes the timpanist for having played the first bar of his crescendo too loudly (bar 786).

Toscanini begins the third movement (*Adagio molto e cantabile*; ♩ = 60, but the tempo in this version is about 44) with deep, flowing beats that never come to a rest. The first clarinet makes mistakes in his solo in the first three bars, but Toscanini remains impassive. Later, to remind the strings to vibrate more intensely, Toscanini sometimes vibrates a finger of his left hand against his chest, a throwback to his cello-playing days, sixty years earlier. Many times in this movement he gives cues only with his eyes, so as not to disturb the flow of the music. At bar 42, on the very last beat of the first 3/4 section (*Andante moderato*; ♩ = 63, but Toscanini's tempo is circa 51), he uncharacteristically but effectively flicks the baton, which is pointed diagonally upward, so as to indicate each of the four sixteenth-notes in the first violin part, and he proceeds directly into the next bar without giving a cutoff. He gently subdivides the last beats of the transition bars 64, 82, and 98. Thereafter, he beats most of the 12/8 section, the remainder of the movement, in four, subdividing only when he senses that the players need a little extra help, as in bars 112, 120 (last beat only), 130, 150, and the third beat of the last bar of the movement; yet his beat is so clear and compelling that even when he makes no subdivisions, one can feel where each note *must* be placed.

The Finale—with the Collegiate Chorale (prepared by Robert Shaw) and soloists Anne McKnight, Jane Hobson, Irwin Dillon, and Norman Scott—is enormously impressive in its cumulative impact. Visually, the force of Toscanini's concentration is overwhelming, but there is little to say about this or that detail. Many musicians who worked with him have said, in one way or another, "Whatever we needed from him, he gave us." And that is certainly the case here. At the beginning of the long orchestral postlude to the *Alla marcia* section, for instance, some of the players apparently forgot to move along at the faster tempo that Toscanini wanted (very fast indeed: ♩. = circa 132), and some confusion ensued. With a less canny and determined conductor, the confusion might have lasted awhile, but Toscanini simply focused his attention on the erring sections and realigned them within a few seconds. He knew, too, that at the end of that postlude, just before the reentry of the chorus, the horns usually need a little extra encouragement for their offbeat heralding notes, and he gave it to them. And he knew that the sopranos in the chorus need a great deal of extra encouragement on their eight-and-a-half-bar fortissimo high A in the *Allegro energico* section; consequently, at that moment he looked as if his life depended on their success. They succeeded. But players and singers need more than important cues, clear time-beating, and encouragement. They also need a guiding sense of direction, especially in as episodic a piece as the Finale of the Ninth. Toscanini provided this as few other conductors have ever been able to do. His conducting was technically dependable and intellectually and emotionally involving.

The performance of the *Tannhäuser* Overture (Dresden version) in the concert of December 4, 1948, offers a good overview of Toscanini's conducting. His beat is very fluid at the beginning; when he reaches the first grandiose tutti (bars 38 *et seq.*), he gives considerable space to the last beat of each bar. During the repeat of the opening statement (bars 70–80), he makes tiny, left-hand gestures in front of his chest, to signal the clarinets, bassoons, and first and second horns to become quieter and quieter, until their sound almost disappears. In the last bar of that passage he looks briefly at the violas, to prepare them for their treacherous entrance in a new meter and tempo during the following bar; and his tiny, preparatory upbeat to the new section is so unmistakable in its intent that the transition is flawless and electrifying. A little glance from Toscanini at bar 172 creates the most furious of fortissimos in the orchestra, and his shaping of the crescendo and accelerando between bars 220 and 242 is breathtaking. In the pianissimo passage (bars 321 *et seq.*), after the huge climax, Toscanini shakes his head and mutters something in the direction of the second violins, who presumably aren't playing softly enough to satisfy him. But the performance is thoroughly remarkable.

On March 26 and April 2, 1949, Toscanini conducted a two-part concert performance of Verdi's *Aida*, with Herva Nelli in the title role, Eva Gustavson as Amneris, Richard Tucker as Radames, Giuseppe Valdengo as Amonasro, and Norman Scott as Ramfis; the performances were broadcast on radio and television and, with a few retakes, were later released on records. Unfortunately, the telecasts show relatively little of Toscanini. The cameras focus on him in parts of the purely orchestral segments and ensemble scenes but do not reveal how the most famous opera conductor in history conducted arias and recitatives; at those moments, the cameras are usually focused on the singers. (The most interesting detail in the *Hymn of the Nations* film, for instance, is Toscanini's sure handling of the tenor recitative "Spettacolo sublime," an excellent demonstration of the equilibrium between leading and following that is required of all opera conductors.) Visually, the *Aida* video is valuable mainly as a demonstration of total musical and dramatic confidence on the part of thoroughly prepared singers performing without scores or prompter but with a great conductor who has worked with them on the opera's every phrase.

Toscanini was the first major Italian conductor, and one of the first in the world, to perform Debussy's music; and we are fortunate to have, as part of the televised concert of March 15, 1952, a visual document of one of his performances of "Nuages" and "Fêtes" from the three orchestral *Nocturnes*. There is not a great deal to be learned here about Toscanini's baton technique; nevertheless, the "Nuages" performance is one of the most fascinating, visually, of all the televised concert items. The piece is in 6/4 time and bears the indication *Modéré* at the beginning; Toscanini evidently decided that that meant moderately in two, rather than moderately in six. But if the basic pace is fast*—much too fast, in my opinion—the performance is neither agitated nor rigid, nor is it too sharply defined. On the contrary, it excellently conveys the music's ambiguity, its atmosphere of vague but pervasive disquiet. Throughout the piece, Toscanini's baton and left hand shape the subtlest inflections in tempo and expression, and his eyes constantly alert the players to difficult entrances and delicate articulations. There is something uncanny about his way of projecting this music's sinuous line: he gives the players all the specific assistance they need, but he makes no stopgap or mood-painting gestures. He seems not to be conducting phrase by phrase—let alone bar by bar—but, rather, to be revealing the piece's whole structure in a single, unbroken line.

The "Nuages" performance is a fine example of one of the most impressive and moving aspects of Toscanini's work: his trust in the

---

* The timing of this performance of "Nuages" is 5:26. Pierre Monteux's recording of the piece with the Boston Symphony and Pierre Boulez's with the Philharmonia Orchestra—neither of them particularly slow—last just under seven minutes each.

people who were doing the playing. His conducting was always helpful in an anticipatory way but never fussy. He laid tremendous responsibility on the players by demanding that they think through the music as he did, and he relied on their collective, professional judgment.

The all-Wagner concert of December 29, 1951, contains an excellent performance of the Prelude and Liebestod from *Tristan und Isolde* and an even more interesting performance, technically, of Siegfried's Death and Funeral Music from *Die Götterdämmerung*. Two of the most celebrated conductors active today have told me of the overwhelming impression made on them by Toscanini's conducting in the *Götterdämmerung* excerpt. It is impressive above all as an example of what Boult—who had seen and admired Richter, Nikisch, Weingartner, Furtwängler, and nearly every other great conductor active in this century—described as

> something that made Toscanini's work different from that of every other conductor. What was it, what power was at work there? I think the main thing about Toscanini's work was that he controlled a higher candle-power, if you like to call it that, of concentration than any human being except perhaps a few great orators. . . . [It] was so intense that nothing could interrupt it. One felt that if there had been an earthquake Toscanini would have gone on with his rehearsal.[3]

Or, in this case, with his performance. There was no earthquake here, but there was dreadful heat from the television lights that had been set up on the Carnegie Hall stage, and the heat left the eighty-four-year-old Toscanini looking and presumably feeling frail and faint. But, as he told a friend, music always gave him even more than he put into it; at this, as at many other unpropitious moments in his career, he quickly mastered himself and the situation.

He generally chose to begin this excerpt as he begins it here: at the dramatic E-minor chord with which, in the opera, the dying Siegfried begins his final soliloquy ("Brünnhilde! Heilige Braut!"; *Sehr langsam*, 3/4). At bar 25 ("Wecker kam"), he begins to beat in nine, to help the players through the complicated rhythmic patterns; but when he reaches the fortissimo at bar 34, he resumes beating in a flowing three-to-the-bar. At the pianissimo (bar 40, where Wagner's indication is *"Das Zeitmass immer etwas zurückhaltend"*—the tempo still a little held back), Toscanini begins to beat in six. He conducts the beginning of the 4/4 section in four, excepting the violas' and cellos' triple-triplet beats, which he subdivides into groups of three. Just before the C-minor key signature, the violas, cellos, and basses play their last three eighth-notes, successively, long and soft, long and slightly louder, shorter (but not short) and more aggressively (the second violins, too, play the last note). Toscanini indicates all this with his right arm.

The C-minor key signature marks the beginning of the Funeral March proper, and the very first bar reveals two important features of Toscanini's interpretation. The French conductor D. E. Inghelbrecht related how Toscanini worked on this bar at a rehearsal in Paris in 1934:

> So long as he does not achieve the same tone-value for the two harsh chords at the beginning, he will persevere. He will explain that [the players] had been wrong in *always* playing the second chord of the first beat and the chord preceding the third beat less strong. Then he will proceed to the fourth beat of the *same* bar, dwelling on the chromatic triplet-figure of the [violas, cellos, and] basses, which he will take neatly to pieces, because it is being hurried, and this always and everywhere, in the attempt of somehow patching it up. "I have given this triplet lesson in vain all over the world," he says.[4]

In this case, however, the lesson was not given in vain: the NBC Symphony delivers the triplets with astonishing variety, a direct result of the astonishing variety in Toscanini's beat patterns. In the first bar, the figure stabs, in the second it begins to subside, and in the third it is calm. Then, five bars before the C-major key signature, as the tension and volume begin to build, Toscanini—instead of pressing forward, as many conductors do at this point—lets the violins hang back on the final triplet of each bar; he gives the figure plenty of room in which to entwine itself around the syncopated fundamental rhythm and the curving melodic line, and the amount of room he gives it varies from bar to bar. The NBC musicians also consistently "achieve the same tone-value for the two harsh chords" that Inghelbrecht mentioned; and at the fifth C-major bar— fortissimo—Toscanini actually conducts the sixteenth-note upbeat to the third beat, to stress that he wants it to be as strong as the on-the-beat eighth note that follows it.

In the passage immediately after the E-flat major key signature Toscanini guides the orchestra along, solidly, nobly; and it is here that we Peeping Toms can clearly see what so many of his musicians talked about having seen in Toscanini's face, especially when he was conducting works by the composers who meant most to him: he *believed* in this music. Fifty-six eventful years had gone by since he conducted the first Italian production of *Götterdämmerung*, but to Toscanini this funeral march was no hackneyed repertoire piece: it was fresh, original, splendid—and it demanded to be given an existence in sound, to be communicated. This was no representation of life; it *was* life. The uncomfortable, perspiring old man standing on the stage of Carnegie Hall managed, at that moment as at so many others, to tap the human and musical wellsprings of the people with whom he was working, and those people, in turn, conveyed their conviction to the listeners.

FOR more than thirty years I have been able to watch and listen to dozens and dozens of well-known conductors working with major orchestras and opera ensembles, often for long stretches—and not just during performances but also at rehearsals, which are more revealing. I was active as a conductor for a dozen years, and I know something about the problems of the profession and about what really goes on in orchestras. I tend not to be impressed by reports of inspiring conductors—there are many such reports and very few inspiring conductors—and I know, from close observation, that in the vast majority of cases the players play better than their conductors conduct. But in conducting as in every other field, there are exceptions; and Toscanini impresses me, as he impressed most of the people who worked with him, as the greatest exception of all.

"Some people become conductors because they like to control things," explained Robert Bloom, who was the NBC Symphony's principal oboist for six years—before the televised concerts took place—"but I never had that feeling with Toscanini. He believed that the music had to go a certain way, and he was going to be the one to make it happen."[5] Toscanini scorned the mystique of the charismatic conductor, yet, paradoxically, he was the most noteworthy example of it: the intensity of his concentration and of his belief in what he was doing created a vortex that pulled players and singers into the heart of the music. And he was a romantic for whom music and the other arts had spiritual and social significance: music-making was a mission, he believed, and the depth of his conviction was as unmistakable in the watchful, serious, unself-conscious expressiveness of his face and in the contained purposefulness of his gestures as it was in the sounds produced by the people he conducted.

No great musician can be explained by his technique. Alexander Kipnis, the celebrated Russian bass, told the American critic B. H. Haggin that a conductor's wife had once asked him, "What is it about Toscanini—what is it he does that my husband cannot do? Does he do something with his hands? Or with his eyes? Does he conduct faster? Or slower?" And Kipnis answered by quoting Gurnemanz's reply to Parsifal, when Parsifal asks, "Who is the Grail?"

"That may not be told," says Gurnemanz, "but if you are chosen for it, you will not fail to know."[6]

Yet there is much to be learned by watching Toscanini—about conducting, about performing, and, above all, about music. The televised concerts supplement, visually, what his recordings have long been telling us aurally: that the things we have heard about the honesty and brilliant simplicity of his music-making are not mere exaggerated tales about the good old days. And they show us that rarest of all creatures, a human being using all of himself to do what he has a supreme talent for doing.

I have incorporated a few paragraphs from my notes for the Toscanini videos (BMG/RCA Gold Seal video cassettes and laser disks 790346/47/51–57) into this chapter, and a few others from an article, "Guardando Toscanini dirigere," that appeared in the *Atti e memorie della Accademia Petrarca di lettere, arti e scienze* (Arezzo, 1982 [1984]); the rest of the chapter was written for this book.

CHAPTER 11

Listening to Toscanini

ORAND Fenyves, who was one of the Palestine Orchestra's concertmasters when Toscanini worked with the ensemble in the mid-1930s, once questioned the conductor about his habit of remaining frozen in concentration for a few seconds before he began a piece, then raising his baton and expecting the orchestra to be ready to start without delay. Toscanini explained that before he could set the music in motion he had to think through the components of the work's structure—in other words, the motivic unit within the phrase, the phrase within the period, the period within the section, the section within the whole piece or movement, and the movement within the entire work—all compressed into a few seconds. Like the boxes with which children play, said Toscanini, the smallest part fits into a slightly larger one, the slightly larger one into a still larger one, and so on. "I have to feel that I contain all the parts of a work in my mind before I can begin to conduct," he said, "and when I do contain them, I *must* begin to conduct."[1]

The explanation sheds some light on the intellectual process that produced the feeling of inevitability common to most of Toscanini's performances. His exceptional, virtually photographic memory, and the extraordinary powers of concentration behind it, were the forces that drove his synthesizing capacity; and his synthesizing capacity was what made him the greatest architectonic conductor in history, at least among those who have left recordings. When he was at the height of his artistic maturity and technical powers, his performances were often and justly praised for their energy, passion, clarity, power, and balance; his greatest musical distinction, however, was his ability to present a work as a coherent unit. Some musicians, even some outstanding ones, wonderfully convey the details of a work but are not very good at giving it direction. Toscanini made all the details proceed, together, toward a common goal. Once in a while, especially in some of the less successful performances of his last seasons, he plowed over a work's particulars in his anxiety to illuminate its structure. It was not a matter of ignoring details but, rather, of marching them along too relentlessly, once he had understood their functions; at those moments, his preoccupation with making the components fit together under a unifying arch swamped all other considerations.

Wilhelm Furtwängler, who is often held up as Toscanini's musical antithesis, had precisely the opposite weakness: he sometimes squeezed so much meaning out of individual harmonic sequences that he lost sight of a work's structure. In his worst recordings, Furtwängler doesn't let us see the forest for the trees; whereas Toscanini, in *his* worst recordings, seems so hell-bent on presenting us with a panorama of the forest that we can no longer make out the individual trees. But original artists like Furtwängler and Toscanini have always made more enormous blunders than their mediocre colleagues. They lay their existences on the line every time they set to work, and they are willing to take apparently foolhardy risks in the unrealizable but inextinguishable hope of bringing off the best possible performance. Serious listeners will almost invariably find a recording by Toscanini or Furtwängler either very, very good or very, very bad and, in any case, impressive in its conviction and intention; rarely did either conductor give a comfortable but unstimulating performance.

Furtwängler intensely disliked most of the Toscanini performances he heard and was upset by his older colleague's overwhelming successes, first in New York, at the time of Toscanini's triumphs with the Philharmonic in 1926 and '27, which put Furtwängler's previous successes there in the shade; and then in Berlin, at the head of the visiting Scala ensemble in 1929 and with the touring New York Philharmonic in 1930. In the aftermath of the latter event, and of the virtually unanimous praise it elicited for Toscanini from German musicians and critics, Furtwängler, who was musical director of the Berlin Philharmonic, drafted an essay in which he demolished or dismissed Toscanini's performances of Haydn's "Clock"

Symphony, Debussy's *La Mer*, the Scherzo from Mendelssohn's Incidental Music to *A Midsummer Night's Dream*, Beethoven's *Leonore* Overture No. 3 and "Eroica" Symphony, Brahms's "Haydn" Variations, and Richard Strauss's *Death and Transfiguration*. Only a few bits and pieces of Toscanini's interpretations received Furtwängler's qualified approval. Toscanini's greatness, said Furtwängler,

> lies in his character. This helps him in the eyes of the world, but it does not, unfortunately, help art. One can say with certainty that if he were a greater artist, if he had deeper insights, a livelier imagination, greater warmth and devotion to the work, he would not have become so disciplined. And this is why his success is disastrous.[2]

In other words, Toscanini was an honorable man and knew how to conduct an orchestra, but he wasn't worth much as a musician or artist.*

Furtwängler's dismay is understandable, however, and not only for professional reasons: he personified a rhapsodic, free-virtuosic approach to music-making, governed by an outstanding musical intelligence and conjoined to the Wagnerian ideal of seeking out the *melos* in every work; whereas Toscanini used his own outstanding musical intelligence in a more stylistically rigorous but no less impassioned attempt to realize the individuality of each work he conducted. (A Furtwänglerian would describe the two conductors' differences in a different way, but I can only describe what *I* hear.) They resembled each other in the degree of their dedication to music—Furtwängler's statement, above, is the only one I can recall ever having come across in which Toscanini's devotion to his work is called into question—and once in a while their musical results resembled each other to a surprising degree; but as interpreters they set out

---

* Toscanini was no more fond of Furtwängler's interpretive point of view than Furtwängler of his, but this did not prevent him from recommending that Furtwängler succeed him as conductor of the New York Philharmonic in 1936. Shortly thereafter, their differences of opinion over how to react to European political developments caused a break in their relations, and by the end of the war Furtwängler had become as much a bête noire to Toscanini as Toscanini had long been to Furtwängler. The musical world lost them within a few months of each other: Furtwängler (born in 1886, the year in which Toscanini had made his professional conducting debut) died in 1954, the year in which Toscanini retired.

from enormously distant points of departure. On the other hand, although Toscanini usually tried not to perform *allegrettos* or *andantes* as *adagios*, he would not have known what to make of the term "objective" as it has been used by uninformed critics to describe his point of view, and he would have been as baffled as Furtwängler by the "authenticity" movement of the last third of the twentieth century. Like every other fine musician, including those involved in the authenticity movement, he thought and felt music in his own distinctive way, and he tried to realize his musical ideas with the resources at his disposal.

Among professional musicians, the overwhelming majority's opinion of Toscanini at his apogee was diametrically opposed to Furtwängler's. It was nicely summarized by another celebrated German conductor, Otto Klemperer, in an article published in a Berlin newspaper in 1929:

One says very little about Toscanini when one says that he can conduct everything by heart. It is more important to say that, in the truest sense, he conducts everything from the heart.* If we wish to distinguish between legitimate and illegitimate manifestations in art, Toscanini is legitimacy personified: he is the king of conductors. His performances are more than beautiful, they are right.

. . . In 1923 at La Scala in Milan I heard a performance of *Die Meistersinger* under his direction, and I can only say that I have never heard so consummate a presentation of this work in any other theater in the world. In New York I heard Toscanini's concerts with the Philharmonic Orchestra, comprising the entire literature from Haydn to Stravinsky. Always the same delightful impression of uncalculated rightness.

Toscanini not only works with the orchestra to the last detail but also rehearses . . . the most subtle shades of expression, which, as he himself says, "can no longer be expressed in words." No one makes greater demands on the orchestra. Nevertheless, I never noticed in his rehearsals, which I had the pleasure of attending, any weariness or resistance in the orchestra. Any resentment would ricochet off his unassailable personality, for it stands above everyone. Over and above the great musician there is a wholly integrated character, and to that we owe the

---

* Klemperer uses the words *auswendig*, from memory, and *inwendig*, thoroughly known from the inside.

rebuilding of La Scala, which, with exemplary musical performances, stands at the summit of opera companies.³

Forty years later—remembering, no doubt, Toscanini's work in its last phase—Klemperer added some valid reservations to his earlier estimate and said that "Toscanini was the greatest conductor of his generation, but Mahler was a hundred times greater."⁴ But he had expressed no such reservations about the Toscanini of the 1920s. The shift in Klemperer's attitude parallels a general shift in critical attitudes toward Toscanini, and that shift was a result of Toscanini's great fortune and great misfortune: his professional longevity.

I recently heard a mediocre recital, given by Sviatoslav Richter, one of the pianists I most admire. All through the program he not only had serious technical problems—not surprising for a man in his mid-seventies—but also betrayed great difficulty in delivering the text with the fine balance between rigor and flexibility that had previously typified his music-making. I went away thinking, at least I know what he is—or was—capable of doing. Later, however, I thought, what if I were a generation younger than I am and were hearing Richter's work for the first time, rather than one of many times over a period of thirty years? Fortunately, he made a substantial number of recordings during his best years—but what if he hadn't? What if only now, or in three or four years, he were to decide to record his repertoire for posterity? What would be the effect on his postmortem reputation?

This is the essence of the Toscanini problem. In 1978 I wrote that the whole question of Toscanini criticism was and would continue to be bound up with his recordings, which, however, could not represent him adequately. His career was half-finished when he made his first records at the age of fifty-three; he made barely four hours of commercial recordings before his seventieth birthday, and most of his well-known recordings were made when he was in his eighties: all the Beethoven and Brahms symphonies, three Schubert symphonies, various tone poems by Debussy and Strauss, four of his five complete Verdi opera recordings (the other one, *La Traviata*, was made when he was seventy-nine), most of his Wagner excerpts, and many works by other composers. This is not to suggest that the very late Toscanini recordings are not to be taken seriously, or that they have no value in themselves. On the contrary, they all testify to the unceasing investigative and analytical passion of an extraordinary musician, and in most cases their inherent musical value and beauty are great. But they do not give much of a perspective on his work.

The reduction in tempo inflection in many of Toscanini's later recordings has contributed more than any other factor to the mistaken view of him as a "literalist," whose notion of realizing a composer's intentions was to give a competent rendition of the written text, but who was uninterested in or incapable of dealing with its implications. Not only was Toscanini as willing as most other conductors of his generation to make major or minor changes in scores that he thought needed improvement through cuts, wind doublings, retouchings in orchestration, or alterations in phrasing and articulation; he was even willing to challenge composers on overall interpretive questions. Conductor Gianandrea Gavazzeni recalls, for instance, Toscanini's telling him that he had heard one of the earliest productions of *Falstaff*, conducted by Edoardo Mascheroni, who had prepared and conducted the world premiere under Verdi's supervision. "If Verdi liked the way Mascheroni conducted *Falstaff*," said Toscanini, "he wouldn't have liked the way I conduct it."[5] But this possibility was not enough to dissuade him from conducting *Falstaff* as he thought best.

Reviews of Toscanini's performances in the first half of his career are as much a hindrance as a help in any attempt to imagine his music-making as it then sounded. At the end of a four-month season that Toscanini conducted in Palermo in 1892–93, the local critic complained that the conductor "did not rigorously observe the metronomic indications."[6] In other words, his performances were perceived as too freewheeling. But a few other critics during those years accused him of being "too metronomical," while the vast majority praised him highly without describing what he did. Nor are secondhand accounts of other musicians' comments on Toscanini more informative than the critics' reports. Alma Mahler said that when she and her husband had heard Toscanini conduct *Tristan* at the Metropolitan Opera during the 1909–10 season, they had found the "nuances"—in other words, the quality and/or degree of expressive freedom—"distressing";[7] but Bruno Walter said that Mahler had told him that Toscanini conducted *Tristan* "in a manner entirely different from ours but magnificently in his way."[8] (Mahler's comment to his friend Julius Korngold, music critic of Vienna's *Neue freie Presse*, is not much more helpful: " 'Yes, [Toscanini] is really something,' he said with respect, but laconically, almost evasively," reported Korngold.9) Some of the composers, instrumental and vocal soloists, orchestra members, assistant conductors, and theater staff members who worked with Toscanini during the first half of his career left useful testimony about his personality and working methods; what each of them said about his interpretations, however, is useful only as a source of technical information (here he doubled the horns, there he allowed the tenor to sing a high C) or as a chronicle of the witness's general impressions.

Thus, only the most reckless of today's commentators would claim to have much of a notion of the performances that Toscanini conducted prior to his early sixties. From 1929, however, when he made his first significant electrical recordings—with the New York Philharmonic and under reasonably natural conditions—until the end of his career, his work was increasingly well documented, through recordings of broadcasts of concerts and opera performances in North and South America and Europe, and through studio recordings with the Philharmonic (1936), the BBC Symphony Orchestra (1937–39), the NBC Symphony Orchestra (1938–54), and the Philadelphia Orchestra (1941–42). The recordings allow today's observers to describe, with at least a small degree of accuracy and fairness, the changes in Toscanini's style during the last twenty-five years of his career. A comparison between, for instance, his 1936 version of Beethoven's Seventh Symphony with the New York Philharmonic and the recording he made of the same work with the NBC Symphony in 1951, ought to demonstrate what sorts of changes took place in his outlook during what was, after all, little more than one-fifth of his career. And since Toscanini is often accused, nowadays, of having misunderstood or even ignored the German musical tradition—as if that tradition were a monolithic entity!—such a comparison should also refer to recordings of the same work by German-school conductors whose roots, like his, were in the nineteenth century. What follows is an attempt at such a comparison. My comments on the first movement are detailed, but I have limited my remarks on the other movements to reflections on tempi and a few other points, in order to avoid turning this essay into an exegesis of alarming proportions. Readers may either follow my analysis closely (before or after listening to the recording, but not while the music is playing) with a copy of the orchestral score in hand, or skim it for nontechnical comments. They should bear in mind, in either case, that even the best recordings, like the best live performances, are imperfect realizations of impermanent visions, and that even the most serious attempts at fairness on the part of a commentator are bound to be influenced by the commentator's prejudices.

Ludwig van Beethoven:
Symphony No. 7 in A Major, Op. 92 (1812)

Toscanini's recordings were both made in New York's Carnegie Hall: (I) New York Philharmonic, April 8–9, 1936 (CD RCA 60316-2-RG); and (II) NBC Symphony, November 9–10, 1951 (CD RCA 60253-2-RG). (Recordings of other Toscanini performances of the symphony have circulated, but these are the only ones the conductor authorized for release.) The other recordings discussed below, listed in the order in which they were made, are Felix Weingartner (1863–1942), Vienna Philharmonic, Vienna, Grosser Musikvereinssaal, February 24–26, 1936 (CD Musica Memoria 30269; other versions forthcoming); Wilhelm Furtwängler (1886–1954), Vienna Philharmonic, ditto, January 18–19, 1950 (CD EMI-Angel CDH 69803); Bruno Walter (1876–1962), Columbia Symphony, January–February 1958 (CD CBS MK 42013); and Otto Klemperer (1885–1973), Philharmonia Orchestra, London, Kingsway Hall, October and November 1960 (CD EMI-Angel CDM 69183). I shall also refer to a version (not available at time of writing) recorded in 1925 or '26 by Richard Strauss (1864–1949) with the Berlin State Opera Orchestra. Parts of Toscanini II were recorded during a radio broadcast of a live concert; but much of it, and all of the other versions, were made during recording sessions.

First movement: *Poco sostenuto; Vivace.* Timings: Toscanini I-11:43, Toscanini II-11:04, Weingartner-11:38, Furtwängler-12:54, Walter-13:00, Klemperer-14:05. (The repeat of the exposition is omitted in all these versions.)

For Toscanini I, two different "takes" of the introduction were released at different times; the second replaced the first and better-known one in copies of the recording issued in 78 r.p.m. albums after approximately 1942. I have not heard the second take, but I know that it was faster than the first, which Toscanini had come to consider too slow. Slow it certainly is: Beethoven's tempo indication is "a little sustained" and his metronome mark is ♩ = 69; Toscanini begins at ♩ = circa 50. (All my metronome calculations were made with a digital metronome; nevertheless, they are approximate, because no performer rigidly maintains a metronomic pace.) Yet the atmosphere is expectant, never stagnant. Throughout the first nine bars—in which the strings use little or no vibrato, except on the big, peremptory tutti chords—the woodwinds and horns play the main motive with subtle expressive inflections: a little rubato in the oboe's last two eighth-notes in bar 4; a minuscule crescendo by the first oboe and clarinet in bar 6 and a poco ritenuto on the last beat of that bar; a tiny caesura before the first beat in bar 9; and a small delay on the third beat of bar 9—after which there is a slight increase in the basic tempo, to ♩ = 54. The strings' volume is noticeably lower on the fourth beat of bar 9 than on the first, as Beethoven requested. In bars 9–12, the violins' and violas' sixteenth-notes are separated but not short; there is no crescendo in their ascending scales, but the quarter-notes at the top (bars 11 and 13) sound like real arrival points, because they are played vibrantly and are held for their full value. The clarinets and bassoons are more expressive in bars 11–13 than they were earlier—in keeping, again, with Beethoven's indication (*dolce*).

A slight accelerando in bar 14 leads to a tempo of ♩ = 60 for bars 15–22. Each scale in this segment is strongly directed toward the last note; while the main motive, which passes back and forth between the second and first violins, is phrased in beautifully poised, full-throated, two-bar arcs of sound. The winds' chords are intense but not so loud as to cover either the violins' melodic figure or the cellos' and basses' scales. At bar 23 the tempo is pulled back to ♩ = 54. The woodwinds' eighth-notes on the last beats of bars 23 and 25 are gently, rather than crisply, staccato; and their sixteenth-note upbeats always lead, with intent but without emphasis, to the following quarter-note. In the same bars, the violins enter softly on G, making no accents and using little or no vibrato; their trills and resolution-notes are clear-voiced but gentle and without crescendo.

As the violins play their sixteenth-note arpeggio at the end of bar 28, with an unindicated diminuendo into the subsequent pianissimo, their tone simultaneously becomes warmer.

In bars 29–33 the tempo is again ♩ = 60; the woodwinds' repeated sixteenth-notes are separated as little as possible—whispered, rather than stated. Toscanini takes the following seven bars faster (♩ = 66): this is his maximum tempo in the introduction, but it is below Beethoven's metronome indication. The winds' chords are lean but not punchy in these bars: they neither cover the activity in the strings nor sound artificially muted. A barely perceptible ritardando accompanies the diminuendo in bar 41, but the tempo in bars 42–52 (♩ = 60) is faster than in the earlier, parallel passage (bars 23–28). The cellos' and double basses' pizzicati (bars 43–48) are calm and vibrant. In bars 53–58 the tempo picks up slightly (♩ = 63). The violins' sixteenth-notes in bar 57 are, again, gently rather than crisply staccato, and from there to the end of the introduction the volume diminishes until the sound almost disappears. In this performance, as in Toscanini II and the Weingartner and Strauss versions, the introduction emerges into the *Vivace* without a jolt; the feat is accomplished by not rushing the tempo of the last bars of the introduction and by observing Beethoven's *sempre piano* mark in the first three bars of the *Vivace*.

In general, however, the performance that most closely resembles Toscanini I in the introduction is Furtwängler's. Not only are his tempi (♩ = 52–54 at the beginning, 56–60 later) not so different from Toscanini's; the overall feeling of expectancy, the attention to contrasts, the care in avoiding *espressivo* playing where understatement is required—all these characteristics were similarly realized by the two conductors. The Vienna Philharmonic did not breathe with Furtwängler quite as remarkably as the New York Philharmonic did with Toscanini, and Furtwängler is somewhat more willful than Toscanini with respect to accelerandos (*e.g.*, bars 32–33 and 49–52—although he never increases the tempo as much as Toscanini does in bars 34–40); but their concepts of the introduction's overall structure and many of its details are very close.

Walter begins much faster (♩ = 64) than Toscanini; he makes a ritardando in bars 7 and 8 until he reaches ♩ = 60 at bar 9, and he stays between 60 and 64 for most of the rest of the introduction. On the last beat of bar 14 he reinforces the crescendo—unnecessarily, in my opinion—by having the double basses play an octave lower than their part is written, whereas he does not get enough sound from the violins in bars 15–22. On the whole, his version of the introduction is feeble. Klemperer's, on the other hand, is strong but excessively wayward. He evades the problem of reconciling the stillness of the first nine bars with the awakening energy of the following passage by taking a fast tempo at the beginning (♩ = 71, even faster than Beethoven's metronome mark) and then drastically applying the brakes when he reaches the last beat of bar 9; from that point until the end of the introduction, his tempo stays at ♩ = 56–59. In bars 15–16 and 19–20 he has the second violins play an octave higher than the written notes, which makes them sound like the Melachrino Strings.

But if Klemperer's version of the introduction differs enormously from Toscanini I, so does Toscanini II, although it goes in the opposite direction. The basic tempo of the first nine bars is ♩ = 58–60, considerably but not shockingly faster than that of Toscanini I; the tempo accelerates to 64, however, at the end of bar 9 and to 68 at bar 14; it accelerates again on the last beat of bar 22, drops to 62–64 for bars 23–31, accelerates in bars 32–33, reaches 68–72 in bars 34–41, returns to 64 in bars 42–48, rushes to 68 at 49–52, drops to 66 during bars 53–58, and drops further, to ♩ = 63, for the last four bars of the introduction. On the whole, the performance is unsteady and often rushed, and its details are neither as polished nor as beautifully meshed as those of Toscanini I.

Even faster and more unsteady than Toscanini II, however, are Weingartner's and Strauss's versions of the introduction, and they are the oldest German-school conductors under discussion. (Weingartner was a pupil of Liszt, who was a pupil of Carl Czerny, who was a pupil of Beethoven, a line of succession that some consider a seal of interpretive authenticity, but that really means virtually nothing. Strauss, for instance, was a sort of honorary grand-pupil of Liszt, thanks to his having been a disciple of Liszt's star pupil, Hans von Bülow; but his performances of this and other works of Beethoven differed greatly from Weingartner's.) In the first nine bars, Weingartner's basic tempo is ♩ = 64–70. He then pushes ahead to 74–76 in bars 10–14, reaches 78 in bars 15–22, drops to 66 for the following eleven bars, reaches the nearly incredible tempo of ♩ = 80 in bars 34–40, makes an enormous ritardando in bar 41, returns to 66 in bars 42–52, pushes ahead to 72 at bar 53, and makes a ritardando in the last four bars. In short, he tends to take the loud parts considerably faster than the soft parts—and so does Strauss. But the details of Strauss's performance seem a bit careless, whereas Weingartner's are carefully worked out.

Beethoven's metronome mark for the *Vivace* is ♩. = 104; in Toscanini I, the exposition starts at approximately 100; it reaches 104 at the first full statement of the main theme (bars 89 *et seq.*) and fluctuates between 104 and 108 for most of the movement—although a few passages are as fast as 116 (*e.g.*, bars 171–178 and from bar 438 to the end).* The first nineteen bars of the *Vivace* are lilting but serene, almost understated, in this version. There is a small caesura before the first beat of bar 67; the flute solo is gentle rather than jaunty or assertive; and the strings' sforzatos in bars 77 and 80 are nudged good-naturedly rather than banged out. The strings don't make a sufficient diminuendo on the forte E that pulls the listener up short at bar 82, thus the note doesn't contrast sufficiently with the diminuendo-less E two bars later. (Klemperer is the best on this detail.) There is another small caesura before the dramatic fermata (bar 88), which is followed by a break and then by a brilliant sweep into the first full-force statement of the main theme. In the following dozen bars the melody soars over the propulsive second violins and violas and over a solid but forward-moving bass line. In bars 101–04 in this performance, the string-woodwind dialogue is a finely balanced, crescendoing line that becomes wilder in the following four bars and culminates in a savage outburst (bars 109–10)—which, in turn, is followed by a sudden, complete drop to a semiserious piano.

---

* No one can be sure what Beethoven meant by writing the movement's principal rhythmic motive two different ways:

♩. ♫ ♪. ♫   and   ♪♫♩ ♪♫♩

At times, he even used the two forms concurrently. There is a case to be made for the hypothesis that, with the first form, Beethoven intended each rhythmic group to begin with the dotted-eighth-note, whereas with the second, he intended each group to begin with the sixteenth-note. But at a *vivace* tempo the strings are hard put to make an audible distinction in articulation between the two forms; the winds can manage it a little better, but the results, nevertheless, are usually unclear. I do not know whether an attempt was made in any of the performances under examination to differentiate between the two versions, but the motive emerges the same in all of them—half-bar by half-bar. On the other hand, Toscanini, Furtwängler, Strauss, and Weingartner avoid accenting every half-bar, whereas Walter and Klemperer often pound on the accents.

Bars 119–23 have what the Germans call *Schwung*—a combination of verve, warmth, and intensity—not only in the tensile melodic line and reinforcing bass but also in the unrushed, cascading scales of the second violins and violas. The strings' chords in bars 124–27 are short but not harsh, and the winds give equal accentuation to each of their repeated eighth-notes in those bars, instead of pairing them in the usual, slovenly sforzato mezzo-forte pattern. (In Weingartner's version, for instance, the second chord in each pair is almost inaudible.) In bars 130–33, the winds play with great warmth, and the strings second them by quietly playing their simple broken triad as a melodic unit with a well-defined beginning, middle, and end. Bars 134–37 are phrased in great, bounding, half-bar leaps. The quarter-note with which each of the following four bars begins is played increasingly shorter, until the sound practically disappears on the pianissimo in bar 141. (Furtwängler, in the same bars, makes the quarter-notes increasingly longer—an equally valid way of helping the diminuendo make its point. Weingartner makes only the last note of the series longer than the others. In the other versions, including Toscanini II, the matter is not addressed.) From bar 152 to the end of the exposition (176), the emphasis in Toscanini I is on Beethoven's wild contrasts between understatement and overstatement.

After its rough introductory bars, the development section begins very gently in Toscanini I (bars 181–94); there is a small caesura before the first beat of bar 185, just as at the related point (bar 67) at the beginning of the exposition. Bars 195–200 pull irresistibly forward, not through a tempo increase but through the strings' ever more incisive rhythmic articulation and the winds' pronounced crescendo. Bars 201–19 are exceptionally energetic, and there is a caesura before the calm (bar 220). In the following passage (bars 222–35), Toscanini and the Philharmonic manage to make a clear distinction between the piano of the solo winds' gently playful melody and the pianissimo of the strings' energizing figure, which is always agogically shaped. The fourteen-bar crescendo (236–49) with which the gigantic retransition begins is extraordinarily well realized. Where Walter and Klemperer inadvertently destroy the tension by having the strings drop considerably in volume at the beginning of each two-bar group of dotted-half-notes, Toscanini aims for and achieves an unbroken crescendo of hair-raising intensity. (Furtwängler's strings drop, too, but very slightly; Weingartner's and Strauss's approaches are similar to Toscanini's in this passage, but they do not reach his level of intensity.) But Toscanini continues to prevent the excitement from boiling over through the four strife-ridden forte bars (250–53), and does not allow the orchestra to unleash its fury until bars 254–63; even there, however, the impact is achieved as much through weight—by slowing the tempo a hair's breadth—as through volume. And in the following four bars, Toscanini maintains the now almost unbearable tension by having the woodwinds and strings, alternately, land massively and vibrantly on the quarter-note—the last and highest note—of every three-note group. This procedure continues, for the strings, in bars 267–74 and is prevented from becoming too heavy by a small tempo increase. Toscanini does not have the strings make the silly, sudden mezzo-piano that Walter calls for at the end of bar 267—in order to make an equally silly crescendo in the following bars. He makes sure, instead, that the tension never relents, and he lets Beethoven look after the volume increase: after all, four wind instruments are added in bar 272, another one in 274, four more in 276, and all the rest plus timpani in 277. No outside help is required! The orchestra makes a small ritenuto in bars 274–77, and the maximum impact falls on the first beat of 278, the beginning of the recapitulation.

The wind chords that intermittently punctuate the first twenty-one bars of the recapitulation are short in Toscanini I; thus the complicated string texture is always clear—or at least as clear as the 1936 recording process permitted. Most of my remarks about the exposition are applicable to the recapitulation, too, although the first violins' sound is not as sustained in bars 332 and 334 as in the earlier parallel passage, nor is the strings' pianissimo at bar 374 as convincing as it was in its earlier manifestation. The coda consists mainly of fragments of the main theme, and Toscanini, from the start (bars 393–400), subtly brings the fragmentation to the listener's attention by making a small but clearly audible break between the repetitions of the main motivic fragment, played by the second violins and first violins, horns and woodwinds. Toscanini and the Philharmonic achieve the long approach (bars 401–22) to the final, prolonged fortissimo passage just as impressively as they achieved the great crescendo in the development section: the gentle entry of the winds' and violins' Es and of the lower strings' repeated motive sets up an atmosphere of expectancy—much more tense, however, than the expectant atmosphere of the introduction. The finely balanced violin swells in bars 404 and 408 give the first hint of the decisive crescendo that is to follow, and the volume and rhythmic tension continue to increase through bars 421–22 (there is a small accelerando in those two bars); they explode at bar 423. Here, too, however, Toscanini had the orchestra hold some energy in reserve. In so doing, he demonstrated his extraordinary sense of proportion: he knew that if the orchestra gave everything in bars 423–26, the following fifteen bars would sound comparatively weak, and the final nine bars would be one of a series of climaxes instead of *the* climax. So he holds back a little there, sustains the tone (but not the volume) to the limit in the following five bars, gives maximum rhythmic weight to bars 432–37, lightens the articulation in bars 438–41, and finally lets the orchestra play *tutta forza* in the last nine bars.

In the *Vivace* as in the introduction, Furtwängler's version is the closest to Toscanini I. He enters it less effectively—by increasing volume and tempo at the third-from-last bar of the introduction— and his basic tempo is slower (♩. = 94–100, with a drop to 92 at the beginning of the coda and an increase to 104 by the end of it), but his concept of phrasing, of the grouping and articulation of melodic and rhythmic figures, and of relative dynamic levels is remarkably similar to Toscanini's. (In bars 142–50, however, Furtwängler's is the only performance discussed here in which a distinction is made between the length of the woodwinds' staccato eighth-notes and that of the cellos' and basses' staccato quarter-notes, and vice versa.) Toscanini II, on the other hand, is worlds away from Toscanini I. Not only is the basic tempo of the later recording somewhat faster (between 108 and 116; usually around 112) than that of the earlier one: the tendency in II is to make all the details fit within a much less flexible superstructure. In this version, the *Vivace* seems at times to be pressed forward as if it were a gigantic scherzo movement in sonata form, which it is not; and a sonata-form movement almost invariably suffers from the perpetual-motion approach that is often appropriate to a scherzo. In the spring of 1990, when I first heard RCA's compact disk transfer of this recording, I found it convincing; several months later, after having listened with care to the 1936 version and the Furtwängler version, I found that Toscanini II did not stand up to the comparison.

Neither, however, do the Walter and Klemperer versions. Walter enters the *Vivace* by making a gradual accelerando through the last seven bars of the introduction, from ♩ = 63 to 76, and he continues to accelerate through the first six bars of the *Vivace*, from ♩. = 80 to 86. Thereafter, his basic tempo ranges from 86 to 92, well below Furtwängler's and very much below Beethoven's indication of 104; even in the coda, Walter reaches a maximum of only 96. Toscanini, Weingartner, Strauss, and Furtwängler evidently believed that drama is essential to any performance of this movement, which is constructed almost entirely of striking juxtapositions of tempo, rhythm, articulation, volume, and phrasing. At Walter's tempo, there can be little if any drama. His version might at least have had a certain wrongheaded epic majesty if he hadn't opted in so many passages (bars 268–73, for example) to clobber the first note of every half-bar; in so doing he rendered the overall delivery ponderous rather than mighty. Many details that ought to have been looked after seem to have passed unnoticed—the lack of shape to the strings' series of dotted-half-notes in bars 309–18, for instance. And Walter makes fussy, antidramatic "preparations" before the fortissimo at bar 323, the first note of 324, the sforzato in 340. The general impression is of tiredness.

Klemperer's version, too, is undramatic. He had the reputation of conducting Beethoven in a rugged, monolithic style; in this performance the *Vivace* is rugged and sometimes monumental, but it is too unsteady to be monolithic. It begins at ♩. = 90 but makes a huge ritardando in the fourth bar. It soon increases to about 86, which remains the basic tempo thereafter; but many jarring fluctuations mar the remainder of the movement: there is even a slowdown to ♩. = 74 in bars 124–29 and another to 76 in bars 401–08. Perhaps too many takes were spliced together, or perhaps Klemperer believed that the piece should sound fragmented. His performance, unlike Walter's, maintains a high energy level, but his treatment of primary and secondary accents is as ham-fisted as Walter's. The performance lacks the quick-mindedness, the lightness of spirit, and the refinement of detail that can be heard in Toscanini I and in Furtwängler's version. And it is not a *Vivace*, however elastically one tries to interpret the word.

Strauss's basic tempi, ♩. = 108–16, are as fast as those of Toscanini II, but he sometimes slows down to 98, and at other times shoots ahead to 122. Weingartner stays within lower parameters: he begins at ♩. = 88–90, takes the first full statement of the main theme (bars 89 *et seq.*) at circa 100, and remains between 98 and 104 until the beginning of the coda (bar 391), when he drops to 90—from which he accelerates to 102 at the end. Weingartner's version is occasionally lackluster: compare, for instance, Toscanini's sweep into the main theme at bar 88 with Weingartner's embarrassingly slovenly sally into it. On the whole, however, Weingartner and Strauss saw the *Vivace* as high drama and communicated it as such.

Second movement: *Allegretto*. Timings: Toscanini I-8:35, Toscanini II-7:57, Weingartner-7:56, Furtwängler-10:14, Walter-10:00, Klemperer-10:02.

The French conductor Louis Fourestier, who attended Toscanini's rehearsals of the nine Beethoven symphonies at La Scala in 1926, reported that Toscanini took great pains to balance the oboes, clarinets, bassoons, and horns in the opening chord of the Seventh's second movement, a tonic ⁶/₄ chord in A minor, marked forte, diminuendo, piano across two-and-a-half bars. "His ear for balance was astounding and exquisite," Fourestier said, "but after all, that is a physiological phenomenon more than anything else. After he had reached his goal and had achieved the diminuendo in the same gradation from each player, he said to the first oboe, 'Your note—your E—make it sing! It's a melody!' *One* note, a melody. *That* was genius!"[10]

   This detail, as audible today in Toscanini's 1936 and 1951 recordings as it was to Fourestier at that 1926 rehearsal, adds a dimension of poignancy to a chord that often sounds threatening or merely empty. Before the chord has died away, however, many listeners previously unfamiliar with Toscanini's performances of the Seventh will be shocked by his basic tempo, which, through the first fifty bars, is approximately ♩ = 63 in the 1936 version and 65–67 in the 1951 version—as opposed to Walter's 50–54, Klemperer's 51–53, and Furtwängler's 53–55. In recent decades, the extremely slow approach of the last three has been accepted on faith as representing "the German tradition." But Strauss's tempo in the first fifty bars varies between 60 and 69, and Weingartner's stays around 66. In his book *On the Performance of Beethoven's Symphonies* (1906), Weingartner

says that the tempo indication, *Allegretto*, "tells us that this movement is not to be taken like the customary *adagio* or *andante*. The
metronome-mark ♩ = 76, however, nearly gives us a quick-march,
which cannot have been the composer's intention here. I have therefore adopted ♩ = 66."[11] Christopher Dyment, who has done much
useful research on Weingartner, has pointed out that, "contrary to
general belief (and the particular assertion of George Szell) Toscanini
was not the first conductor in modern times to take the second
movement of the Seventh Symphony at a true *allegretto*; . . . the two
conductors' tempi for Beethoven's slow movements and scherzos
were in general almost identical."[12] (Unlike Toscanini, however,
Weingartner seems not to have paid much attention to the movement's opening chord, which is scandalously out of tune and unbalanced in his recording.)

Weingartner was still adopting 66 as his basic tempo thirty years
after the publication of his book, but he often exceeded it considerably, after the first fifty bars; so did Toscanini in his later version. But
in Toscanini I the musical discourse unfolds naturally, whereas Weingartner's version and Toscanini II sometimes flow too quickly—
especially in the A major and C major sections (bars 102–49), in
which Weingartner fluctuates between ♩ = 69 and 80, and Toscanini II between 79 and 92! (In the same passage, Toscanini I remains
in the 63–66 range, Klemperer's tempo is 63–64, Furtwängler's 57–
70, and Walter's 54–66.) In the slower versions of the movement,
every bar becomes a phrase. Furtwängler attempts to resolve the
problem by shortening the staccato eighth-notes in every second bar
of the main theme, thereby lightening the texture; but because the
pattern is repeated so many times, the effect soon sounds forced.
Still, Furtwängler avoids the ponderousness of the Walter and Klemperer versions.

Third movement: *Presto; Assai meno presto*. Timings: Toscanini
I-7:00, Toscanini II-6:56, Weingartner-7:58, Furtwängler-8:37, Wal-
ter-8:15, Klemperer-8:43.

Toscanini I and II resemble each other much more in the last two
movements than in the first two; but in the Scherzo (third movement) they bear little resemblance to any of the other versions under
examination. Beethoven gave this movement the fastest tempo and

metronome indications—*Presto*, $\rfloor$. = 132—of any of his symphonic scherzos: the nearest contenders are those of the "Eroica" and the Ninth, both marked $\rfloor$. = 116. Toscanini I varies between about 128 and 132, and Toscanini II stays for the most part very close to 132. Furtwängler's tempo is 124–28, with many ritardandos and accelerandos, including a few sections as fast as 132; Weingartner's is 122–26, Strauss's 114–22, Walter's 112–20, and Klemperer's 106–12—with points as low as 100 in the return of the Scherzo, after the first playing of the Trio. Neither of Toscanini's accounts gives the impression of being rushed: however energetic the pulse, the texture is always light and boisterous, and the playing is thoroughly joyful. There are moments, especially bars 117–35 and parallel passages later, that are almost irresistibly dancelike. Toscanini II is less subtly inflected and sometimes harsher in articulation than Toscanini I, but there seems to have been little difference in overall intent. I find Furtwängler's version the best of the others in the body of the movement, but with too unsteady a tempo for a Scherzo. Weingartner and Strauss seem to lack the devilish sense of fun that Toscanini and, occasionally, Furtwängler communicate. Walter's performance is enervated, whereas Klemperer's demonstrates, again, that a high energy-level can be maintained even at a slow tempo—but it has no lilt.

The part of the symphony in which both Toscanini I and II are most distant from all the other versions is this movement's Trio. Beethoven's indication is *Assai meno presto; presto* is one of the fastest tempo indications used by Beethoven, and *assai meno* means "much less." The metronome mark is $\rfloor$. = 84. In Toscanini I the Trio starts at 84–90 and slows to 72 at the fortissimo (bars 211–26); during the repeat, however, the basic tempo drops to 80 and the fortissimo tempo to 69. Something similar happens in Toscanini II, but at a still faster pace: the first time around, the basic tempo is $\rfloor$. = 88 and the fortissimo passage slows to 80; the second time around, the basic tempo is 80 and the fortissimo 78. Again, I prefer the 1936 version, but I wish that Toscanini had taken his second-time-around tempo the first time around, too. Klemperer, whose tempo for the Trio hovers between 51 and 56, with a drop to 49 at the fortissimo, was scandalized by Toscanini's approach: "He took the trio much too fast. So far as I know, it's an old Austrian pilgrims' song, an Ave Maria. He didn't understand that. It only makes sense when it is taken slowly. It should be a contrast to the scherzo."[13] The *Assai meno presto* indication, however, clearly tells performers that the Trio is meant to be fast, although not as fast as the body of the Scherzo. Beethoven could much more easily have written *allegretto* or *andantino*, had he wanted the Trio to emerge as a metaphysical glimmer, rather than playfully.

Weingartner's basic tempo in the Trio is circa $\dot{\textrm{d}}$. = 50, Walter's is 48–52, and Strauss's 48. Furtwängler's version is the most deflated of all: it drags along like a slow-motion nightmare at a basic tempo of 44 (about one-third his tempo in the Scherzo), dropping to 42–43 at the fortissimo, and slowing down to below 30 by bar 240.

Fourth movement: *Allegro con brio.* Timings: Toscanini I-6:50, Toscanini II-6:44, Weingartner-6:35, Furtwängler-6:51, Walter-6:45, Klemperer-8:37.

Toscanini may be odd man out in the Scherzo, but Klemperer wins the title in the Finale. The timings of all the other performances are remarkably similar, but Klemperer's is 25 percent longer than the longest of the others. Beethoven's metronome indication is $\textrm{d}$ = 72; Klemperer thunders through the movement at $\textrm{d}$ = 55–62. Again, he maintains a high energy-level, but the performance is entirely lacking in brio. Weingartner's basic tempo is 70–74; he never falls below 68 and occasionally reaches 82. Strauss stays between 70 and 80, and does a great deal of pushing and pulling toward each extreme. (He also makes a huge cut, presumably to avoid making the recording run onto another side of a 78 r.p.m. disk.) Furtwängler is the most wayward: his basic tempo, $\textrm{d}$ = 69, is close to the metronome mark, but he frequently shifts between the distant limits of 58 and 84, thus forcing himself to execute brusque forward and backward handsprings. Bars 14–21, for example, are ground out rather determinedly in Furtwängler's version, but the following sixteen bars are fast and cutting. Walter's performance, like Toscanini I and II, takes Beethoven's metronome mark as a valid basic tempo and rarely sinks below it; sometimes, however, it rushes to 84, whereas Toscanini I never goes beyond 76, and Toscanini II's maximum is 79. The movement's dominant characteristic is its rhythmic unity; if one strays far from the fundamental pulse, one destroys that characteristic. Among all seven versions, Toscanini I is the most successful in maintaining unity without sacrificing the expressive individuality of any of the piece's elements. It is, at various times, vibrant, joyful, playful, threatening, violent, refulgent, and triumphant—always in a state of flux but always solid. Thus, as in every other movement, my first choice is Toscanini I.

WITH the exception of the third movement's Trio, which Toscanini—by accepting approximately the tempo indicated by Beethoven—conceived differently than anyone else, his approach to the Seventh Symphony differed no more startlingly from that of his German colleagues than their approaches differed from each other's. In this case, Toscanini's interpretations have many points of contact with Weingartner's, Strauss's, and Furtwängler's, far fewer with those of the two Mahler disciples, Walter and Klemperer; in other German classics, other combinations of similarities and differences emerge.

The contention that Toscanini's tempi became faster and more rigid as he aged is often correct; and in this case, too, the tempi in the 1951 recording are generally faster than those in the 1936 version. But in the introduction to the first movement and throughout the second, the tempi in the later version fluctuate much more than in the earlier one—too much, in my opinion.

Regarding Toscanini's overall approach to interpretation, the only conclusion to be drawn from this mass of information is the one that Gavazzeni—who heard most of the Scala productions during the 1920s—drew years ago. Toscanini's performances, he said, were "always in a state of flux, as a result of his conviction that a great musical text is never merely a substance to be poured out, but rather a living organism."[14] Anyone who wants to begin to understand Toscanini must first recognize what Gavazzeni called the "evolutionary quality of his operation, which was tireless, never sated, never still."

This chapter has been written specifically for this book.

APPENDIX *I*

An Opera Premiere in 1902

I N 1990, I found, in an antiquarian bookshop in Florence, a copy of the libretto (by Luigi Illica) of Alberto Franchetti's opera, *Germania*. The edition was printed especially for the world premiere, which took place at La Scala on March 11, 1902, and the original owner of this copy made notes as the evening proceeded. The notes give an idea of what went on at a successful opera premiere in those days, and what the members of the audience were listening for. Page 15: "This passage strongly conceived, first call for the composer"—in other words, the audience had shouted the composer's name or "Autore!" (approvingly) for the first time. Page 18: "Very beautiful melody." Page 19: "Patriotic call to the students. A real people's anthem"; "Weber's well-known song [a musical quotation]"; "first [outburst of] enthusiasm / encore"; "second call for the composer." Pages 22–23: "[The scene of] Palm's arrest is extraordinarily effective"; "four curtain calls for the composer" at the end of the prologue. Page 28: "Scarlatti-like quality." Page 30: "The entire wedding scene has most agreeable music." Pages 32–33: "This entire love duet is a delightful musical poem." Page 35: "One of the most vigorous, most thoroughly thought-out fragments of the opera." Page 38: "sorrowful aria, deeply felt"; "two calls for the composer." Pages 41–42: "Jane's tale [is] in classic Italian style"; "two curtain calls for the author" at the end of Part I. Page 48: "Full of austere, elegiac majesty." Page 53: "Stupendous fragment, full of pathos." Page 54: "The finale [of Part II] brings to mind the third act of *Asrael* [another of Franchetti's operas]"; "three curtain calls for the composer." Page 55: "Encored [symphonic interlude]—the orchestration is powerful." Page 62: "Melodic bit stupendous." Page 64 (end): "Three curtain calls for the composer." Our anonymous chronicler does not once mention the performers—and to think that the lead tenor was Enrico Caruso and the conductor Arturo Toscanini!

Opera in the Italian Provinces

TRANSLATION OF the contract between the Municipality of Ravenna and the impresario who was to organize the spring 1894 opera season at the town's principal theater:

KINGDOM OF ITALY, CITY OF RAVENNA

Ravenna, this Twentieth day of April eighteen hundred ninety-four (1894).

With the present private contract the Administration of the Teatro Alighieri of Ravenna has agreed and agrees to give the De Comis Agency of Milan, represented by Mr. Aristide De Comis of Milan, present, who accepts, and who, insofar as this contract is concerned, has chosen and chooses to make his [legal] home at that of Mr. Petroncini, Alessandro, Superintendent of the Teatro Alighieri[,]

the Concession of the above-mentioned Theater for the coming spring season, with the following conditions.

1. The Impresario Mr. De Comis, Aristide, undertakes to present the opera-ballet Roi de Lahore of Maestro Massenet.

There must be no fewer than fourteen performances, which is to say twelve by subscription and two not by subscription; of these last two, one will be given to raise funds for a local Charitable Institution.

2. The said Opera-Ballet will have to be mounted with the greatest possible decorum and in keeping with the importance of the production and of the Teatro Alighieri, care being taken that the properties, sets, lighting, costumes etc. be sumptuous and worthy of the production.

3. The principal parts in the above-mentioned Opera will be taken by the following artists;

Ferrani, Cesira—Soprano
Cardinali, Franco—Tenor
Sammarco, G. Mario—Baritone
Quaina, Maria—Mezzo-Soprano
Sabellico, Antonio—Bass.

The Entire Company of Singers and dancers, including the Conductor and Rehearser of the Opera in the person of Mr. Toscanini, Arturo, must be in town not later than 28 April current to mount the opera without fail by the evening of 10 (Ten) May next, barring cases unforeseen by the Administration, so that the last performance not take place after 3 June next.

4. The dates of the performances will be determined by common accord between the Agency and the Administration, but always at the rate of four per week.

5. At the benefit performance for a local Charitable Institution, the Agency must provide gratis the entire company of artists, that is, singers, dancers, music, sets, properties, and costumes, and the Administration will cover only the expenses of attendants [*i.e.*, ushers and service personnel], orchestra players and chorus members from the city, as well as the electric and gas lighting.

6. The Agency must, if possible, make use of chorus members of both sexes and of orchestra players from the town, so long as they are deemed suitable by the respective conductors, and the Agency must also provide at its own expense [replacements for] those players and choristers of both sexes who are not deemed suitable by the theater's Administration, the total number to be approved at #50 choristers of both sexes and #60 orchestra members including the stage band.

If subsequently, during the period of rehearsals, or even in the course of the performances, a player or chorister should be lacking, either because of illness or because the number is insufficient, the Agency must replace him or provide one, again at its own expense, subject to the Administration's approval.

7. All the players and choristers, as well as the members of the Corps de Ballet, will have to stay in town through the last performance.

8. In the event of illness on the part either of the [solo] artists or of orchestra members or choristers, or members of the ballet, the agency must replace them with others who are equally suitable, to be chosen among those available and ready and willing to take their parts.

9. The Corps de Ballet will be made up of:
Prima Ballerina of high Italian rating—Miss Pezzattini, Bice.
#24—Twenty-four—Second Ballerinas
#12—Twelve—Coriphées
#12—Twelve—Boys
#40—Forty—Extras
Mr. Rando, Giovanni, will be the ballet master.

10. The fees owing to the singers, to the Maestro Conductor of the Opera-Ballet, to the Ballet Master, to the members of the orchestra, to the male and female choristers, whether local or outsiders, to the Chorus Master, to all the Artists who make up the Ballet, to the stagehands, Theater attendants, extras, Firemen, also at the rehearsals, as well as the tax payable by the Impresario, will all be paid by the Agency[.] Likewise, the expenses for the rental or purchase of those costumes indispensable for the opera-ballet, the related properties and sets, the electric and gas lighting for the stage, the gas lighting for the

auditorium, service rooms, and dressing rooms, at the rehearsals as well as at the performances, the lighting necessary for the theater's boxes, the [candle]wax for the use of those persons who have the right to have it [presumably, boxholders had the right to use candlelight in the boxes, where social life went on during performances], the gas lighting for the theater's external lights, the taxes set and to be set by the government, and all other ordinary and extraordinary and unforeseen expenses, be they required before the production opens or in the course of the performances, with nothing excluded or withheld, are declared to be entirely attributed to the agency, so that the Administration will have nothing further to expend beyond the settlement in the measure undertaken as follows:

11. As to the said daily expenses, the agency must, after every third performance, pay the sums due, to the Theater's representative, in order that they be distributed to those to whom they are owed, in accordance with the note that has already been given to the Agency by the Administration.

12. The Agency must give not fewer than ten copies of the libretto of the Opera-Ballet to the Administration.

[The agency] must also give free admittance to the Theater's doctor, surgeon, bookkeeper, and Chief Technician.

The Doctor and the Surgeon will also have the right to orchestra seats, while the bookkeeper will sit at a desk, which the Agency will make available to the above-mentioned gentlemen.

13. The Theater Administration promises and undertakes to pay, by way of participating in the expenses, the sum of Twenty-eight thousand Italian Liras, which it will pay into the hands of the Impresario, Mr. Aristide De Comis, in four installments.

The first, amounting to ten thousand Liras (£10/th), on the day on which the entire Company of Singers and dancers, including the Conductor, arrives in town—The second, amounting to six thousand Liras (£6/th), on the day after the third performance.

The third, amounting to six thousand Liras (£6/th), on the day after half of the obligatory performances have been given—The fourth and last, amounting to six thousand liras (£6/th), after the last of the obligatory performances, in all cases only if the agency has fulfilled its obligations to the Theater Administration as per the present contract.

Furthermore, the De Comis Agency will be given all the proceeds from ticket sales for standing room in the orchestra and gallery, subscriptions [*i.e.*, boxes], chairs and single or reserved seats [*i.e.*, in the orchestra and gallery], with the exception of the three indicated at #12.

The theater's Café and that of the Gallery will earn nothing for the agency, because they are rented from the Theater Administration by a special contract.

The normal ticket prices per evening have been established as follows: Entrance Ticket [*i.e.*, standing room] 2 Liras—reserved seat in addition to entrance ticket Liras—2-Two—Front-section orchestra seat in addition to entrance ticket Liras 4 (Four)–Gallery [in addition to entrance ticket] 0.75 Lira.

The prices as stated above may be changed in certain cases and always by agreement with the Administration, which, however, immediately concedes [this right] for the evenings of the days on which races are run[.]

14. The Impresario is absolutely forbidden to subcontract or cede to others the aforementioned proceeds in whole or in part, with the exception of the gallery, and also to cede the contract to others, while the Theater Administration intends to recognize only De Comis, Aristide, as impresario and to hold him responsible for all the obligations undertaken through the present contract.

15. To guarantee to the Theater Administration that all the above-mentioned obligations will be strictly observed, the Impresario Mr. De Comis, Aristide, has deposited with the Municipal Treasury the sum of six thousand Liras (£6/th) consisting of Southern Railway shares [variously enumerated], all of which have Coupons for the first trimester of 1894, which sum may be realized by the Theater Administration, with no authorization whatsoever, in the event that the Agency falls short of the obligations that it has assumed, and only after it has been found that these have been fully satisfied will the deposit be returned to the said Mr. De Comis, Aristide, and the agency could under no circumstances take exception or make demands of any sort if the Theater Administration were to make use of the said deposit as stated above[.]

16. The Agency must pay all expenses deriving from this contract, and registration fees, where necessary, and the relative penalties.

In confirmation of which, the parties, alternating among themselves the obligation of payments of any damages, interest, and extrajudiciary expenses whatsoever, now undersign [signatures].

The performances were successful, yet subscription and single-ticket sales earned only 14,818.50 liras (excluding the benefit performance); thus, the municipality's 28,000-lira subsidy to the impresario was almost twice as great as the amount realized at the box office. At the going rates, the fees of the singers, conductor, orchestra, chorus, chorus master, corps de ballet, and ballet master must have amounted to over 35,000 liras, to which must be added the costs of set, costume, and prop rentals; transport; stagehands' fees; and all the other house expenses listed in the contract. The impresario's profits were probably not great.

Notes

1: TOSCANINI AGAIN (pp. 3–17)

1. Adrian Boult, *Thoughts on Conducting* (London: Phoenix House, 1963), 2.
2. Peter Heyworth, *Conversations with Klemperer* (London: Faber and Faber, 1985), 120.
3. Interview with Carlo Maria Giulini by the author, Milan, 1977.
4. This and the following quotations of Rodolfo Celletti are taken from "Tant pis pour Monsieur Toscanini," in Celletti's *Memorie d'un ascoltatore* (Milan: Il Saggiatore, 1985), 57–71.
5. David Wooldridge, *Conductor's World* (London: Barrie and Rockliff, 1970), 315.
6. Guglielmo Barblan, *Toscanini e la Scala* (Milan: Edizioni della Scala, 1972), 159–61.
7. Teodoro Celli and Giuseppe Pugliese, *Tullio Serafin—il patriarca del melodramma* (Venice: Corbo e Fiore, 1985), 37.
8. Maurizio Modugno, "Quand'ero viola di fila" (interview with Carlo Maria Giulini), in *Vita italiana—cultura e scienza*, vol. 2, no. 2, April–June 1987, 79.
9. Simonetta Puccini, ed., *Giacomo Puccini, lettere a Riccardo Schnabl* (Milano: Emme Edizioni, 1981), 211.
10. Ibid., 46.
11. G. Pozza, in *Corriere della Sera*, Milan, April 15, 1903.
12. Interview with Erich Leinsdorf by the author, Toronto, 1972.
13. B. H. Haggin, *Conversations with Toscanini* (New York: Da Capo, 1989), 135.
14. Interview with Gianandrea Gavazzeni by the author, Bergamo, 1972.

3: "WORTHIEST AMONG THE WORTHY":
TOSCANINI IN TURIN (pp. 27–49)

1. Interview with Erich Leinsdorf by the author, Toronto, 1972.
2. This and all subsequent documents quoted come from Turin's Archivio Municipale, Repertorio Gabinetto del Sindaco.
3. *Il pianoforte*, Milan, vol. 5, no. 6, June 1924, 175.

4: BACKGROUND TO THE REBIRTH OF LA SCALA (pp. 50–59)

1. Barblan, op. cit., 337–38.
2. Celli and Pugliese, op. cit., 46–47, 52.
3. Carl Krebs, *Meister des Taktstocks* (Berlin: Schuster und Loeffler, 1919), 215–16.
4. Walter Mocchi, "Ventennale," in *La verità*, Rome, October 31, 1942, 371.
5. *Il pianoforte*, op. cit., 167–68.
6. Barblan, op. cit., 346.

5: TOSCANINI AND MUSSOLINI (pp. 60–99)

Legend for material found in the Archivio Centrale dello Stato, Rome (ACS): CO = Corrispondenza ordinaria; CPC = Casellario politico centrale (central political files); DGPS = Direzione generale di pubblica sicurezza (general administration of public safety); DPP = Divisione polizia politica (political police division); FP = Fascicoli personali (confidential files); MI = Ministero dell'Interno (Ministry of the Interior; the political and other national police forces were under this ministry's jurisdiction)

NA = National Archives, Washington
SAC = St. Anthony's College, Oxford

1. Harvey Sachs, *Toscanini* (New York: Lippincott, 1978), 5–8.
2. Ibid., 132–36.
3. Ibid., 139–40.
4. Ibid., 144.
5. Ibid., 154.
6. Maria Labia, *Guardare indietro: che fatica!* (Verona: Bettinelli, 1950), 117.
7. Harvey Sachs, *Music in Fascist Italy* (New York: Norton, 1987), 34.
8. ACS SPD CO, no. 7661, June 6, 1924.
9. Ugo Ojetti, *I taccuini* (Florence: Sansoni, 1954), 156–57.
10. Sachs, *Toscanini*, 174; and ACS SPD CO, no. 7666, undated.
11. Sachs, *Toscanini*, 179.
12. Arnaldo Fraccaroli, *La Scala a Vienna e a Berlino* (Milan: Corriere della Sera, 1929).
13. E. A. Teatro alla Scala, *Cronistoria della stagione 1928–29* (Milan, 1929), 142.
14. MI DGPS DPP FP 51/B, no. 446.

15. Sachs, *Toscanini,* 209.
16. Barblan, op. cit., facing 360 *et seq.*
17. Indro Montanelli and Marcello Staglieno, *Longanesi* (Milan: Rizzoli, 1984).
18. Wanda Toscanini Horowitz, interviewed by Edward Downes, Metropolitan Opera broadcast, March 25, 1967.
19. Mario Labroca and Virgilio Boccardi, *Arte di Toscanini* (Turin: ERI, 1966), 137.
20. Letter of November 6, 1967; copy in Fondo Respighi, Fondazione G. Cini, Venice.
21. Elsa Respighi, interviewed on RAI, August 1977.
22. Sachs, *Toscanini,* 209–10.
23. Ibid., 210.
24. Barblan, op. cit., facing 360 *et seq.*
25. Sachs, *Toscanini,* 213.
26. Reprinted under headline: "L'incidente provocato da Toscanini in una nota de *L'assalto,*" in *La tribuna,* May 19, 1931.
27. *Il popolo d'Italia,* Milan, May 16, 1931.
28. "In margine: Effetti salutari di uno schiaffo," in *La tribuna,* May 20, 1931.
29. Barblan, op. cit., facing 360 *et seq.*
30. MI etc., no. 346.
31. Sachs, *Toscanini,* 214.
32. Josef Szigeti, *With Strings Attached* (New York: Knopf, 1967), 347–48.
33. Clara Clemens, *My Husband Gabrilowitsch* (New York: Harper, 1938), 206.
34. Lia Pierotti Cei, *Il signore del golfo mistico* (Florence: Sansoni, 1982), 293.
35. SPD SAC, nos. 088760–61.
36. MI etc., no. 435.
37. Ibid., no. 434.
38. Ibid., no. 413.
39. Ibid., no. 433.
40. Ibid., no. 419.
41. Ibid., no. 418.
42. Ibid., unnumbered.
43. Ibid., no. 415.
44. Ibid., no. 378.
45. Ibid., no. 339.
46. Ibid., no. 375.
47. Ibid., no. 358.
48. Ibid., nos. 365–66.
49. Ibid., nos. 328–32.
50. Ibid., no. 343.
51. Ibid., no. 323.
52. Emil Ludwig, *Talks with Mussolini* (London: George Allen and Unwin, 1932), 211–12.
53. Nino D'Aroma, *Mussolini segreto* (Bologna: Cappelli, 1958), 304.
54. MI etc., no. 308; nos. 304–5.

55. Ibid., no. 310.
56. Ibid., no. 288.
57. Ibid., no. 283.
58. SPD SAC, nos. 088788–89.
59. MI etc., no. 4.
60. Ibid., no. 40.
61. Ibid., no. 3.
62. A. Della Corte, *Toscanini visto da un critico* (Turin: ILTE, 1958), 319–20; and Friedelind Wagner, interviewed by the author, 1978.
63. *Il regime fascista*, Cremona, September 1, 1938, no. 207.
64. Della Corte, op. cit., 321.
65. MI etc., no. 39.
66. Galeazzo Ciano, *Diario 1937–1938* (Bologna: Cappelli, 1948), entry for September 7, 1938.
67. MI etc., no. 29.
68. Sachs, *Toscanini*, 267–68.
69. SPD SAC, no. 088801.
70. MI etc., no. 26.
71. Sachs, *Toscanini*, 270.
72. Gaetano Salvemini, *Memorie di un fuoruscito* (Milan: Feltrinelli, 1960), 178.
73. Gaetano Salvemini, *L'Italia vista dall'America*, E. Tagliacozzo, ed. (Milan: Feltrinelli, 1969), vols. I and II, 165.
74. Tito Silvio Mursino (alias Vittorio Mussolini), "La settima sinfonia," in *Il messaggero*, Rome, April 17, 1943.
75. Sachs, *Toscanini*, 280–81.
76. Ibid., 281.
77. Arturo Toscanini, "To the People of America," in *Life*, September 13, 1943.
78. Salvemini archives, Rome.
79. Gaetano Salvemini et al., "An Italian Manifesto," in *Life*, June 12, 1944.
80. Sachs, *Toscanini*, 283.
81. Barblan, op. cit., 370.
82. Armando Borghi, "Esilio americano," in *Il mondo*, May 14, 1957.
83. Sachs, *Toscanini*, 288.
84. Sachs, *Toscanini*, 288–89.
85. RAI–2 (TV), "I giorni della Repubblica," June 3, 1986.
86. Arturo Toscanini, unpublished letter of May 16, 1941, from Riverdale, York, private collection.

6: "COME BACK, THOU BOLD SINGER!":

TOSCANINI AND BAYREUTH (pp. 100–19)

1. Barblan, op. cit., 324.
2. Ibid., illustration opposite 49.
3. This and all subsequent quotations not otherwise credited are from documents in the Richard Wagner Museum, Bayreuth.

4. Kurt Söhnlein, *Erinnerungen an Siegfried Wagner und Bayreuth* (Bayreuth: Mühl'scher Universitätsverlag, 1980), 83–84.
5. Telephone interview with Friedelind Wagner by the author, 1987.
6. Private collection, Rome.
7. From Toscanini Legacy, in the New York Public Library, Library and Museum of the Performing Arts, Lincoln Center.

10: WATCHING TOSCANINI (pp. 148–59)

1. B. H. Haggin, *The Toscanini Musicians Knew* (New York: Da Capo, 1989), 158.
2. Boult, op. cit., 54–55.
3. Ibid., 52.
4. D. E. Inghelbrecht, *The Conductor's World* (London: Peter Nevill, 1953), 19–29.
5. Interview with Robert Bloom by the author, Toronto, 1971.
6. Haggin, op. cit., 72.

11: LISTENING TO TOSCANINI (pp. 160–80)

1. Interview with Lorand Fenyves by the author, Toronto, 1971.
2. Wilhelm Furtwängler, *Notebooks 1924–1954* (London: Quartet, 1989), 46.
3. Otto Klemperer, *Über Musik und Theater* (Wilhelmshaven: Heinrichshofen, 1982), 50, reprint of article in *Das Tagebuch*, Berlin, May 25, 1929.
4. Heyworth, op. cit., 30.
5. Conversation between Gianandrea Gavazzeni and the author, Florence, 1991.
6. Review reprinted in L. Frassati, *Il Maestro* (Turin: Bottega d'Erasmo, 1967), 20.
7. Alma Mahler, *Gustav Mahler* (London: John Murray, 1973), 146.
8. Bruno Walter, *Theme and Variations* (New York: Knopf, 1947), 278.
9. Julius Korngold, from transcript of excerpt from unpublished memoirs, "Postludien in dur und moll."
10. Conversations between Louis Fourestier and the author, Nice, 1971.
11. Felix Weingartner, *On the Performance of Beethoven's Symphonies* (New York: E. F. Kalmus, n.d.), 106.
12. Christopher Dyment, *Felix Weingartner* (Rickmansworth: Triad Press, 1976), 82.
13. Heyworth, op. cit., 116.
14. Gianandrea Gavazzeni, *Non eseguire Beethoven* (Milan: Il Saggiatore, 1974), 96.

About the Author

Harvey Sachs was born in Cleveland, Ohio, in 1946. He received musical training in Cleveland, New York, and Toronto, and was active for a dozen years as a conductor, mainly in Canada and Italy. His internationally acclaimed biography, *Toscanini*, was first published in 1978 and has appeared in ten editions. He is also the author of *Virtuoso* (1982) and *Music in Fascist Italy* (1987). Articles by Sachs have been published in the *New Yorker*, the *Atlantic*, the *Times Literary Supplement*, the *New York Times*, the *New Republic*, *Grand Street*, the *Guardian*, *La Stampa*, *Corriere della Sera*, *Le Nouvel Observateur*, and many North American and European music journals. He is a Canadian citizen and lives in Tuscany with his wife and son.